ROBERT MCNAIR WILSON

MONARCHY

OR

MONEY POWER

OMNIA VERITAS

ROBERT MCNAIR WILSON

MONARCHY OR MONEY POWER

Published by Omnia Veritas Ltd

OMNIA VERITAS

www.omnia-veritas.com

Table of Contents

Preface 9

Chapter I
   The Origin Of Nations 11

Chapter II
   The Nature of Kingship 18

Chapter III
   The Doctrine of Money 24

Chapter IV
   TURGOT 31

Chapter V
   King and Banker 44

Chapter VI
   Tribune and Banker 52

Chapter VII
   ROBESPIERRE 56

Chapter VIII
   BONAPARTE 73

Chapter IX
   NAPOLEON 86

Chapter X
   The New Feudalism 92

Chapter XI
   The Great Betrayal 105

Chapter XII
   MAMMON 147

Chapter XIII
   "The Hungry Forties" 159

Chapter XIV
   DISRAELI 170

Chapter XV
   "Dutch Finance" 176

Chapter XVI
   Empress of India 180

Chapter XVII
   CHAMBERLAIN 185

Chapter XVIII
   Imperial Patriotism 192

Chapter XIX
   Germany 197

Chapter XX
   King and Parliament 207

Chapter XXI
   Credit 213

Chapter XXII
   MILNER 219

Chapter XXIII
   The King's Grace 253

Chapter XXIV
   Counter-Attack 257

Chapter XXV
   Stewardship 274

Preface to the second edition (of Monarchy or Money Power) 277

Introduction to the Second Edition..................................279

Re-Dedication "God is marching on" – President Roosevelt..286

Turgot and the Ancien Régime in France

By Douglas Dakin, Lecturer in history, Birkbeck College, University of London..311

The Assignats

By Harris, Seymour Edwin..322

ROBERT MCNAIR WILSON

Preface

NEXT to the weather, finance is now the most talked about subject in the world. But discussion remains difficult owing to the confusion which exists in many minds about the nature of money. In the following pages an attempt has been made to describe the money system so that its principles may be grasped easily by anyone above the age of sixteen years.

I wish to thank my friend C. Featherstone Hammond for the great help he has given me.

R. MCNAIR WILSON,
January 1st, 1934

Robert McNair Wilson

Chapter I

The Origin of Nations

EVERY society or association, whether of insects, animals, or men, is based on a surrender of individual function. The worker bees, for example, are strictly females; the brain cells of the human body have lost, wholly, their powers of reproduction. To speak, therefore, of the hive or the body is to speak of associations founded on individual loss or, in scientific phrase, on differentiated function.

It is evident that, in such associations, an attempt by any individual or group of individuals to resume the surrendered function must result in great danger to the organism. (The disease cancer, for example, is the resumption by a group of body cells of the function of uncontrolled reproduction.) Such resumption of surrendered function is therefore revolt, and must be prevented or suppressed if the organism is to live. The two methods employed in nature to effect the prevention and suppression of revolt are gain and fear. The member of the pack or herd is early made aware that, by itself, it must perish, and is, in addition, taught that acts of insubordination are visited by death.

The pack, therefore, lives and fights as one creature. Weakness, wherever it shows itself, is ruthlessly eliminated. The old are thrust aside to make way for the young, and the unfit for the fit. For gain and fear, even in their humblest manifestations as the pulsations, expansions, and contractions of a unicellular creature, enforce always and everywhere their law of death, called, properly enough, the law of the jungle.

That this law applies to the physical bodies of men cannot be disputed. But it is significant that, from the earliest times, men as opposed to the whole creation of brute beasts have exalted another law of association - namely, the surrender of individual function at the call of duty, using that word to signify neither gain nor fear, but the denial of them both in the name and for the sake of a virtue of life apprehended by the soul of man.

The history of men is the history of duty. The merit of the ancient civilizations resides in their experience of duty, called patriotism, and exhibited not only at the behest of the gods, but even, as in Aeschylean tragedy, in opposition to them. Man, as patriot and patrician, out grew his gods, whose Olympian mirth rang false in ears about to die; he prepared himself thus for a new revelation of duty that is to say, for a fuller law of life in contradistinction to the natural law of death.

It was to men thus prepared for His coming that the Lord Jesus Christ gave this law:

"Thou shalt love the Lord thy God with all thy heart, and with all thy soul, and with all thy mind, and with all thy strength: this is the first commandment.

And the second is like, namely this: Thou shalt love thy neighbour as thyself. There is none other commandment greater than these."

The Christian law, therefore, presented duty in two complementary aspects, as duty to God and duty to men. It made duty synonymous with love, and so raised it from the devotion of the pagan to his fatherland to the Christian's adoration of the Father. Patriotism assumed a new quality of brotherhood. Above all, man's duty was comprehended in the Divine love which was at once its sanction and its law. Christian civilization consequently recognized two necessary means to the performance of the Christian's office - namely, the Church and the State. Both, as the vehicle of the Christian Law, were of divine appointment, and the divinity of the one was part of the divinity of the other and inseparable from it.

The history of what are called the Dark Ages is the history of the development of the Christian state. From the beginning, the character which this state ought to assume was clearly recognized by the Church, which did not dispute that the Grace by which the King should reign belonged to him as the direct gift of God, without any intervention whatever. In actual fact the disturbed condition of Europe consequent upon the fall of Imperial Rome was such that there were no states in the modern acceptation, but only a multitude of nobles, the feudal barons. In these circumstances it was inevitable that the first step towards the Christian state should be a dominion of the Church over all the barons.

This was achieved when, on Christmas Day of the year 800, Charles the Great was crowned Emperor of the West in Rome by the Pope. The Empire of Charlemagne embraced all Europe - that is to say, the whole of Christendom - and that shining truth blinded many eyes to the fact that it did not represent the Christian state as originally conceived, but represented merely an approach towards this Christian State. For the essential quality of the Christian State is its sovereignty - that is to say, its political independence. This is evident when the break-up of Charlemagne's Empire is studied. His Empire in the end fell to pieces primarily because it was an association of barons rather than a kingdom.

This distinction deserves the most careful attention. It was the teaching of the Church that the resources of nature belonged only to God, but existed so that men, by making use of them, might be enabled to fulfil their duty. An essential office of the Christian state, therefore, was to secure to men the use of natural resources, and this implied the provision of such leaders of agriculture and industry as would guarantee the most efficient employment both of material and of craftsmanship, and of such leaders as could, if necessary, organize the country's defence. These leaders, with the bishops and priests, must, from the nature of the service demanded of them, become a privileged body, possessed of rights deriving from and dependent on their duties. But the human story had afforded too many examples of the usurpation of rights for private advantage to make it expedient to leave such a body uncontrolled by any superior authority.

Again and again individual leaders, whether clerical or lay, had succeeded in forming parties, usually with the help of moneylenders, and by such means holding the State to ransom, to the grave scandal of Christian men and the heavy disadvantage both of the Church and the temporal authority. It had been recognized in the earliest time, as has been said, that kingship supplied the means of solving these difficulties. That remedy could not be applied until Europe had emerged into the Middle Ages. The story of the Middle Ages is the story of the fight for Kingship, in which the Church, no less than the laity, played a part.

The object was to establish Kings secured in their office on the one hand by the grace of God, and on the other by the loyalty of the People, so that power might be secured wherewith to curb the intoxication of privilege and the influence of money. It is evident that the People cannot exert such power of itself, for, in truth, there are no People unless there be also a King. People without Kings are ever sundered into parties and factions of which the richest inevitably becomes the most powerful. The triumph of the richest party is the occasion of the rewarding of its financial backers. (It must be insisted that a King who is dependent upon the support of a party cannot reign in such a way as to protect his people, for he too, in that case, will fall immediately into the usurer's hands.) It is the Grace of God which arms the King with his strength and raises him above all his People to be their father; it is by this Grace of God therefore, manifested in the King's Grace, that Democracy must live if it is not to perish.

The difficulty which all the medieval Kings experienced in greater or less degree was the establishing of themselves in the People's love. The King needed the People as much as the People needed the King, but it was ever the object of interested parties to hold them asunder. And so was witnessed a perpetual struggle between, on the one hand, King and Church, anxious alike to hold their servants and ministers in subjection to duty, and, on the other hand, unruly servants and ministers, barons and prelates, seeking means of sustaining themselves in revolt against both spiritual and temporal authority, and so very often becoming allied to the financial powers.

Money from an early time showed itself the enemy of Kingship, in which it recognized the bulwark against its operations. Money became concerned, like the rebellious nobles and prelates who were often its tools, to hold the King and his People apart and make them both dependent upon its own power. It was from this danger that Richelieu delivered France at the moment when, in England, a triumphant oligarchy based upon the City of London was hurrying King Charles I to the scaffold.

By a curious misconception the growth of French Nationalism is held by many Catholics to have inflicted injury upon the Church. This view the writer, as a Protestant, is unable to accept. For it seems to him that the French monarchy under Richelieu and Louis XIII attained finally to the position which, from the beginning, the Church herself had accepted as the rightful place of Kings. Richelieu effected the union of King and People, and by means of it brought every unruly element in France into subjection, so that the Church in temporal affairs and the nobles became the servants of the King, were yoked to duty, and were excluded from any privilege not deriving from that duty. The nation was born.

Protestants, on the other hand, it may legitimately be argued, have done less than justice to the Church for her careful fostering, through many difficult centuries, of the Christian State.

Protestants are accustomed to hail the coming of the nations to maturity as a victory over the Church, whereas in fact it was the direct result of the Church's mothering. If the Mother, by holding back when the time for restraint was passing away, was in part responsible for the conditions of lawlessness, both religious and secular, which preceded the Reformation, that was a fault much less disastrous in its consequences, as will be seen, than the doctrine suggested by some of the reformers - namely, that the People is its own Sovereign. Richelieu built his new France on the foundations of *God-wealth* and duty; in England the idea of Commonwealth - that is to say, a society based upon the mutual gain of its members - was made to serve until such time as the Throne had been restored. Even its defenders do not now contend that Cromwell's rule was based upon consent. Its real base was a military party enjoying a substantial backing of financial support. This, perhaps, is the reason why Cromwell himself wished at one time to assume the Royal dignity.

Chapter II

The Nature of Kingship

A NATION under the Feudal System was a spiritual rather than a political conception, seeing that its object was to enable men to perform their duties to God and to their fellows. By God's Grace and the people's love the King reigned, and by virtue of that Grace and that love the King held under subjection all those, whether churchmen or nobles, who were the leaders of his people, compelling them to discharge their offices towards people and preventing them from asserting against his authority any right which did not find its sanction in duty. The King himself was God's lieutenant; his office was a stewardship, and he could not and did not suffer that any should alienate his land by sale or mortgage or export his money, the means of exchange of his people, beyond his dominions. His nobles derived their titles and their lands from him, on account of service, and though bishops and archbishops were subject in spiritual matters to the Pope, they were subject in all temporal affairs to the King, who possessed and exercised the power to advise the Pope, if need be, about their behaviour. Thus the law of duty was upheld worthily before all men, and men were persuaded that, apart from duty, no right can exist or lawfully be sustained.

The reign of Louis XIV of France, by common consent, furnishes the most notable example of an effective Kingship. It began in the welter of parties called the FRONDE, when all powers of rebellion and irresponsible ownership which had re-asserted themselves at the death of Richelieu were ranged against the young King's power. It was carried to heights of dignity and splendour of which the palace of Versailles remains the monument. From first to last the power of money was arrayed against it.

No man possessed a clearer understanding of the nature of the King's office than Louis XIV, and the advice which he bequeathed to his son has lost none of its interest during two centuries.

"Armies, Councils, and all human activities," he wrote, "would be a weak means of maintaining us on the Throne if everyone thought he had an equal right to it with ourselves and did not reverence a Higher Power of which our own is a portion. The public respect which we render to this Invisible Power might, in fact, be called justly the foremost and most important part of our policy, had it not a nobler and more disinterested motive as a duty... Consecration, although it does not confer on us our royal position, does not fail to make it manifest to the people and to render it more August, more invaluable, and more sacred."

Nor was he inclined to overstress the hereditary principle he made a sharp distinction between legitimacy and heredity:

"Empires, my son, are only preserved as they have been acquired - that is to say, by vigour watchfulness and labour... Courage and victories are the election and suffrages of Heaven itself.

... Although in the matter of transgressions Kings are men as much or even more than they are in other things, I do not fear to tell you that this is not so much the case when they are Kings in very truth, because an overmastering and dominating passion, that of their interests, their greatness, and their glory, stifles every other in them... And to speak truly to you, my son, we are wanting not only in gratitude and a sense of justice, but also in prudence and a good sense, when we fail in veneration of Him of Whom we are only the lieutenants. Our submission to Him is the law and example of what is due to us."

He added:

"I have given some consideration to the condition of Kings - hard and rigorous in this respect - who owe, as it were, a public account of their actions to the whole world and to all succeeding centuries... I made a beginning (of my reign) by casting my eyes over all the different parties in the State... Everywhere was disorder... There was no governor of a city who was not himself difficult to govern; no request was made without some complaint of the past or some hint of discontent in the future which I was to expect or to fear... The finances which give movement and action to the great organization of the monarchy were entirely exhausted, so much so that we could hardly find the ways and means... At the same time a prodigality showed itself among public men, masking on the one hand their malversions... and revealing them on the other in insolent and daring luxury... The Church... was threatened with open schism... by Bishops established in their sees and able to draw away the multitude after them... Cardinal de Retz, Archbishop of Paris, whom for well-known reasons of State I could not permit to remain in the Kingdom, encouraged all this rising sect from inclination or interest. The least of the ills affecting the order of Nobility was the fact of its being shared by an infinite number of usurpers possessing no right to it or one acquired by money without any claim arising from service rendered. The tyranny exercised by the nobles over their vassals and neighbours in some of my provinces could no longer be suffered, or suppressed save by making severe and rigorous examples... The administration of Justice itself... appeared to me the most difficult to reform. An infinity of things contributed to this state of affairs, the appointments (to judicial office) filled haphazard or by money rather than by selection and merit... All this collection of evils, their consequences and effects, fell principally upon the people, who, in addition, were loaded with impositions."

The King, as has been said, knew the remedy and applied it. He crushed opposition and made of the rebellious nobles and Churchmen humble servants of the people. And he devoted himself to daily toil:

"Two things," he wrote, "were, without doubt, absolutely necessary: very hard work on my part and a wise choice of persons capable of seconding it... I will warn you, my son, that it is toil by which one reigns and for which one reigns... The only thing I felt was that I was King and born to be one. I experienced next a delicious feeling hard to express, and which you will not know yourself save by tasting it as I have done."

The whole of this Royal philosophy is summed up in the phrase: *L'etat c'est moi*. There was no Frenchman but must perform his duty; there was no privilege but must be derived directly from duty. The King made it his first business to purge his realm of men who had acquired advantages without earning them, and to abolish such offices as were no longer useful to government or to the people. Even the growing power of Money felt the weight of his authority:

"I did a thing," he wrote, "which seemed even too bold, so greatly had the gentlemen of the law profited by it up till then, and so full were their minds of the importance they had acquired in the recent troubles through the abuse of their power. From three-quarters I reduced to a half all the new mortgages which were charged upon my revenue, which had been effected at a very extortionate rate during the War and which were eating up the best of my resources. The officials of the corporations had acquired the greater part of these mortgages and looked upon it as good business to treat their debtor as harshly as possible in his most vital interests. This action of mine was perfectly just, for a half constituted a substantial premium on the sums advanced... It was just that public utility should take the place of all other considerations and reduce everything to its legitimate and natural order... The interests of the State must be the first consideration... The good of the State makes the glory of the King."

Money acquired under Louis' rule a national complexion; it served the ends of the State.

CHAPTER III

THE DOCTRINE OF MONEY

BOTH in England and France, during the Eighteenth Century, the Monarchy transgressed against these principles of Louis XIV though in England the fault was not the King's. The House of Hanover, from its origin, was dependent on the Whig party; the House of Bourbon from its corruption under the Regent Philippe d'Orleans and again under Louis XV, became enervated by pleasure and more and more dependent on the good graces of moneylenders. The Whigs drew a great part of their support from the merchant bankers of the City of London, whose financial operations extended over the whole world; the French nobility and higher clergy, as a consequence of their extravagance, fell into the hands of the Swiss and Dutch bankers. Thus, in these two countries, the internationalism of Money challenged the power of the Throne and began to exert influence on national policy.

So far as Money was concerned there was neither England nor France. Close relations existed already between the banking houses in all European centers. Thus the firm of Thelusson and Necker financed the grain trade in France and England and was connected both in France and England with the trade with the East Indies. This Swiss firm of Geneva had offices both in Paris and London. It made numerous loans to Louis XV and was interested at the same time in loans made to the British Government.

This house, along with many others, discovered in the markets of America, India, and the East a rich field of enterprise. It was contended by these bankers that money, like water, must be free to find its level - that is to say, that they themselves must be free to obtain the largest possible profit irrespective of any national need. It was a claim which Louis XIV would have heard with lively indignation and would have answered by demanding how the advantage of a section or a party should be placed above the advantage of France. Louis XV, on the contrary, sold titles and conferred privileges without regard to service. In consequence he lost the support of his people. France returned to a condition in which parties and factions divided the realm to the advantage of international finance. The Seven Years' War against Frederick the Great and his ally England revealed the ruin which had been wrought. The French arms were everywhere defeated and humiliated, and England seized the opportunity to possess herself of India and Canada. The bankers in their counting-houses, meanwhile, were haunted by the fear that a King of the type of Louis XIV would arise with enough popular backing to sweep away their privileges, and put a stop to their operations in so far as these operations bore heavily upon his people.

The history of the banker Jacques Necker deserves close study as illustrating the precautions of Money. This man, from his counting-house in Paris, in the latter years of the Eighteenth Century took steps to widen as much as possible the breach between Throne and People. With that end in view he made himself the patron of those liberal writers who were finding audiences among the hard-pressed farmers and industrialists. It was an easy matter to persuade these people that Louis XV's faults-which were real enough-were the sole cause of their distresses, and that sovereignty belonged not to the King but to the People. Necker entered into association with the philosophers Voltaire, Montesquieu, and the others, and kept open house in Paris for the entertainment of would be popular leaders of every kind. He was a learned man, big and smug, with a troublesome sense of his own moral worth. The humanistic doctrines of Jean Jacques Rousseau, a fellow Swiss, met with his approval up to a point, and he spent money, of which he possessed enormous quantities, in helping to make them better known.

While Necker was pursuing these ends in France, William Pitt the elder, the son of a wealthy East India merchant, was at work in England defeating the attempts of the young King, George III, to escape from the control of the Whigs and become the leader of the nation. The dice, here, as in France, were loaded against the King. It was Pitt and the Whigs who had wrested India and Canada from France. Pitt was the City of London's man, and employed against his Sovereign the same weapons of newspaper and philosophic propaganda of which Necker was making such deadly use in Paris. The English people were roused against the young King who wished to make peace with France. When the King succeeded in making peace, he was attacked with extreme violence, notably by John Wilkes, and the peace became little more than an armed neutrality.

Far from feeling any patriotic resentment against Pitt, Necker tried to arrange a marriage between his own daughter Germaine and the English minister's son. The truth was that England seemed to be a safer place for plutocracy than France. England was mistress of the seas and therefore able to protect overseas trade; England possessed a Royal House which, in spite of the young King's exuberance, was still insecurely seated; the governing power in England was largely in the hands of the Whigs, who were largely in the hands of the bankers; above all, England possessed the immense overseas Empire which had formerly belonged to France. So excellent a combination of advantages the field of overseas operations, the means of communication, a large home population containing a minimum of peasant proprietors and therefore easy to mobilize for industrial work, a huge public debt, and a weak Monarchy was to be found nowhere else in the world. The English, in addition, being patriotic and good fighters, could be counted on to protect their country, and, being honest, to pay their debts. Their island position made it exceedingly improbable that they would be successfully invaded. London, therefore, suffered the calamity of becoming the financial center and the financial magnet of the world. Money came home, not indeed to roost, but to pause in its flight. The English people were flattered by the opportunities afforded them of getting rich of which a very few availed themselves and by the spectacle of a great Empire and the sovereignty of the seas. They were yoked, at the same time, to the car of Mammon and brought to understand that there is an inexorable economic law which decrees that the wages of an unskilled labourer must remain at the subsistence level and that all other wages must be determined in relation to that level.

Agriculture in England shared with industry the distresses arising out of the growth of the bankers' power. At the beginning of the Eighteenth Century the greater part of England had been covered with open fields in which numbers of small farmers held isolated strips of land. They lived on these strips of land and enjoyed a high degree of independence. But they produced no profits. On the plea that efficient methods of farming could not be introduced while these common holders continued to cumber the ground, Parliament passed a number of Enclosure Acts which had the effect of compelling the cultivator of the strip to merge his rights in those of his richer neighbours. The rich man now planted hedges and dug ditches, and the poor man found himself faced with charges, as a shareholder in the land, which he was quite unable to pay. He had to sell his rights to pay his debts; from independence he sank at once to the position of a hired labourer on the land that had formerly maintained him and his family. The yeomen, worthy backbone of England, were broken and destroyed and their places taken by merchant farmers - wholly dependent on the banks. Agricultural wages were now brought down at once to the barest level of subsistence.

Such were the conditions in England during the latter half of the Eighteenth Century. The conditions in France were worse because, as has been said, money was much more reluctant to remain in that country. French agriculture visibly declined; French industry languished; the condition of the peasants and workpeople became so distressing that men of goodwill were everywhere shocked by it. The King tried to raise further loans in order to help his people - for Louis XV, though a debauched liver, was a man of kindly nature subject to severe pangs of conscience - only to find that, as he was told, his credit was exhausted. Even the imposing spectacle of Versailles, once so powerful a magnet of money, had lost its attraction.

In these circumstances French hatred of England was roused to boiling point. Was it not England who had filched away India and Canada? England who had driven French ships from the sea? England who was sucking the wealth out of Europe as a vampire sucks blood? The King ascribed his poverty to this cause; so did the peasant. Neither King nor peasant was aware that Englishmen as a whole, had derived no advantage and were suffering the same distresses as their neighbours.

Money, in fact, concealed its operations so successfully that the hatred engendered by its operations was felt not against itself but against Englishmen and Frenchmen. Necker took occasion to deplore this exhibition of nationalist feeling. He was accustomed to call himself a good European and to suggest that it was the mission of bankers to bring nations closer together. This was the cue for the philosophers, economists, journalists, and wits who thronged his wife's salon and enjoyed his own lavish hospitality. They deplored the senseless luxury of

Versailles, which, as they urged, had to be paid for by the tears and sweat of the people, and shook their heads over the King's rising indignation against the excellent people of England. In London the same sentiments were being expressed, in the same language, by Necker's partner the Swiss, Thelusson, and his fellow bankers. What a pity French nationalism was so troublesome and so blind!

CHAPTER IV

TURGOT

So swift was the flow of wealth out of England to those American colonies where the labour of negro slaves was enabling huge profits to be obtained in short periods of time, that King George III determined to bring some of the wealth back again by means of taxation. The Stamp Act was passed.

The effect was terrific. No more deadly threat to the system of international finance could have been imagined. Pitt uttered protests no less vigorous than those which came immediately from the other side of the Atlantic. The King's right to impose taxation of any kind on colonists was sharply called in question, and in the following year, 1766, the Stamp Act was repealed.

But George III was obdurate. In 1767 he secured the passage of an Act to tax American Imports, and again found himself assailed by the City of London as well as by the colonists. The opposition became violent; in 1770 this Act also was repealed, only the tax on tea remaining.

But the bankers were in no mood for compromise. They continued to agitate with all their might. The King, unshaken in his resolution, reaffirmed his right to impose taxation on the colonists. In 1770 the people of Boston rebelled; in 1775 the American War of Independence was made inevitable by the colonists' formal denial of the King's right.

That year, in France, witnessed the death of Louis XV and the ascent of the throne by his grandson, Louis XVI, a young man imbued, like George III, with high ideals, and like him determined, if possible, to rescue the people by restoring the Royal authority. Louis XVI chose as his foreign minister Vergennes, a man firmly of opinion that France's troubles sprang out of the triumph of England. Vergennes' sole idea was to resist English influence throughout the world. He saw a golden opportunity in the troubles in America.

The bankers, especially Necker, were rejoiced at this turn of events; for the behaviour of the King of England filled them with consternation. If investment in the British Overseas Empire was to be subject to tax, where were they? Necker, acting in secret, made it possible for King Louis and Vergennes to send help to the American colonists; at the same time he paid a visit to his London office, taking his wife and daughter with him. As the agitation against the war in America and in favour of the Colonists was still going on in London, he had no need to hide his views. He found his English colleagues hopeful that King George III would receive a severe lesson, but not anxious that war should break out between France and England. These were his own views. It was essential, as he thought, that the King of England should be taught his place in relation to finance; but not at the expense of an upheaval such as a great European war, with its attendant outbreaks of patriotic fervour, must occasion, since such a war would inevitably, for a time at any rate, heal the breach between the King of France and his people and so restore to the King his sovereign power. Necker returned from London in an anxious frame of mind.

His anxieties were not lessened by when he heard about the activities of another of King Louis' ministers, the Comptroller General Turgot.

Anne Robert Jacques Turgot was fifty. His grandfather had served Louis XIV with distinction; his father, as *Prévôt des Marchands*, had instituted an excellent system of sanitation for the City of Paris. Service was in young Turgot's blood; he showed his capacity for service when, in 1761, he was appointed by Louis XV Intendant of Limoges. This was a poor and backward district; he set himself the task of being the friend of the people placed under his care.

"Everything," he declared, "in these God-forsaken provinces reflected the image of ignorance and of barbarism in the middle of the Eighteenth Century."

He wrote immediately to his subordinates:

"Do not neglect to instruct yourself on the state of agriculture in each parish, the quantity of lands in waste, the reclamation of which these are susceptible, the principal production of the soil, the object to which the industry of the inhabitants is applied...."

The information which Turgot gathered showed him how harshly the taxes pressed on the poor and how wrong it was that the 130,000 clergy and 140,000 nobles in France, who, between them, owned the larger part of the land, were privileged that is to say, exempt from taxation. He wrote letter after letter to Versailles urging that the burden of taxation in his province should be reduced by at least 700,000 livres (£28,000). But the King was without resources and did not dare to offend the nobles and their creditors the bankers.

A famine occurred in Limoges. Turgot took active measures to feed his people and quickly find that the lords of the grain trade, over which Necker presided, had discovered ground of offense. On May 14, 1770, he wrote to Versailles:

"In times of scarcity it is humane and even just to bring the law to the help of the over-burdened farmer. The landlord, whom the scarcity enriches, cannot, without showing most odious greed, attempt to draw, from the cruel circumstances when his tenant is now placed, a profit still more exorbitant than before."

Turgot held the view that agriculture was the bedrock of national prosperity, and declared:

"Finances are necessary; for a State must have revenue; but agriculture and commerce are, or rather agriculture animated by commerce is, the ultimate source of these revenues. If State finance is injurious to commerce it is injurious to itself. These two interests are essentially united... Government ought to remove those obstacles which retard the progress of industry... (for example) the high rate of interest charged on money. This (high rate of interest) offers to all possessors of capital the mean of living without working, encourages luxury and idleness, and withdraws from commerce (and so renders unproductive for the State) the wealth and work of a large number of citizens.

"High rates of interest, further, prevent the nation from engaging is branches of commerce which do not yield one or two per cent. more than these rates... and condemn to be left uncultivated all the lands of the kingdom that cannot yield more than five per cent., since, with the capital needed to develop these lands, one could, without working, procure the same return."

Turgot, in short, as an opponent of the doctrine that money must find its level, was an enemy of international finance. He saw, clearly enough, that if money was poured out in America and India, it would become ruinously dear in France, and that the consequences must be a starvation of French agriculture and industry, unemployment, poverty, and a home market incapable by reason of its lack of purchasing power of absorbing home production. He saw further that the goods which could not be sold at home would have to be sold in foreign markets if producers were to live. Thus he became an active opponent of the bankers' doctrine of the supreme importance and value of the export trade as opposed to the home trade.

The fact that Louis XVI, on coming to the throne, had chosen this man as his financial adviser excited, as has been said, a lively anxiety in the minds of financiers all the world over. They would have been more anxious still had they been able to read Turgot's first memorandum to his King:

"So long," he wrote, "as finance shall be continually subject to the old expedients in order to provide for State services, your Majesty will always be dependent upon financiers, and they will ever be the masters, and by the manoeuvres belonging to their trade, they will frustrate the most important operations. Thus the Government can never feel itself at ease, it can never be acknowledged as able to sustain itself, because the discontents and impatience of the people are always the means made use of by intriguing and ill-disposed men in order to excite disturbance."

Turgot's policy consisted of No bankruptcy; no increase of taxes; no loans. In the impoverished condition of France he urged the King to practice a rigid economy. He added:

"I feel all the danger to which I expose myself. I foresee that I shall be alone in fighting against abuses of every kind, against the power of those who profit by these abuses, against the crowd of prejudiced people who oppose themselves to all reform and who are such powerful instruments in the hands of interested parties for propagating the disorder. And this people for whom I shall sacrifice myself are so easily deceived that, perhaps, I shall encounter their hatred by the very measures I take to protect them against exactions."

Louis XVI promised his new finance minister his wholehearted support. Turgot immediately decided to remove the restrictions on the free sale of wheat throughout France, so that in times of famine, such as he had experienced at Limoges, wheat might be brought easily from districts where it was plentiful to districts where it was scarce. The effect of this measure was to cause an immediate fall in the price of bread at a moment when, thanks to a bad harvest, the price was very high. Necker and the other bankers who financed the grain trade were filled with alarm. Necker at once composed a pamphlet against Turgot's policy and caused it to be widely circulated.

The pamphlet failed to influence the King. Immediately riots began to break out in many departments. The first of these occurred at Dijon on April 20, 1775. After that Pontoise was affected, then Versailles, then Paris. It was observed that the rioters were liberally supplied with money, both gold and silver, and that their sole object was to destroy wheat. They pillaged the bakers' shops in Paris and flung masses of bread into the Seine while shrieking for cheaper bread. The *parlement* of Paris, in which Necker's influence was strong, looked on without concern. Turgot saw his expectations fulfilled. With the King's concurrence he put down the riots and compensated those who had suffered loss. But he realized that the forces ranged against him were as powerful as they were full of resource and cunning. His best endeavours failed to establish the identity of the fomenters of riot.

The battle between King and bankers was now joined in France as well as in England. Turgot urged Louis to purge France of privileged persons and so restore the system of service:

"Privilege," he wrote, "was founded at a time when the nobles, as a class, were under special obligations to render military service which they fulfilled in person at their own expense. Now, on the one side, this personal service having become more inconvenient than useful is fallen entirely into disuse; on the other side all the military power of the State consists in a numerous army, kept up and maintained at all times by the State. Such of the nobles as serve in this army are paid by the State; and not only are they under no obligation to serve, but on the contrary it is the common people alone who are compelled to serve since the establishment of the militia, from which the nobles and even their valets are specially exempt."

"Another reason operates to make privilege most unjust and at the same time contemptible. It is that, by reason of the ease with which nobility may be acquired by paying for it, the body of the noble corresponds to the body of the rich, and the cause of the privileged is no longer the cause of distinguished families against the common people, but the cause of the rich against the poor. The reasons we might have had to respect this privilege when it was confined to the ancient defenders of the State certainly cannot be entertained when the privilege has become common even to the race of financiers (revenue farmers) and contractors who have plundered the State."

Turgot proposed a tax on land to be paid by all holders no matter what their station. He proposed further the supersession of the obsolete *parlements* by local authorities of a representative character and the abolition of the rights of ancient trade guilds and corporations whereby industry and commerce were held in thrall. It was a return to Royal feudalism; everyone possessed of any sort of privilege was threatened. Suddenly, therefore, the financiers found themselves supported by a host of courtiers, higher clergy, nobles, lawyers, and craftsmen, all of whom desired to see Turgot and his schemes brought to ruin. France was in an uproar; even the King's Cabinet was divided, but the King stood firm:

"I have read with care," Louis XVI wrote to Turgot, "all the memorials which you have submitted to the Council, and the six projects of edicts which I have already approved. The want of unanimity is my Council upon these proposals, and the opposition they have met with outside, have given me much to think about; but the projects appear to me too useful and conformable to the public welfare not to be published and maintained by my whole authority... There are so many private interests opposed to the general interest. The more I think of it, my dear Turgot, the more I repeat to myself that there are only you and I who really love the people."

Necker was anxious and so were his colleagues in London, for while the King of France was endearing himself to his people by his wise and just policy, the King of England looked like bringing the American colonists to submission. An attack by the colonists on Canada had failed, and though the English had been forced to evacuate Boston, Washington was in great anxiety that New York would fall into their hands. His troops were far from satisfactory and, as he wrote himself, "Money is much wanted."

A flight from the dollar was, in fact, in progress, for the very last thing that any of those who had sought profit in America desired was to lose their money:

"The resources of domestic loans," wrote Washington at a later period, "are inconsiderable because there are, properly speaking, few moneyed men, and the few there are can employ their money more profitably otherwise; added to which the instability of the currency and the deficiency of funds have impaired the public credit."

In these circumstances Necker and his friends overcame their repugnance to a war between France and England. If France and perhaps Spain also supported the American colonists openly, they argued, the odds were that the policy of King George III would fail. Moreover the King of France would be plunged so deeply in debt by reason of his expenditure on ships and troops as to be unable to pursue his policy of reform. The reasoning was sound; but nothing could be done so long as Turgot continued to enjoy King Louis' support. Necker devoted himself, therefore, in the first instance, to the ruin of the minister. Three separate means to this end were employed. In the first place, as has been said, it was represented to the King, through his Foreign Minister, Vergennes, that the moment had come to make England restore some of the possessions she had taken from France, and notably Canada. Vergennes himself was sincerely convinced of the justice of this view, and had already crossed swords with Turgot in the King's Council because the Controller was opposed to war. The King confessed himself sorely tempted to make war and argued, with reason, that reforms which were difficult to accomplish in the existing state of affairs would present far less difficulty to a King who had achieved the glory of victory and the restoration of lost provinces.

The second line of attack was made by Necker himself. He drew up a memorandum on the budget which his adversary had produced for 1776, in which he criticized Turgot's powers as a financier. As Necker was a multi-millionaire with the reputation of a financial wizard, these criticisms might be expected to influence the King to whom they were submitted. Incidentally Necker offered, if he himself was appointed Comptroller, to arrange for the King the loans which would be necessary in the event of a war with England. (Turgot had arranged a loan with the Dutch on the definite understanding that there would be no fresh expenditure of any sort.)

Finally Marie Antoinette was enlisted against Turgot. The Queen did not like the minister; but she had not made any open attack upon him. It was now represented to her that the disgrace of the young Comte de Guines, to whom she was attached, was due to Turgot's influence with her husband. This was not, in fact, the case. De Guines, who was French Ambassador in London, had been recalled at the instance of Vergennes because he had acted indiscreetly in his dealings with the English Cabinet. Marie Antoinette implored the King to dismiss both ministers. Louis promised to make de Guines a duke, but refused further to commit himself.

"M. Turgot," wrote the Swedish Ambassador to his King, Gustavus III, "finds himself threatened by the most formidable league composed of all the great people of the kingdom, of all the parlements, of all the financiers, of all the ladies of the Court."

Louis XVI was by no means the henpecked husband which it has pleased some historians to call him. He remained unshaken in his view that Turgot's reforms were necessary. But he felt himself incapable, in the weak state of the Monarchy, of carrying out these reforms against the united opposition of clergy, nobles, and financiers to say nothing of his own Court. Reform, he declared in effect, is impossible without glory, and glory can only be won in a war with England. Turgot replied in a series of letters in which he used plain language. In the last of these he urged:

"Do not forget, Sire, that it was weakness that brought the head of Charles I to the block... You, Sire, have been sometimes believed to be weak, but I have seen you, in trying circumstances, show real courage. You have said yourself, Sire, that you lack experience, that you have need of a guide. For such a guide, intelligence and energy of character are both required...

"See, Sire, how you stand: with a ministry weak and disunited; outside, all minds in fermentation, the parlements leagued with all the discontented parties, the revenue short of the expenditure, the greatest resistance being made to an indispensable economy, no harmony in your council, no fixedness in its plans, no secrecy kept about its decisions..."

Louis dismissed his minister and made de Guines a duke as he had promised.

"What gratifies me most, I must confess," wrote the Marquise du Deffand, an old lady of the Court, "is the triumph of M. de Guines. What joy M. Necker will feel!"

She was not mistaken. Necker was summoned to take charge of the King's finances. A loan was forthcoming and the war with England began. Turgot's reforms, those dealing with the corn trade among the others, were flung on the rubbish heap.

Chapter V

King and Banker

EVERYTHING happened as the financiers had arranged. The American Colonists obtained their independence thanks, in large measure, to French help; France obtained very little; George III was humiliated, lost his popularity, end began to show signs of having lost his reason as well. America, France, and England emerged from the struggle staggering under the weight of a load of debt which promised to keep all three in chains to the bankers for generations. So far as America and England were concerned there was nothing more to be said. But in France the case was different. Louis XVI, in spite of having dismissed Turgot, had not abandoned his plans. And he was able to offset his sorry financial plight with the satisfaction felt by his people at the spectacle of England's humiliation.

That spectacle had aroused the greatest enthusiasm from the moment of France's entry into the war in 1778. The King was entitled to congratulate himself that he had not erred in contending that glory was essential to the upholding of his authority. But just as he began to adopt a firmer tone, his new Finance Minister, Necker, sprang a surprise on him. Without asking his King's consent, this man published a statement of his King's accounts, private as well as public, under the insolent title of *Compte Rendu*. The object was to show that, under Necker's thrifty stewardship, the King's income was fully adequate to meet the King's expenses-and that, consequently, there was no need to make the privileged classes contribute a penny of taxation. The inference was that France's financial troubles were due, not to the policy of the financiers in sending money out of the country, nor to the exemptions from taxation granted to the Church and the nobles, but solely to the extravagance of the King himself.

In fact, Necker had falsified his accounts to show a balance when, actually, there was a deficit. This was not discovered till later. The appearance of *Compte Rendu* caused a tremendous outburst of excitement, and gave delight to clergy and nobles as well as financiers. The people of Paris, now falling under the influence of Necker's paid writers and agitators (he kept a Press of his own), hailed this false balance sheet as a revelation from heaven and bared their teeth against the King, who, whatever his mistakes, had no wish except to do them good. Louis began to see that Turgot had told him the truth when he wrote in reference to one of the ministers who had helped Necker to compass his fall:

"He does not see that, after having isolated me, after having prejudiced your Majesty against me, and having compelled me to leave you, the whole storm directed now against me, will come in time to burst upon himself and that he will end in failure, dragging with him, in his fall, your authority."

Turgot died in the year *Compte Rendu* was published; it was too late to summon again that stout heart. The King dismissed Necker and banished him to his estate of Saint-Ouen, twenty miles from Paris. The capital began to snarl against the palace; thousands of citizens wore green cockades, green being the colour of the banker's livery. Necker, in his retirement, began to write a history of religion, but his friends in Paris carried on his work by means of a vigorous propaganda, the object of which was to suggest that the American War of Independence was a revolt of free men against the tyranny of a King. All that the banker's hirelings wrote and spoke against George III of England applied with equal force to Louis XVI of France. The free men of the City of Paris were duly edified, and when the young Marquis de Lafayette came back from America made a hero of him. Lafayette announced himself a Liberal, adopted airs of patronage towards the King and Queen, and spoke without ceasing of *my friend Washington*. King Louis began to see that the glory of the American adventure had been filched away from him.

The cost of the adventure, on the contrary, was fixed upon his shoulders. He was quickly made aware that his dismissal of Necker had roused against him the wrath of the world's bankers. He found himself unable to borrow, and tried to revert to Turgot's plan for a tax on the privileged classes. The roar of execration which greeted this project showed how effective had been Necker's propaganda. It was no longer the King's minister who was attacked, it was the King. What, cried the clergy and nobles, the *parlements* and financiers, is France to be sacrificed to the wild extravagance of Versailles? Did not the excellent M. Necker show that the revenue was large enough to pay all the necessary expenses? The King shrank before the blast. In a kind of despair he heard all the privileged asserting what they called their rights in tones of menace.

The great lords laid heavy hands on the countryside; the army was purged of plebeian officers; the Church asserted her right of ordering the civil estate of all Frenchmen.

Sectionalism, in short, tore the nation asunder as it had been torn asunder during the Middle Ages. Monarchy, stripped of prestige and penniless, was compelled to look on. Every attempt which the King made to raise a fresh loan was met, by the bankers, with blank refusal. They had him firmly in their clutches and were in no mood to allow him to escape. Despair descended on Versailles; but the darkness in the King's mind possessed, in addition, a tragic quality because he was utterly alone. Even his wife was out of sympathy with him; his brothers were frankly hostile. These could not see, as he saw, that the root-cause of all their troubles was the breakdown of the system of service occasioned by the feebleness of the King's power.

Louis was not a brilliant man; his mind moved slowly. But the operations of his mind were just and temperate. He realized the religious devotion of his people and the immerse love of country surging in their hearts; he felt their attachment to the sacred soil; he knew their patience and courage in adversity. He knew, too, how swift was the movement of the French mind. If he could show his people a Kingship animated by a lofty patriotism, old and yet new, unhampered by privilege and inspired only by the service of God, they would belong to him once more. It would be possible then to purge the Church of the scandals which were repelling honest men and to raise up again the sense of reverence even in instructed minds. Like his ancestor Louis XIV, he willed a liberal-minded Monarchy in association with a liberal-minded Church; unlike Louis XIV, he lacked the means to make his vision effective.

In his extremity he sent his wretched minister Calonne to address the *parlement* of Paris and the Assembly of the notables—bodies consisting wholly of privileged persons and therefore implacably hostile. Calonne was to urge that a tax on land had become an urgent necessity and to point out that Necker's statement of the royal accounts was false as well as insolent. The minister discharged his task; he was met in both instances with a contemptuous refusal to listen to his proposals.

But Necker felt himself wounded by the plain and true statement that he was a liar. He composed hastily a *Mémoire jusficatif* and sent it to the King. Louis forbade him to publish it. He disobeyed. The King banished him to a distance of one hundred miles from Paris. The banker's friends saw to it that he was presented to the public as a holy martyr in the cause of French liberty. Once again there were demonstrations in his favour in Paris. His daughter Germaine, recently married to the Baron de Staël-Holstein, the Swedish Ambassador in France, rushed of to Versailles to pour out her grievance to the Queen, who, however, received her coldly and refused to interfere. Madame de Staël, from that moment, vowed hostility to the Royal Family. She held her father in such adoration that she was unable to see the smallest fault in anything which he said or did. She kept open house at the Swedish Embassy in the Rue du Bac, and entertained there all the people who were opposed to the King—nobles, churchmen, financiers, philosophers, journalists, and wits. The King's half-uncle, de Narbonne, an illegitimate son of Louis XV, was already one of her lovers; Talleyrand, Bishop of Autun, was another. These gay fellows looked forward to the day when Louis would be compelled to come hat in hand to the banker, whose daughter's favours they enjoyed, and when they, in consequence, would gather up the reins of government.

The King, meanwhile, found a new Finance Minister in the person of Lomenie de Brienne, Cardinal Archbishop of Tours. Brienne was sent to address the *parlement* and the Notables, but met with no better success than his predecessor. The King found himself at the end of his resources. In these critical circumstances he tried to act alone. He exiled the *parlement* from Paris and imposed his land tax. Nobody paid it. Worse still, this assembly of persons privileged to pay no taxes while the poor were bowed to the earth by the burdens placed on them became heroes of the Parisian mob. It says much for the skill with which Necker conducted his propaganda that it succeeded in convincing thousands of good citizens that the harpies who were devouring their vitals were their best friends and that the King, who was trying to make these harpies disgorge, was a tyrant and a spendthrift.

Louis was now defeated; he had but a few thousand pounds in his coffers and no prospect of receiving any more. In bitter humiliation he sent for Necker. Instantly in a single day the funds increased in value by thirty per cent. Necker recalled the parlement, and it was greeted by the Parisians with showers of roses. The banker told the King that he must forthwith summon the States General, the Parliament of the Nation.

Louis was not averse from that step, for he felt that he had nothing to fear from Frenchmen, once his ideas were made known to them. But he reckoned without his Necker. It was no part of the banker's plan to allow the King to reestablish relations with the people. On the contrary, he proposed that the States General should be wholly subservient to himself, should take its orders from him, and should set up at once a constitutional Monarchy on the English pattern with himself as Chief Minister. The State General consisted of three houses, the Clergy, the Nobles, and the *Tiers État*. These Estates sat separately and voted as bodies, so that if any two of them were agreed the third was bereft of power.

Now that he was in supreme command, Necker troubled no longer to keep up the pretence that the King's income was sufficient for his expenditure. Thanks to the huge burden of debt incurred in the American War, the Budget, on the contrary, was hopelessly unbalanced, and a large part of the debt belonged to Necker himself and his friends. The project of the tax on land, therefore, found favour, suddenly, with the man who had been its most bitter opponent. To the consternation of his friends, the Clergy and Nobles, Necker informed the Assembly of Notables that the land tax must be collected. They drove him forth as they had driven forth Calonne and Lomenie de Brienne before him.

Next day they woke up to find that this was no longer the helpless King of France with whom they had to deal, but a master who knew how to exact obedience. Suddenly the newspapers which had made heroes of these privileged persons changed their tune. The Notables were called robbers of the poor and drones in the hive. The mob put away its roses and doubled its fists. When Necker appeared before the *parlement* of Paris he was met with cringing submission. By all means let his Majesty take such steps as seemed good to him. The banker returned to Versailles and suggested to the King that, as the population of France had doubled since the last meeting of the States General, more than 160 years before, the number of members of the *Tiers État* or Commons, ought likewise to be increased. The King agreed. Necker congratulated himself that everything was perfectly in train.

For he saw that the huge body of Commons would not submit to being outvoted by the combined Clergy and Nobles. The Commons would inevitably demand voting by head instead of voting by Chamber. They would thus acquire the same dominating position as the Commons of England. Most of Necker's friends were likely to be found in the Commons' house.

Chapter VI

Tribune and Banker

NECKER had made only one miscalculation, but that proved to be serious. He had reckoned without a man; Providence sent Mirabeau. Mirabeau was the second son of a doctrinaire father, who had lived, all his life, in violent opposition to that father, to his relations, to his King, to his fellows. Gabriel Riquetti, Comte de Mirabeau, was steeped in debaucheries, but had carried out of a wasted youth a heart very easily moved and a brain swift in action and vast in its powers of understanding. Mirabeau was huge, his face possessed a great broadness which supported handsomely his wide, high forehead. Hair, like Samson's, rioted on his head so that, when he was angry, he looked like a lion. But he was not often angry. On the contrary, his big, hooked nose surmounted lips of a singular proudness of expression. The man had noble stamped on his face; he possessed all the vices which have been imputed to his caste; but he was great, nevertheless, of spirit, deep of wisdom, generous of enthusiasm, and reckless wholly where personal interests were concerned. Such a man was bound to hate Necker; actually the smug manner of the banker produced a kind of madness in the tribune's mind. The two men choked in each other's company.

Necker addressed the States General after the King, but failed to enlighten them. Within a few days his calculations were justified; the Commons had opened an attack on the Clergy and the Nobles and had demanded voting by head. King Louis tried to keep out of the quarrel, and might have succeeded had not the citizens of Paris taken a hand in the dispute. Necker's Press in the capital had begun to demand that the King should compel the Clergy and Nobles to sit and vote with the representatives of the people. There were riots. The Commons became nervous and then defiant. They declared themselves a National Assembly and denied the King's right to dissolve them. Louis summoned the three estates to a Royal Sitting and again addressed them. He unfolded his own plans - namely, the complete abolition of all privileges, equal justice for all Frenchmen, equal opportunity, equal service. He bade the estates continue to sit separately as before. It is possible that he would have been obeyed in spite of Mirabeau's dramatic outburst that the Commons sat by the will of the people, had not Necker chosen the occasion to tender his resignation.

The banker had foreseen this move of the King to carry his policy and re-establish relations with his people. He had provided against it. The moment his resignation became known Versailles and Paris too were in uproar. Angry crowds demonstrated before the palace, and the King heard expressed by them the view that he was about to dismiss the States General and institute again his despotic methods. The excitement became so great and the crowds grew so menacing that Louis feared a riot. He sent for Necker, agreed to the condition that the three Estates should sit together and vote together, and restored the banker to his office. Necker was borne from the palace shoulder-high by his supporters, who became delirious in praising his wisdom, his courage, his patriotism, and his moderation.

Mirabeau observed the scene with growing uneasiness. He saw Necker's game and he detested it. The hero who arrived by means of famine, we one of the curses which he hurled at the banker. He wrote secretly to the King offering help and advice. But Louis shrank from a man possessed of so evil a reputation. The tribune therefore used his eloquence to attack and discredit the minister in the Assembly. Necker's reputation waned in Versailles.

It remained as high as everhigher than everin Paris. Paris began to complain that the Parliament at Versailles was going to sleep. It was falling under the influence of the Court. It was learning manners and forgetting the people. Mirabeau saw the hand of Necker in this propaganda. But he had no weapons with which to defeat it. He wrote again to the King, but received no answer. He began to absent himself from the Assembly, where the chief subject of discussion was the Declaration of the Rights of Man.

"**What is wanted,**" cried Mirabeau, "**is a declaration of duties.**" The King held the same opinion. Necker had foiled his attempt to establish relations with his Parliament; Necker was exciting the Parisian mob against him. He resolved to fight with such weapons as remained to him. Troops were ordered to approach Paris and Versailles. On July 12,

1789, the King dismissed Necker and ordered him to leave France instantly. The banker departed from Versailles the same night, with Madame de Staël and her husband in pursuit as soon as they learned the news. Next morning Paris went mad. Everyone wore green, and even the trees in the Tuileries gardens were stripped of their leaves to supply *Necker cockades*. The mob attacked the Great State prison, the Bastille, entered it by a ruse, and on July 14 razed it to the ground. The Town Council of Paris turned itself into a kind of Government, and as the Commune enlisted a National Guard with Lafayette the hero of the American War, as its General.

This was revolution. Louis despatched messengers after Necker bidding him come back. Meanwhile, at Lafayette's order, he came himself to Paris of the day after the riot, gave his approval to the Commune and the National Guard, and actually pinned on his breast the new cockade which Lafayette had made.

By this bitter humiliation was the King of France taught the power and resource of Money. His brother of England had already undergone a punishment which, if less severe, was not less difficult to endure. In 1780 Dunning had carried, by 233 votes to 215 in the House of Common, a motion: *"That the power of the Crown has increased, is increasing, and ought to be diminished."* Since then, as has been said, George III had tasted the bitterness of defeat at the hands of Washington and later at the hands of the Whigs and the City of London. His Civil List had been drastically overhauled and he himself had, temporarily, lost his reason and been placed under restraint.

Chapter VII

ROBESPIERRE

NECKER had reached Bâle on his way back to Geneva when King Louis' messengers found him. He and his wife and daughter set out, next day, to return to Paris.

It was a triumphal march. Those French country folk whom this man had pillaged during years, and from whom he had snatched the reforms prepared for them by their King and his minister, Turgot, displayed an overflowing gratitude. The banker addressed to them, at every posthouse, pious words of exhortation. They responded by filling his carriage with flowers and his ears with praise. He drove direct to Versailles. Next day he made his entry into Paris and showed himself to the people from the balcony of the Hôtel de Ville. Madame de Staël swooned with joy.

A fortnight later the nobles who were members of the Assembly renounced their privileges in a sitting which was characterized by every sort of manifestation of hysteria, and the Feudal System was pronounced dead and buried. But these same nobles showed themselves reluctant to subscribe to a loan which Necker floated a few days later and to which, as a piece of window-dressing, he himself subscribed about £100,000.

The failure of the loan and the impossibility of collecting any taxes, after the abolition of the system of taxation, occasioned the banker grave anxiety. He addressed anxious letters to the Assembly informing its members that the Government was bankrupt and that it was impossible to pay the interests due on the loans. Nobody gave any attention to him; worse still, he convinced himself that the King was awaiting a favourable opportunity to leave Versailles and betake himself to some part of his realm farther removed from Paris and its mobs. He played again the card which, until now, had never failed to achieve success. It was suggested in the capital that the Assembly was once more forgetting its mission and that, in consequence, it would soon fall a victim to Royal tyranny. The King, the rumour ran, meant to go to Rouen and to summon the Parliament to follow him. Once he got safely away the chains would soon be fastened again on his people's necks.

Lafayette, who kept in touch with Madame de Staël, began to speak of going to Versailles and bringing King and Assembly back with him to Paris. The National Guard took up its General's cry. It was repeated in the streets, until the gutters resounded with it. When Paris learned that the Queen had presented herself at a banquet given by the officers of the Guard and had bidden the officers remove their tricolour cockades and wear again the Bourbon white, the tide of wrath apparently overflowed, for a mob of women, largely of the prostitute class, and all liberally supplied with wine, marched out to Versailles shouting like the mobs which had demonstrated against Turgot for bread, which, clearly they did not want. The King ordered his carriages; the people of Versailles, the same who had carried Necker shoulder high, refused to let them pass. After a hideous night, during the course of which the mob broke into the palace and threatened to murder the Queen, Louis and Marie Antoinette were compelled to accompany the women to Paris. Lafayette had marched out his National Guard with the avowed object of protecting the King; he offered no resistance to the mob's fury.

The Assembly followed the King; Versailles was deserted. The banker made sure now that his demands for money would be attended to. He was not mistaken. With the mob howling in the galleries the representatives of the People descended swiftly to earth. Madame de Staël's lover, Talleyrand, Bishop of Autun, having proposed that the nation should possess itself of the lands of the Church, these were immediately seized to serve as security for further borrowing. Necker had won. He had the King under lock and key in the old palace of the Tuileries; he had the Assembly held in living fear of the Parisian mob, which he alone could direct; and here was a rich harvest in the shape of the plunder of Mother Church ready for his honest reaping. He made haste to thrust in his sickle.

He urged that the Church lands should be made over to the bankers in exchange for a loan to the Government to be issued by the bankers, to be redeemable on a fixed date and to carry interest.

Holders of the loan were to possess the right to change their paper for land. The bankers, in other words, were not disposed to trust the Government's bare word. Mirabeau criticized the project by asking why the Government should lend to itself and pay interest for so doing. Was not the land of France the property of the French people? Why pledge it to bankers in exchange for their paper? Let the Government pay its creditors in its own paper, giving these creditors the right to change the paper for land if they so desired. No interest would require to be paid on such paper, and redemption would lie with the holders of the paper, who could use it as money or turn it into land at their discretion. Is the land not there? Mirabeau asked. Is it not the good soil of the father-land? What better security can any man desire?

Necker's plan, in other words, was a fresh loan from the bankers secured on the Church lands. With the proceeds of this new loan the Government could pay its debts to Finance. The advantages, as the banker saw them, were a safe investment yielding a good rate of interest; the repayment of earlier and less well secured loans; above all, no possibility of an increase in the quantity of money in circulation which would have the effect of lowering the value of all investments. Mirabeau cared nothing for these ideas. He was out to serve France, not international finance. He saw in Necker's scheme chains for Government and people. The interest payments on Necker's new loan would prevent expenditure on the reforms which all, Louis XVI included, knew to be urgently necessary; they would place the Government in the position of hopeless debtor to the bankers, who would be free to invest their interests abroad, and thus further reduce the quantity of money in France. Finance, in short, would take the place of the Church as the largest landowner in the kingdom and so obtain, virtually, the sovereign power.

But the Assembly distrusted Mirabeau and feared Necker, who had the mob of Paris at his back. Necker's propagandists were shouting the word inflation from the housetops and demanding why the wages of the poor should be paid in worthless paper." The Assembly, which was unskilled in money matters, was stampeded. With the bogey of inflation before its eyes, and the yelping pack of banker's scribes and orators at its heels, it voted for Necker's plan.

The banker experienced a great relief, for, in truth, the standing loans which he and his friends had made to the King were much too big and much too unsafe for his liking. Necker proceeded with the help of the Church lands to set his house in order. But he had reckoned without the French people. The new loan was an act of deflation because it enabled the Government to pay its debts without creating any fresh money, and so was the means of transferring a large block of purchasing power to the bankers. The effect was to increase the existing stringency and to cause hoarding of coin in anticipation of a crash. The bankers were trying to get their money out of France; notes no longer commanded any confidence. A money scarcity began.

"If Necker remains another month," Mirabeau cried, "there will not be an ecu in circulation in the country."

The situation grew desperate; commerce came to a standstill; the cities were threatened with famine because nobody would accept Necker's bank notes, and all the coin had disappeared. In these circumstances the demand that the Government should be allowed to pay its debts directly in the new landpaper was revived. Mirabeau took it up; the Assembly rallied to him. "This paper," he cried again, "is circulating land. What better security do you want?" Necker's heart sank. He saw his loans being repaid in paper which would possess little or no international value, since its backing was the soil of Revolutionary France. He would no longer possess the least hold over the Government, for the Assignats, as the land notes were called, would bear no interest and be irredeemable in money. France's wealth would be attached to the soil, so to speak, and would no longer be available for transference to other lands offering higher rates of interest and better security. He protested, argued, threatened. Mirabeau tore him to pieces. The mob, obedient so long, went over to the enemy, and the banker sank under a tornado of execration. He fled from France and with difficulty gained his native Switzerland. Politics had conquered finance.

Mirabeau, almost alone among his contemporaries, understood what had happened. Necker, as he saw, had fallen victim to his own plotting. He had shaken so successfully the confidence of the French people in their King that the King's credit was no longer good. There was the explanation of the hoarding of coin and the refusal to give goods for paper. Recovery depended, therefore, on a restoration of the King to his people's affection and respect. If that could be achieved, the new land-paper would circulate freely because faith in it would be established.

Louis would then possess the means of getting rid of his debt and of giving effect to all his projects of reform.

Mirabeau set himself to accomplish for the King what the King could not, by any means, achieve for himself. He constituted himself the Royal mentor, and wrote letter after letter explaining his policy. The King was to assume his rightful place as the leader of the Revolution; the Revolution was to be shown in its true character as a restoration of the God-system of service. The tribune himself wooed and won the Paris mob, charming it by his eloquence. He exalted the Monarchy as the lively foundation of government and urged, again and again, that King and Nation were necessary to one another, so that if they became separated, catastrophe in the shape of the rule of force and fear must follow.

The Assembly heard this doctrine with patience if not with pleasure. Nobody, as yet, dreamed of abolishing the monarchy, but many people hoped to rule it. Mirabeau advised the King to leave Paris openly, go to Rouen or Compiégne and summon his Parliament to follow him, on the ground that the state of feeling in Paris made calm deliberation impossible. For a short time it seemed that Louis might follow this advice. The King has been blamed severely for not following it. But it may very well be that he was right in thinking that the estrangement from his people, which Necker had brought about, was of such a character that action in accordance with Mirabeau's advice would have been the signal for civil war. The opportunity, if it was an opportunity, passed quickly. Mirabeau died. Louis with his wife and children tried to leave France, was arrested at the frontier, and became the prisoner of his Government.

It was a Liberal Government, under the influence of Madame de Staël, Necker's daughter. Its object was to restore sound finance by a discreet use of the Royal authority. Madame de Staël's lover, Louis de Narbonne, was Minister of War. With her help he planned a campaign against Austria and compelled the King to fall in with his plans. The land-paper money fell sharply in value, and Necker in Geneva began to anticipate the time when, the paper having become hopelessly debased, it would be necessary to appeal once more to high finance. The war proved disastrous; the German armies under the Duke of Brunswick advanced on Paris. A panic-stricken mob attacked the palace, broke through the King's defenses, and murdered his guard. The Royal Family was shut up in the Temple prison. Less than a month later, when Brunswick was only a few days' march from the capital, a system of organized massacre revealed the fact that power had passed into new hands. The party of Madame de Staël was swept away; in its place appeared the Republican party with an admixture of Radicals including Danton. Danton recruited a new army and drove back the invaders. The Assignat (land-paper money) appreciated sharply in value, so much so that the Government felt itself free of financial embarrassment. It was believed everywhere that the Revolution had reached its climax and that a stable Republic would be established. The policy of terror was relaxed and its alleged authors who showed anxiety to disavow their activities fell into disgrace.

Immediately, the Assignat began to depreciate again. Farmers looked doubtfully at the notes they had been eager to accept only a few weeks earlier, and hoarding of wheat and other foodstuffs caused prices to rise sharply. What had happened? The earnest Republicans (called the Girondins) who were in control of government could not supply an answer. The enemy threatened no longer; the King was safely under lock and key; priests, nobles, and bankers had been driven beyond the frontiers. France had glory, security, the wealth of her matchless soil. Why then this strange lack of confidence?

Mirabeau could have supplied the answer namely, that France was no longer a nation, but merely an agglomeration of factions not greatly different from the factions of the barons. Department was in arms against department, province against province, city against city. So much so, indeed, that the Government was making plans to introduce a form of federal-ism under the pretext of strengthening local authorities. The grievances of Lyons, of Bordeaux, of Marseilles, of Toulon, of La Vendée, bulked larger in many minds than the afflictions of France. All these places had their rights. Having determined the Rights of Man in general, the Government was busy determining also the rights of this man and that. Duty was a word tarnished for want of use. In these circumstances, since confidence is inspired only by service, a universal want of confidence was inevitable. What Necker had destroyed was not merely faith in the Throne, but faith in the purpose of life of which the Throne was the expression. By preventing the King from abolishing privilege, he had robbed him of the exercise of his office and with him all his subjects. Lacking the sense of divinely imposed duty, men remembered their grievances, nursed their wrongs, and reverted to the use of force. They were ready no longer to sacrifice themselves. That readiness, in the last issue, is the foundation of credit, whether financial or other.

The Republicans, in their bewilderment, had glimpses of this truth. They tried to substitute for the King's authority what they called the sovereignty of the People. God, it was declared, had bestowed His Grace on the Nation, so that each citizen might render service to his fellows in the double capacity of sovereign and subject. Unhappily for this doctrine, the discovery was soon made that there are as many Peoples as there are parties in the State. If the Republicans claimed to represent the People, and so to exert a natural sovereignty, exactly the same claim was made by the Radicals. It was a competition for power in which success chiefly depended on efficient organization and a plentiful supply of money. The People in other words, had to be coaxed or bribed or terrified into giving their support. Such a state of affairs possesses nothing in common with responsible nationalism; it is essentially self-seeking and mercenary. Its foundation is not God but brute force and greed.

The fall in the value of the Assignat, therefore, was a true reflection of the political and moral situation. Credit-money, as has been said, depends on the character and security of the people by whom it is issued. Both character and security were suffering deterioration by reason of the substitution of the idea of benefit for the ideal of service. The farmer, for example, no longer felt it incumbent on him to feed the towns. As he did not like the look of the Assignats he planted less and took his ease. When appeals were addressed to him to play a citizen's part, he retorted by asking if liberty did not belong to him. Prices rose and the mob of Paris grew threatening.

Was this the Sovereign People? The leaders of the mob, Danton and his friends, removed any doubt on the matter by demanding that the tyrant Louis XVI should be brought to trial.

The Republicans began to lose their nerve. Action against the King, as they now saw, could have no other effect than a further shaking of confidence and credit. The value of the Assignat would fall; the hoarding of foodstuffs would increase and the cities, in all probability, would starve.

What would happen then no man could tell. The Government, therefore, tried to prevent the King's trial. Instantly they were accused of treachery. The names which, under Necker's guiding hand, they had flung at King, priests, and nobles were flung at them. It was asserted by Robespierre at a later period, that Danton, who led the attack on the Republicans, was in the pay of foreign banking houses. It is certain that he served their ends. The King's trial effected a further fall in the purchasing power of the Assignat; his execution continued the process. The Government passed from anxiety to despair. Their money was ceasing to command confidence and they had a great European war on their hands. So evil did their plight seem that revolt against their authority was everywhere stimulated. Both Lyon and Marseilles declared for the King's son, *Louis XVII*. The inhabitants of Toulon handed that great naval base over to the English. Metz fell and German and Spanish armies crossed the frontiers. Famine threatened the capital.

Danton led his mob against the Republicans and they were swept away to prison. He took their place, but failed utterly to restore authority or attract food to the cities. It seemed that France must infallibly succumb to her enemies both foreign and financial. This was the opinion of these enemies. Necker, for example, felt that the time was at hand when a Regency under Marie Antoinette must be instituted, and urged his daughter, who was with Narbonne in England, to rejoin her husband at the Swedish Embassy in Paris. Danton, the ferocious, began to use mild language and to talk of bringing the Revolution back into peaceful courses.

Suddenly the accusation that he was in English pay began to be whispered. Why, it was asked, had he attacked so persistently French policy in India and elsewhere if not because the English financial houses with interests in India had bribed him? A wave of panic swept the Parliament, and within a few weeks of his victory over the Republicans Danton himself was gently, it is true, removed from power. Robespierre and Carnot replaced him.

They were a strange couple, Robespierre small, fragile, rather timid; Carnot big, burly, with a plentiful self-assurance. The odds were against agreement between these two; perhaps, even, against toleration of the one by the other. Certainly they did not like each other. But they loved France. The idea that France should yield to her enemies, or ask succour of them, was hateful to both. Carnot undertook the conduct of the war without, Robespierre that of the war within.

Robespierre was reputed a mild little man. He had earlier in his career relinquished a legal appointment held by him in the town of Arras because it entailed the duty of signing the death warrants of criminals. That was in keeping with his record as the *best boy* at the Jesuit school at which he had been educated and at which, because of his merit, he had been chosen to deliver the address of welcome to Louis XVI when the King visited the school. He set himself, with conscientious thoroughness, to discover ways of pulling France together and averting the threatened famine. Within a few weeks he discovered that the accustomed means to that end had been destroyed. There was no longer in the land any discipline, religious, moral, or political. Loyalty had perished with the King; glory possessed so little attraction that desertions had seriously reduced the strength of the army; even patriotism had grown cold, so that the majority of Frenchmen despaired of the State. What force remained whereby men's allegiance might be bound and their service compelled? Robespierre glanced at the empty throne; he must find a substitute for that excellent power by which the tribes of France had been wrought into the French nation, and men held in duty to God. He was a party leader. Only force remained to him.

He set up the guillotine and, instead of the ministry of the King's grace, proclaimed a new ministry of fear. First the Republicans, then the Queen, were hurried to the scaffold. They were followed by a great crowd of persons accused and persons suspected. Lyon, Bordeaux, and Marseilles were brought to submission. Thanks to the genius of an officer of artillery, named Napoleon Bonaparte, the British and Spanish fleets were driven from Toulon harbour and the town retaken. The foreign armies were driven across the Rhine, the Alps, and the Pyrenees.

Robespierre sent his agents into the disaffected districts. They brought with them their red guillotines, their firing parties, and their executioners, until France sickened with the horror of it all. But the cities were fed and the armies disciplined. The name of France grew terrible again in Europe, and the Assignat rose in purchasing power so sharply that this paper money was taken gladly throughout the length and breadth of the land.

The guillotine, then, was an efficient substitute for the throne. Fear could achieve some of the results which loyalty had achieved. It could whip opponents into submission; it could compel service and impose silence. In these respects it resembled God's grace more nearly than ambition or glory or greed. But the resemblance ended there. Even Robespierre knew that fear could not be continued indefinitely. He began, in the spring of 1794, to speak of milder measures, and marked the expressions of joy which greeted these hints. He sent the worst of the butchers, who had - so he said - exceeded his orders, to the guillotine.

Danton tried to come back on the wave of moderation. Instantly Robespierre recoiled. Was the alternative to fear the rule of greed and corruption? He accused Danton of treachery, of taking foreign pay, of robbery of the People. Danton also ascended the guillotine. The Reign of Terror began. It marks the madness of Robespierre, for it proceeded from the idea that fear, often enough renewed, can beget love. He called it the purge of virtue, suggesting that it was the terror to end terror. It grew fiercer from day to day. And from day to day the paper money appreciated in value and the power of the French arms increased. Robespierre passed from politics to ecstasy. His grace of fear assumed, in his mind, a mystic quality. He began to see himself as the Scourge of God. He ordered a solemn festival in which France, under his leadership, should acknowledge The Supreme Being. The Palace of the Tuileries looked down gloomily on a small figure in a sky blue coat and nankeen breeches, with powdered hair and prim, beautifully laundered cravat, calling upon God to bless the guillotine's office.

That was a figure of dread as well as a figure of mockery. Robespierre had achieved mightily for France. He had saved her from invasion, from civil war. He could not save her from himself. His acknowledgment of God, indeed, was a gesture of despair. By it, he confessed that above fear there his love, above force there is loyalty, above Man there is God. What he had accomplished horribly, by the slaughter of thousands of victims, Kingship, during centuries, had achieved without violence.

As he preached and prayed, there were gathered round him men, once the creatures of his will, who had resolved already on his ruin. Like him, they reeked of innocent blood; unlike him, they were corrupt, the agents of the wolves and vultures of finance. Because there is a term set to fear, these fellows triumphed. Robespierre was flung under the knife. This man who had possessed all the riches of France, who had known no woman, who had tasted no wine, left behind him as the sum of his worldly goods a small shelf of books and an Assignat to the value of five francs.

On the morrow of Robespierre's execution the Assignat began to depreciate in value. Its fall now was swift and catastrophic, for the new rulers, the vicomte de Barras and his crew, dared not employ fear, and possessed no other means of commanding obedience. France would certainly have perished by invasion but for the discipline imported into the armies during the reign of Robespierre. These armies of the Revolution, therefore, were the inheritors of the guillotine.

Could the sword maintain what the ax had failed to maintain?

The Government was not concerned to answer this question. So long as they were able to hold the foreign armies in check, they felt confident of being able to maintain themselves in power, if only because the Parisians were weary of violence. Barras was hopelessly corrupt and so were his associates. They looked upon office primarily as a means of getting rich and buying pleasure.

This attitude spread to all sections of the community. Service was put away, except in the armies; greed was exalted into the chief end of man. Rights were insisted upon. Confidence naturally and inevitably declined. People did not like the look of those in authority, and so fought shy of money the basis of which, as they believed, was the character of their rulers. The value of the Assignats fell from thirty per cent. in January 1795 - six months after Robespierre's death - to twenty per cent. in April 1795, and to one per cent in November 1795. These figures display one of the differences between a nation and an agglomeration of factions.

It must not be supposed, however, that the fell of the Assignat was due solely to lack of confidence. It was too quick, too catastrophic for that, for the paper, after all, retained the land security, and France had triumphed so signally in the field that all the European Powers were ready to make peace with her. What was it, then, apart from the bad character of the new rulers, that destroyed within a few months a paper money on which fourteen armies had been supported and by means of which France bad been preserved from ruin?

Chapter VIII

BONAPARTE

BETWEEN the years 1630 and 1640 the goldsmiths of the City of London set up a special organization for collecting and sorting coin. They paid the bookkeepers of the merchants 4d. per cent. per day to leave the merchants' money with them. As soon as they got the money they picked out all the full-weight, unclipped silver pieces, replaced them by underweight, clipped pieces, and then returned the money. The good pieces were now melted down, in spite of the severe penalties attaching to this crime, and exported. "Here," says A.E. Feavearyear, "was the beginning of banking in England."

Banking elsewhere began in much the same fashion. It was ever the wish of Kings and their people to prevent loss of money - and so deflation - by export of the precious metals; it was ever to the profit of bankers to export these metals. Bankers, therefore, from the beginning found themselves in opposition to the national interests.

In the second half of the Seventeenth Century trade with the East offered investors a rich new field of enterprise. The East India Company in 1676 paid a bonus of 100 per cent. A few years later its stock was quoted at 360. Since the natives of India did not wish to buy English woollen goods, but did wish to acquire, in exchange for their produce, English silver, silver money began to be exported in great quantities. The embargo upon the export of coin had not been raised; but bullion produced from English coin could be passed through the Customs by swearing that it had not been so produced.

The outflow of silver continued through the Eighteenth Century. When London triumphed over Paris as the financial Center of the world, French silver began to flow across the Channel. The outbreak of the French Revolution was followed immediately by a great increase in this tide.

There was, as has been said, a virtual disappearance of metallic money from France, due in part to hoarding and in part to export by financiers and bankers who wished to have their treasure in a place of safety. These people saw in the death of Robespierre the opportunity for which they were anxiously waiting. Now was the time to regain their power in France by lending to the French Government.

But no Government which possesses a stable paper currency needs to borrow. The destruction of the Assignat became, therefore, the chief object of finance. Barras and his friends were instruments to this end of a type very agreeable to the masters of money. They were open to bribery in its worst and most unconscionable forms, and they were bribed. Robespierre had enforced the law giving the Assignat an exclusive monetary privilege - that is to say, forbidding the use in competition with the Assignat of gold and silver as money. Barras showed himself less irreconcilable. Because the premium on the metals exceeded that on the exchanges it paid to import gold and silver into France. The financiers, French and English, contrived to place these metals in competition with the land-paper, which at once lost value. Everybody distrusted the Government; everybody, therefore, wished to be paid in coin. In April 1795 a law was passed permitting free dealings in gold and silver; this law was a further blow at the value of the Assignat. More gold and silver came in to earn profits for finance. The Assignat became so unpopular that its value almost wholly disappeared. France was now given over to army contractors and moneylenders, who grew rich while the mass of the population went hungry and the poor starved.

In England, on the other hand, the enterprise of the financiers in sending silver to India and gold and silver to France, in order to earn the largest possible profits, brought about an acute lack of money, a matter of grave concern seeing that England was at war with France.

"In August 1795," says Mr. Feavearyear, *"another and a greater cause of drain was added to the Government borrowings. The value of France's paper currency, the Assignat, which had been tumbling headlong for some months, reached zero for all practical purposes early in 1795. The French Government thereupon determined to restore the gold standard. There was immediately a great revival of confidence among the French people. They began to transfer their savings home again. Gold, which had been driven out by the Assignat, rushed back.*

Metal from France which had helped the Bank of England to replenish its stock after the collapse of 1793 was now drained away from it. By 1796 the reserve was down to 2½ millions."

This spectacle of the Bank of England repaying, in time of war, the enemy's gold is a remarkable one. Guineas, as it happened, could not be exported legally in any circumstances; but, as Mr. Feavearyear testifies, "there was little difficulty in getting them away and large quantities were going." How much of this gold was French and how much English cannot be determined, but, as has been said, it was profitable to send gold into France.

The Bank of England reduced its commercial discounts. Money began to earn larger profits in London, and very soon some of the French gold - again in spite of the state of war - recrossed the Channel. Most of this gold was, later, withdrawn from the Bank of England by the provincial banks.

The French Government displayed more activity in face of the drain of gold from France than had been displayed by the English Government when gold was leaving London. Now that the Assignat had disappeared, money in France was very scarce. (St. Cyr, for example, reported that the Army of the Rhine and Moselle had been compelled, from want of metallic money, to abandon its espionage, and the Army of the Rhine had been compelled to resort to requisitions because the farmers refused to accept paper.) In these circumstances the war indemnities imposed by General Bonaparte in Italy, as the result of his successful campaign against the Sardinians and Austrians, were a matter of great importance. Bonaparte sent back 23,000,000 francs in gold and silver during 1796, and it was some of this money which found its way to London. The conqueror of Italy was not yet in a very strong position, but he complained bitterly, in May 1796, that he was unable to pay his soldiers and that the Government had not kept its promise to send him back 31,000 francs for the upkeep of his artillery. Later in the same year, when he felt more secure, he addressed sharper remonstrances. Barras became anxious, and it was decided to take such action against England as would convince Bonaparte and the French nation that the rumours about the export of gold to London were unfounded. At the end of 1796 a fleet was ordered to sail from Brest towards Ireland. It achieved nothing and soon returned to its home ports. This demonstration was followed, on February 25, 1797, by a descent on the Welsh coast. Upwards of 1,000 men were landed but none showed fight. The Frenchmen proved to be convicts put into uniform for the occasion.

These gestures achieved their object. French public opinion was satisfied. In England the effect was different. A run on the banks took place. The Bank of England appealed to Pitt, who sent an urgent message to King George III at Windsor. The King hurried to London. On February 26, a Sunday, a Council was held at the palace and it was resolved that the Bank should stop payment in gold. Next day *The Times* adjured the nation to stand firm and accept the Bank's notes. The effect was to put an end to the excitement and to tie up the French balances of gold. The notes were made legal tender and regulations were enforced to prevent a return of silver, which, had this not been done, would have earned large profits and might have brought about a depreciation of the paper pound in the way in which the depreciation of the paper Assignat had been effected. The boot was now on the other leg. France was back on gold; England was on sterling paper. The Continental speculators lost their interest in London and busied themselves in trying to repatriate their capital - an enterprise now rendered very difficult.

The chief obstacle to the prosecution of the war against France - namely, the necessity of paying in goldwas now removed from the English Government. Notes were issued according to the needs of the population, and a period of prosperity began which had the effect of attracting gold from the hoards within the country and also from the countries of Europe which felt themselves threatened by France, notably Portugal. The Bank was able to increase its reserve of gold and by means of its reserve to finance the enemies of France on the Continent. The Bank, in other words, obtained gold at relatively low rates, and lent the gold again at high rates.

Meanwhile, Bonaparte returned in triumph from Italy and set sail with a great fleet for Egypt with the avowed intention of cutting the Suez Canal and so opening a short route to India. This threat to the basis of the international financial operations of London was met by loans to the Austrians, who were eager to re-conquer Italy, and by the despatch of troops to India. Nelson's victory at the Battle of the Nile, however, quickly dispelled the anxiety. Bonaparte's fleet was destroyed and Bonaparte himself shut up, with his army, in Egypt. The Austrians crossed the Alps, drove the French out of Lombardy, and laid siege to Genoa as a preliminary to the invasion of France. Money flowed again into London and was duly distributed to the quarters where the highest rates of interest were obtainable.

These events engaged the attention of Bonaparte. He had been a close friend of Robespierre's younger brother, Augustine, and had observed with astonishment the rise in the value of the Assignat during the Reign of Terror. Before he began his campaign in Italy, he had reached the conclusion that France's greatest need was a King, and had even suggested bringing back the Bourbons. Unhappily for this idea the brother and heir of Louis XVI, who called himself Louis XVIII, was receiving a pension from the English Government, and had threatened to employ the help of England in quelling his rebellious subjects. Behaviour so unkingly made restoration impossible. The campaign in Italy convinced Bonaparte not only that he was a soldier of exceptional ability, but also that his was the only head upon which the crown of France could possibly rest. Long before anyone even of his own family had the least suspicion of what was in his mind, this man, as his actions show, was preparing to ascend the throne. In Italy, at a moment when the French Government was persecuting the Church, he showed respect to Pope and Cardinals and refused to allow any kind of sacrilege. Emigrant nobles and priests obtained his protection. His proclamations to his soldiers and to the French people were couched in the language of a King.

"The French nation," he declared later, *"needs an hereditary chief. I feel so deeply the necessity of conferring this boon on France that my reason has marked out the work of securing it as one of my duties no matter on what head or in what family the French may choose to place the dignity (of the crown). I would even urge the restoration of the Bourbons if, today, they possessed in Europe any other title to consideration, any other power than that which they derive from the despicable salaries they receive from England, and if Frenchmen had not such good reason to fear that their return would bring down on the heads of their subjects the contempt in which their feebleness is held and would result in the destruction of our existing institutions at the hands of followers and hangers-on who hold these institutions in detestation."*

Bonaparte saw the Revolution as Mirabeau had seen it - namely, as a purging of the Feudal System of its abuses.

"At the beginning," he said, *"the Revolution took its course under the leadership of Louis XVI. The great mistakes of the Three Estates and the evil counsels of foreigners, but especially the false advice of England, which knew better than anybody what an advantage France was gaining through real liberty, destroyed the fine beginning."*

The reference is to Necker, whom Bonaparte looked upon as the architect of ruin, and who, as he continued to believe, acted throughout in the interests and on the advice of his partners in the City of London. Money, Bonaparte held, had come to the rescue of privilege, and by destroying the Throne had prevented the real Revolution. He himself was determined to carry this real Revolution through by re-establishing the Throne. That, as he knew, meant curbing the power of Money, which would certainly, unless he was prepared to come to terms, offer him a bitter opposition.

He saw clearly the forms which opposition would take. Money, as he knew, never comes into the open, but acts always through agents who may or may not be aware of the objects they are serving. There was international money already behind every foreign enemy; there was international money behind Louis XVIII and the whole Royalist party; there was international money behind the Jacobins. Barras and his friends had been speculating in London with the gold won in the Italian campaign. Whoever would reign in France, therefore, as King must be able to command the love and loyalty of those who cannot be bought - namely, the peasants. He must be capable of driving back the foreign armies, of restoring the altars and recalling the emigrants, and of establishing the principles of equal service, equal justice, and equal honour.

He must be able, too, to show that legitimacy and heredity are not the same thing, but that, on the contrary, a King reigns by that Grace of God which is bestowed only upon him who shows himself capable of uniting the nation and compelling all men to service. France knew now that popular election could not bestow sovereigntythe Reign of Terror had proved it. She knew that, without Kingship, a people is at the mercy of force, which will express itself either in terms of greed or in terms of fear.

That Bonaparte attempted this task is proof of his courage, for the idea of service was gone wholly out of fashion and all were persuaded of their rights. He relied, however, on the common people, those countryfolk who had shown themselves ready to die for France and to follow anywhere a leader of whose patriotism they were persuaded. These were the people whom Necker, by his propaganda, had inflamed against Louis XVI and Marie Antoinette so that, for a time, they had supposed the banker to be their deliverer. Bonaparte employed every means at his command to bind them to himself, using most of all the means of a call to service. Thus, for the guillotine which Robespierre had set up, he presented a new symbol, the man in the grey coat, the hero of Arcole and Lodi and Rivoli Himself.

When he returned from Egypt the people called him Saviour. A few weeks later, when he made an end of Barras and leaped into the saddle as First Consul, they gave him a new title - namely, The Man. The year 1799, and with it the Eighteenth Century, was passing away. Consul Bonaparte surveyed a world in which, as he could see, the system of service was everywhere in melancholy decline. In the old monarchies a privileged class glared with hostile eyes at the merchants and bankers who already were disputing their privileges. In England, the reign of George III, which had begun so bravely, was fallen under eclipse. The King, since his humiliation in America, no longer dared to act against the wishes of the City of London.

Financial houses exported and imported the precious metals without regard either to the law or to the state of war. Their operations went unpunished because those who should have punished them were partners in their enterprises, and were reaping handsome rewards. Privilege was not challenged in England because the bankers and merchants were sure already of entry into the privileged classes. The case of France was not greatly different from that of England. In France, also, financial houses were setting the law at defiance, while the Middle Class established itself in the places of power. But this movement was not apparent to spectators in England and in Europe. The terror inspired by Robespierre lingered side by side with the resentments which Louis XVI and Turgot had engendered. The aristocracies hated the Revolution because it had begun by an attempt to abolish privilege and restore service, and had ended by the abolition of aristocracy itself; the Money Power hated it because, under Turgot, Mirabeau, and Robespierre, it had denied the right of money to seek the most profitable investment. The old order, therefore, was everywhere joined to the new in opposition to *Revolutionary France*, though, in fact, the principle of the old order - namely, service was the same as the principle of the Revolution as expressed by Louis XVI, and was, like it, wholly opposed to the principle of the new order.

There is no doubt that, at first, Bonaparte expected to find support among the English people. No man cherished a livelier admiration for England and for her institutions. In England, as he often insisted, a clear distinction had always been drawn between heredity and legitimacy, so that James Stuart had been replaced on the throne by William of Orange and Anne had been succeeded by George. In England, too, Kingship had survived and embodied Revolution. The First Consul of the French Revolution knew that, though London has become rich, a bitter poverty held in its grasp the English worker, both in agricultural and industrial. Would the English people in their misery join him against the common oppressor?

"All thing are possible for humanity," he told the English Ambassador two years later, "to England and France united."

Bonaparte had thought, now, of disputing England's command of the sea. The Battle of the Nile had taught him that, in his own words, "with the incessant efforts of ten years and the employment of all my resources I should not be able to equal your navy." What he wanted was peace and co-operation so that he might carry through his plan of ascending the throne of France and completing the Revolution.

Fortune helped him. The year 1799 was *lean* so far as the harvest in England was concerned. It became necessary to import large quantities of wheat from the Continent, and when the wheat was paid for the exchanges went against England. A flight from the pound occurred. Golden guineas began to be melted for export to countries where as gold they commanded e better price. They were replaced by paper; the note issue increased from about 12,000,000 to nearly 16,000,000 and the cost of living rose sharply. The speculators in wheat made fortunes; the poor were brought to the verge of starvation. The circumstances were thus favourable to the proposal of peace which reached London from France, for peace promised a reduction of expenditure by the Government and a cheapening of the price of wheat.

Peace was concluded at Amiens, and London and Paris were illuminated. Bonaparte, who had defeated all his enemies, recalled the exiles, and re-established religion, heard a solemn *Te Deum* in Notre Dame. The Londoners took the horses from the carriage of the French Ambassador and drew it through the streets. The price of bread in London fell and the exchange moved in favour of London. Gold began to return to its headquarters.

Chapter IX

NAPOLEON

HAVING made peace with the whole world, Bonaparte set about his task of preparing himself and the French people for the return to the God-system. It was ordained by him that money should not be exported from France on any pretext whatever except with the consent of the Government, and that in no circumstances should loans be employed to meet current expenditure whether civil or military.

The object was to withhold from finance the power to embarrass the Government as it had embarrassed the Government of Louis XVI. When a Government, Bonaparte declared, is dependent for money upon bankers, they and not the leaders of that Government control the situation, since "the hand that gives is above the hand that takes".[1] He did not allow anyone to forget the shipments of gold to England organized by Barras at the expense of the army of Italy, and at a moment when France was denuded of metallic currency.

"**Money,**" he declared, "**has no motherland; financiers are without patriotism and without decency: their sole object is gain.**"

---

[1] This was among his favourite quotations.

Money reacted against Bonaparte with all its strength. Necker remained in Switzerland, but his daughter, Madame de Staël, was in Paris. She reopened her *salon* and entertained nightly the diplomatic corps and the Liberals. She spent the resources of a lively wit in making fun of the "dynasty of Ajaccio" - a particularly deadly form of attack on a man who was about to declare himself the anointed of God. A second line of attack consisted in showing Bonaparte as an ignorant provincial. Madame de Staël and her friend, the beautiful Juliette Recamier, wife of the banker of that name, proclaimed them-selves citizens of Europe, and cried that Bonaparte's methods were shutting France in an "iron cage". Men, they urged, must be free to follow their own ideas. (This meant that rich men must be free to move their money about.) Men must be free, too, to produce, to buy and to sell where and when they chose. (This meant that bankers must be free to stimulate the export trade by foreign lending.) Madame de Staël committed herself to the shrewd opinion that, had her father's system of loans not been kicked out of court by Mirabeau, the leaders of the Revolution would never have got their paper money (Assignats) and so would not have been able to finance the wars which kept the foreign invaders out of France.

People who did not understand the object of these opponents of Bonaparte were surprised at the way in which he reacted to their opposition. He made no secret of the fact that he feared Madame de Staël's tongue. As he very well knew, she had only to set France laughing and his ascent on the throne would be impossible. He banished her and with her the Liberals who played her game. He established a censorship of the Press, having first shut down all the newspapers which were definitely in the hands of his enemies. He became a journalist himself, and, day after day, preached his own gospel of service to the French people.

These activities awoke anxiety in the City of London, where, as Thiers points out, there was dismay at the refusal of the French Government to contract any loans. The friendly spirit towards France and her new leader was changed to hostility, and the London Press opened a vigorous attack. Bonaparte protested that England and France were at peace; he was told that in England the Press was free. Then he protested that the conditions of the Treaty of Amiens had not been fulfilled in the matter of Malta, which England had contracted to evacuate, and was informed that Malta would be evacuated when he removed his troops from Holland.

The English people, at first, felt no animosity against France and took no part in the campaign, but it was clear, nevertheless, that very soon war would be resumed unless Bonaparte made the trade treaty for which London was clamouring and so abandoned his isolationist policy. His Ambassador in London, Andréossy, warned him that -

"In a country where the main interest is business, and where the merchant class is so prosperous, the Government has to appeal to the merchants for extraordinary funds and they have the right to insist that their interests should be considered in the policy which is adopted."

In spite of this Bonaparte refused to discuss a trade treaty. War was declared by England, and shortly afterwards the First Consul ascended the throne of France as Napoleon I. He submitted himself to his people to be elected, but insisted that consecration should come from the Church at the hands of the Pope himself. Then, in order that it might not be supposed that Heaven's appointment came indirectly through the Church, he put the crown on his own head.

Napoleon's sovereignty, therefore, was by the Grace of God, and it is an error to look upon it in any way different, in its quality, from that of Henry IV, Louis XIV, or Louis XVI. Napoleon himself never ceased to proclaim that he reigned by Grace and not by election, and he considered this distinction fundamental.

Money was face to face now with Kingship. Money proceeded, immediately, to enlist Kingship on its side. This was easy, for the old Monarchies, as has been said, desired nothing so much as the final overthrow of the man they looked upon as the child of the revolution. The doctrine, again, that God's Grace does not necessarily descend from father to son was hateful to people who believed that birthrights cannot in any circumstances be alienated. Add to this that the old Monarchies were bankrupt and so compelled to live by borrowing from the masters of money. Thus the descendants of the coin-sorters and melters of the City of London, once held in contempt as thieves of the King's currency, became kings of kings and lead the forces of European nobility against the man who was upholding spiritual as against material value, the nation as against greed, loyalty as against fear.

They had good hope of compassing his down-fall. None believed that he could finance war on a great scale now that the resource of paper money had been denied him by the destruction of the Assignat. Where would he obtain the indispensable gold and silver to feed and equip a great army? Pitt counted already on a coalition of England, Austria, Prussia, Russia, Spain, Sweden, and numerous small States. Some 600,000 men would be put into the field. All the resource of England's wealth - that is to say, of the world's wealth - would be placed at the disposal of this overwhelming force. Could the Corsican muster 200,000? Could he arm them? Could he feed them? If the lead bullets did not destroy him the gold bullets would soon make an end. He would be forced, like his neighbours, to come, hat in hand, for loans and, like them, to accept the banker's terms.

He was far from happy himself. He had just acquired Louisiana from Spain and was about to buy Florida. What ships he possessed were on the high seas as part of an expedition to San Domingo. He saw the seas swept clear of the tricolour flag and France imprisoned within the seas. He could not put his hands on £2,000,000, so empty was the Treasury and so depleted the nation's stock of metallic money. London waited with interest to see how the puzzle would be solved. It was learned with surprise that Napoleon had sold Louisiana to the United States for £3,000,000.

"**One has only to consider**," Napoleon remarked, "**what loans can lead to in order to realize their danger**. Therefore I would never have anything to do with them and have always striven against them. At one time people asserted that I did not issue loans because I possessed no credit and could find nobody who would lend me anything. That is quite false. That surely implies a very scanty knowledge of human nature and an ignorance of stock exchange methods if people imagine that I could find no one ready to lend. It was not part of my system." (Las Cases, 1816, September 7.)

Chapter X

The New Feudalism

NAPOLEON defined his system as the application of the resources of Government, including finance, to the uses of his people for the greater glory of God. He set agriculture first, "for that is the soul of the people." Industry came second, "for that is the people's comfort." The export trade ranked as a bad third.

"In France," he told Las Cases at St. Helena, (1816, June 23.) "we are still far behind on those delicate matters (of finance) which remain unperceived or ill-understood by the mass of Society. And yet how much progress we have made and what clearness of thinking has become possible as a result of my recognition of this order of importance in the nation's activities - namely, agriculture, industry, and foreign trade. Agriculture is the soul, the foundation of the Kingdom: industry ministers to the comfort and happiness of the population. Foreign trade is the superabundance; it allows of the due exchange of the surplus of agriculture and industry... Foreign trade, which, in its results, is infinitely inferior to agriculture, was an object of secondary importance in my mind. **Foreign trade ought to be the servant of agriculture and home**

industry; these last ought never to be subordinated to foreign trade."

This system is the exact opposite of that of the masters of Money. The Money System (let it be urged again), by its transferences of credit to the most profitable foreign borrowers, is able, if its plans are not carried out, to deprive the home markets, in all European countries, of their purchasing power and so to compel producers to export the goods they cannot possibly sell at home. Foreign trade, therefore, comes first; if it languishes, the country dies. Both industry and agriculture, as has been shown, are therefore bent to the uses of the export market. A rise of wages which makes it impossible to compete in foreign markets is tantamount to the ruin of the nation.

Napoleon never could understand why the other European Kings failed to grasp a point of such supreme moment to themselves.

"In the great cause of which I saw myself the chief and the arbiter," he told Las Cases on another occasion, "one of two systems had to be followed: either to make Kings listen to reason from the people or to conduct the people to happiness through the instrumentality of their Kings. As it is well known that, once the People are in full cry, it's no easy matter to restrain them, I thought it wiser to count on the wisdom and intelligence of rulers. I supposed that I was entitled to believe that those rulers were possessed of enough intellect to see where their own true interest lay. I was wrong.

"The Kings gave no consideration to the position in which they stood. In their blind fury they let loose against me forces which I had studiously refrained from arousing against them. (1816, March 11.)

"Peoples and Kings misunderstood me. Yet I had restored thrones, I had recalled nobles. These thrones and these nobles may again find themselves threatened. (Let them remember that I fixed and consecrated the reasonable limits of the People's rights.) Vague, peremptory, undefined claims may once more be made... Such work as mine is not done twice in a century. I saved the Revolution as it lay dying; I held it up to the people shining with fame. I inspired France and Europe with new ideas which will never be forgotten... France's finances are the best in the world. To whom does she owe them? If I had not been overthrown I would have made a complete change in the appearance of commerce as well as of industry. The efforts of the French people were extraordinary. Prosperity and progress were growing immeasurably.

Enlightenment was making giant strides. New ideas were everywhere heard and published, for I took pains to introduce science among the people... If I had been given time there would soon have been no more artisans in France; they would all have become artists."

He was not given time. Pitt completed his coalition, and Austria, Russia, Sweden, and Spain attacked France. Napoleon defeated these enemies in the campaign which ended at Austerlitz; but he lost the Battle of Trafalgar and with it his last faint hope of maintaining himself at sea. Meanwhile, during his absence from

Paris, the men whom he had placed in charge of his funds had allowed themselves to be seduced by financiers, notably the banker Ouvrard, and had embarked on a huge speculation in Spain. Their calculations were unsound and a financial panic occurred in the capital.

Napoleon returned in triumph and sent for the culprits. Inevitably he saw the hand of international finance - that is to say, of Money - in the trouble. Ouvrard and the others were stripped of all their possessions and sent to the prison of Vincennes. Napoleon founded the Bank of France with himself as its president, but so great was his suspicion of finance that he refused to entrust even to this bank the care of the Treasury account, lest secrets of his policy might leak out and be made the basis of speculation.

Napoleon was now his own banker and could direct the stream of credit wherever he chose. International finance found a great part of Europe closed to its operations, and the hatred against the Corsican entered on a new phase. In 1806 Prussia was induced to declare war on him, and a new coalition consisting of that country, Russia, and England took the field. The army which Frederick the Great had led so gloriously was destroyed at Jena, and this year Napoleon entered Berlin instead of Vienna. From Berlin he promulgated his Continental System, the object of which was to strike at England's foreign trade with the Continent and so, since England was compelled to import wheat, to bring about a drain of gold from London. Loss of gold, Napoleon felt sure, would cause the financiers to become peacemakers; and he had no doubt about their influence with the English Government. Further, loss of gold would prevent the financing of armies to fight against France. The campaign extended from Germany to Poland and ended, when the Russian army had been defeated at Friedland, in a reconciliation between the Emperor of the French and the Emperor Alexander of Russia.

This was a new and very severe blow to London. The period was now ended during which Napoleon might have been England's friend. The English people, thanks to the policy of their masters, were in real danger and were under the necessity of defending themselves. Thus patriotism was summoned to repair the damage wrought by gold. It was not summoned in vain. Englishmen have never, in their history, failed to sacrifice themselves for their country, or are they apt, on the day of sacrifice, to ask questions about the policies which have made sacrifice necessary. The common people rallied round the Throne, ready to spend their blood.

Napoleon bad only one object now - namely, to drain gold out of London. The means to this end, as has been said, was destruction of the English export trade; success depended on the possession of the European seaboard from the mouth of the Baltic to the Straight of Gibraltar. Denmark and Spain became, therefore, the chief object of French interest. Napoleon had established relations with the rulers of both countries and had little doubt that he would succeed in bending them to his will. In the case of Denmark success was certain; the Prince Royal was bitterly hostile to England. But Canning acted with promptitude;

Copenhagen was bombarded, without even the delay necessary to make declaration of war, and the Danish fleet brought to English waters.

Napoleon now seized Portugal and placed the House of Braganza in the trying position of having to decide between him and England. The House of Braganza, with the spectacle of Copenhagen before its eyes, decided for England and took ship for its overseas empire of Brazil. Shortly afterwards Napoleon possessed himself of Spain. The Peninsular War now began, because it was essential, if gold was to be prevented from flowing out of England, that the Mediterranean as well as the Baltic should be kept open to English ships.

England, in other words, could not afford to finance both her import trade and her foreign allies; and as her foreign allies were necessary to the defeat of her great enemy, and so to the defeat of his system, the export trade was a matter of life or death. But even this fact did not hinder the financiers from keeping a careful eye on their private interests.

Napoleon had placed his brother Louis on the throne of Holland. This young man quickly fell under the influence of the Dutch bankers to such an extent as to allow the import of English goods in great quantity. The trade, which was exceedingly lucrative, was financed by, among others, Sir Francis Baring. All went well until the price of gold began to rise sharply on the London market. The price of foreign currencies in terms of the English paper money increased at the same time by over twenty per cent. Sir Francis Baring and his friends experienced a lively anxiety. Were their Dutch and German debtors to be enabled to repay them in depreciated sterling? A further shock awaited them. Napoleon, they learned in February 1810, meant to depose his brother Louis and annex Holland to his Empire. In that case they would not get paid at all.

Baring opened negotiations with Napoleon through his, (Baring's) son-in-law, Pierre-Cesar Labouchère, the head of a great Amsterdam banking house. The banker Ouvrard, who had been in prison in Vincennes since 1806, was liberated by the French Emperor and became involved in the scheme, in which also Fouchè, Napoleon's Minister of Police, was intimately concerned.

Napoleon's object was to hoist the bankers with their own petard. He knew that Sir Francis Baring exercised a great influence in London both over the Government and over the City. He proposed to enlist this influence in the cause of that peace with England which he so urgently desired. King Louis of Holland was instructed by his brother to forward to his Dutch ministers a letter setting forth the plans of the French Emperor and to urge these ministers forthwith to send Labouchére into England with proposals that peace be made.

"He" (Labouchére) the letter ran, "shall inform the English Government that the destiny of Holland depends on the arrangements made by England to arrive at a speedy peace with France or at least to bring about a real change in the measures adopted by the said

Government in the attitude adopted towards the commerce and shipping of neutrals.

"Labouchére shall use the channels he may find most convenient to inform the English Government of this state of affairs, and he is at liberty to state that he is authorized by the Dutch Government in the matter.

"He shall then try to show the English Government how greatly it is to England's interest that Holland should not fall under the sovereignty of the French Empire. If he find the English Government persuaded of this fact, or if he succeed in making them realize it, he shall try to persuade them to contribute to the maintenance of the political existence of Holland by showing readiness to join in the negotiations for a general peace."

Labouchére reached London on February 6, 1810, and went at once to his father-in-law, Sir Francis Baring, a director of the East India Company, who had already secured that he would be received immediately by the Marquis Wellesley, Canning's successor in office. This had not been difficult, for Wellesley was indebted to Baring for his position, his fortune, and he credit.

Wellesley received Labouchére on the evening of February 7, the day after his arrival. He received him again on the 12th and told him in so many words that the fate of Holland was a matter of indifference to the British Government.

Baring was in despair. He turned his attention immediately to the inflation of the English note issue which was evidently proceeding as was indeed essential to the safety of the country during a state of war and one of his friends, Francis Horner, in this same February 1810, called for returns of the quantity of bank notes in circulation at various dates, the rates of exchange with certain countries, and the price of gold. On Horner's motion a Committee of the House of Commons was appointed, with the unanimous assent of the House, to inquire into the high price of gold bullion. The Bullion Committee, as it was called, at once began its sittings.

"With the exception of Sir Francis Baring," says Feavearyear, "the Bullion Committee called no witnesses who had made any particular study of currency theory. The witnesses were nearly all chosen for their knowledge of the facts of the trade and monetary position. They were bullion and exchange dealers, bill brokers, country bankers, officers of the Mint, the Customs and the Clearing House, and the principal directors of the Bank. Only two or three of them were asked their opinion regarding the effect of paper issues upon the exchanges and the price of bullion. It is not too much to say that the leading members of the Bullion Committee had made up their minds beforehand upon the theoretical question."

The Bullion Committee had the effect of frightening the Cabinet so much that, in March, Baring felt able to reopen his negotiations with France. Napoleon had seized a part of Holland and was about to marry the Archduchess Marie Louise of Austria. Fouchè and Ouvrard both perceived unlimited opportunities of wealth. Labouchére was told to stand by in Amsterdam, and from that city to transmit to Baring in London the messages he would receive from Paris. Napoleon was not told about what was happening and Labouchére was not told that Napoleon had not been told. Baring, therefore, fell into a trap which two of the cleverest rogues in Europe, Fouché and Ouvrard, had set for him in the hope of making great profit for themselves. Ouvrard acted as messenger and, in the middle of March, carried this note to Labouchére in Amsterdam:

"It appears that he (Napoleon) is now, though only on the occasion of his marriage, ready to yield on the following points. Malta, Sicily, Naples, the Ionian provinces, the Hanseatic towns, Holland, Portugal, and the greater part of the Spanish colonies."

Labouchére wrote to Baring on March 21, and enclosed a note for Wellesley dictated by Ouvrard which ran:

"From a conqueror he (Napoleon) is becoming a preserver; the first result of his marriage to Marie Louise will be that he will make an offer of peace to England. It is to this nation's (i.e., England's) interest to make peace, for it has the command of the sea; on the contrary, it is really to the interest of France to continue war, which allows her to expand indefinitely and make a fresh fleet, which cannot be done once peace is established. Why does not the English Cabinet make a proposal to France to destroy the United States of America, and by making them again dependent on England, persuade Napoleon to lend his aid to destroy the life work of Louis XVI?... Peace will allow England to pour her industrial products over the Continent. If only for this motive it is to her (England's) interest to conclude peace and to flatter Napoleon's vanity by recognizing his work and his imperial title."

Ouvrard carried the letter and its enclosure to London. He saw Baring, who, at midnight on April 5, 1810, was received by Wellesley. Wellesley took council with Canning, and on April 14 the two statesmen agreed that the proposed American settlement and the outlet for English goods which peace with France would afford offered a very favourable basis for England and should be submitted for the Cabinet's approval.

The Cabinet discussed the proposals and approved them. Wellesley at once hurried to Baring's house to give him the good news. Baring was not at home. The minister called three times before seeing him.

Baring could now congratulate himself that the Bullion Committee had not sat in vain. He had expressed himself freely before the Committee about the Bank of England, saying that it had allowed mere clerks with no business experience to open credits to the tune of £10,000 each, a charge which alarmed the country. He had good hopes of seeing the note issue made convertible to gold. If that happened and peace with Napoleon was concluded the Dutch would be able to pay and would be compelled to pay in gold.

Unhappily Napoleon found out what was afoot and took somewhat strong objection to the plan of a joint attack on the United States. He arrested Ouvrard, dismissed and exiled Fouchè, and published the whole story, to the grave distress of Wellesley and Baring. The Bullion Committee, meanwhile, reported early in June 1810. The report was shelved. The Bank continued to issue notes and the price of gold continued to rise.

But a year later, in May 1811, the report was debated in the House of Commons the question being: "Ought the convertibility of the notes into gold to be restored within a period of two years?" This was the Committee's recommendation. Had it been carried out it would almost certainly have lost the War to England, for the power of England to finance her allies and feed her people would have been seriously weakened. It was rejected by 180 votes against 45.

A measure of the sincerity of Baring and his friends was furnished by the financial crises which occurred in 1811, just before the debate on the Bullion report. This crisis would have swept away many financial houses had not a measure of relief in the shape of an issue of £6,000,000 of Exchequer bills been carried out.

"It is possible," says Feavearyear, "that the issue of Exchequer bills prevented a wholesale collapse of credit and a rapid deflation of note issues. The opponents of the Bullion Committee accused the latter of inconsistency in condemning the Bank for inflation while they raised not the slightest protest against this issue of Government paper. After all, the Exchequer bills were issued in March 1811 to counteract a shrinkage of credit, and a shrinkage of credit was just what the Bullion report had recommended in 1810..."

How often have Governments come to the rescue of the Financial System only to be told later that they have been playing the prodigal and living beyond their means!

Napoleon had the satisfaction of exposing the patriotism of Money to the world and of revealing what a great extent the English Cabinet was able to be influenced by the City of London. He was to pay dearly and soon for his pleasure. There we no more agitation against the issue of notes while the War lasted. On the contrary, every available ounce of gold was invested in the armies of Russia, Prussia, and Austria, paper promises by these countries to pay being accepted in London at very severe rates of discount. The bankers won. Louis XVIII was restored by British arms and British diplomacy to the throne of his ancestors. Loans were placed at his disposal, though Napoleon had left a France which enjoyed a credit balance.

A year later the man whom every King and every banker in Europe called usurper won back his throne with 800 men and without the firing of a single shot. On this occasion he had no option but to raise a loan for the defense of France. The City of London accommodated him with £5,000,000. With this sum he equipped the army which Wellington defeated at Waterloo.

Chapter XI

The Great Betrayal

THE fall of Napoleon marks the triumph, throughout Europe, **of the Money System**. Every financial house in 1815 held large quantities of paper, acquired at low rates. **Every financier was concerned** to get back as quickly as possible to gold, was concerned, that is to say, **to secure that what he had bought for little should be made worth much.**[2] He was concerned, in addition, to establish the Money System on its sure foundations of freedom of investment and convertibility.

Money, in other words, claimed the right to exercise powers which, until now, had been vested solely in the Sovereign. It demanded the repeal of the laws against exporting gold and silver; it demanded that notes should be convertible into gold. Thus, it demanded power to change at its discretion the value of the King's money as measured in goods and services. Even the King himself had not exercised such a power without long and grave consideration. Money's claims, which have not changed, may be thus recapitulated: (1) *Money must be free to find its own level - namely, those investments,*

---

[2] The same thing took place at the conlusion of the American revolution, the American civil war, the first war and the second war.

whether at home or abroad, where the highest profits are obtainable with a reasonable degree of safety (The trade mechanism by which this claim is asserted is explained below.) (2) *The export of gold, when it occurs, must not be compensated by any increase of the supplies available in the home market, but must, on the contrary, be allowed to exert its effect on the home market - namely, the production of an insufficiency of money.*

Such insufficiency of money causes, as will be shown, a fall in prices and so compels employers to reduce wages in order to earn profit. Convertibility of paper into gold secures that exported gold cannot be replaced by paper since gold cannot be printed.

The basis of this system, of course, is starvation. The home producer is held, all the time, in a vice. He cannot earn profits unless he can produce as cheaply as his competitors in foreign markets. He must therefore cut wages or close down. But he cannot hope to dispose of all of his goods in a market starved of purchasing power by reason of the low wages. He must therefore produce, as far as possible, for export. Thus a system the object of which in its beginning was to supply the needs of Englishmen (or Frenchmen or Germans) is bent now to a different object namely, the supply of goods cheap enough to compete successfully in foreign markets. No country is allowed to live to itself; on the contrary, every country is played off against every other country, so that the rewards accruing to Money may everywhere be as high as can possibly be obtained short of provoking violence among the wretched victims of the system. This end is achieved by means of the gold standard.

It is necessary that a clear understanding should be arrived at about the nature of the gold standard, about the claims which are made on its behalf, and about the purpose which, in fact, it serves. It is claimed for the gold standard that it keeps the prices of goods throughout the world uniform and steady. This, if it were true, would be a great service, because, as everyone knows, a large number of contracts are made on the assumption that the price of goods will be uniform throughout the world and will remain more or less steady from day to day. A sheep farmer, for example, finding that the price of wool 1S 2d. a lb., can form some idea of how much rent he can afford to pay, what scale of wages he can offer to pay his shepherds, and what state of life he can maintain himself. But if, as has happened in this year 1932, the price of wool falls to 2d. a lb., these calculations will be upset. It will now require many more pounds of wool to obtain the money necessary to pay rent and wages than were required when the price was 1S. 2d. a lb. In consequence the farmer will be compelled either to lose his capital and then go out of business, or to go out of business at once, or to persuade his landlord and his shepherds to take less. This persuasion will be easier in the case of his shepherds than in the case of his landlord, for wage-earners do not possess long contracts and have, usually, no savings to fall back on if they lose their jobs. In fact, therefore, a fall in prices entails, as a rule, either a fall in wages or unemployment. It has this further effect, that the farmer, because he ceases to earn an income, ceases also to pay income tax. The Government's budget, therefore, becomes upset by the fall in prices just as the farmer's budget was upset.

But a farmer is not solely a producer. Like everyone else he consumes goods and materials for example, food, clothes, railings, sheep-dip, motor-cars, wireless sets, and so on. When he loses his income he cannot afford to buy, and consequently the people from whom he was accustomed to buy find themselves in the same position as he is in. They have to reduce their prices in order to sell their goods at all and must, in consequence, reduce their wages also. If their employees refuse to accept smaller wages, then they have no option but to close down, with a resulting increase of unemployment and lowering of the yield of the income tax at the very moment when the Government is being urged to make provision for the out-of-work.

Now it is claimed for the gold standard that it prevents such a fall in prices as has occurred in the price of wool. On the face of it, this claim would seem to be unjustified, seeing that the whole world was upon the gold standard when the price of wool began to fall. But it is argued, against this view, that gold standard cannot properly blamed because it was not being worked in accordance with what are called the rule of the *game of the gold standard*.

In these circumstances a clear idea of the *game of the gold standard* is necessary. The game is based on the exchange of goods between one country and another. Each country, like each individual, is both a producer and a consumer in its relations to other countries. It exports its own goods and it imports other people's goods, and, generally speaking, exports pay for imports.

Thus, England may send a quantity of coal to France and may at the same time take a quantity of wine from France. The coal will pay for the wine and the account will be squared. Obviously, however, this *balance of trade* may not always work out so exactly. England, for example, may send more coal-value then she takes wine-value, and in that event France at the end of the year will find herself on the wrong side of the ledger. How is France to square her account? She could square her account, of course, by sending to England more wine or some other product of her farms or of her factories. But Englishmen may not be disposed to buy her products, because, for instance, they can get similar products at a cheaper price elsewhere. In that case it will be open to the French to reduce their prices or, if they do not wish to do that, to buy less coal from England in the future until the accounts square themselves.

The gold standard, however, offers a third method out of the difficulty. France can send gold to England to square her account, because gold is accepted readily all over the world as a means of payment. (Every currency is convertible into gold at a fixed rate and the owner of gold can buy any currency at a fixed rate.)

Now this payment by means of gold would be no more than a simple squaring of accounts were it not that the money of every nation is based upon gold. All that would happen, if monies were not based on gold, would be that when the account was squared England would have more gold and France less. There would be no effect on French prices and there would be no effect on English prices.

The effect on prices of both French goods and English goods, which would, in actual fact, follow the squaring of the account by means of a payment of gold, depends on the rule that *when gold leaves a country an amount of the money of that country equal to the amount of the departing gold must be removed from circulation.*

This rule, as will be shown later, was imposed in England by Act of Parliament in the year 1844. Under the Bank Act of 1844, the Bank of England must, if and when gold leaves the country, withdraw from circulation at once pounds, shillings and pence equal in value to the departing gold. The truth of this statement is not affected by the fact that the Bank has the right to issue a certain amount of pounds, shillings and pence against which it does not hold gold. For this so-called FIDUCIARY ISSUE is much too small to meet the needs of the country. The Fiduciary Issue is like a belt which will not nearly encircle a man's waist. In these circumstances the exact size of the belt is of small importance, for it is useless in any case until substantial additions have been made to it. If the quantity of money in use in England were limited to the amount of the Fiduciary Issue the entire trade and commerce of the country would come to a standstill. In other words the size of the Fiduciary Issue was fixed, deliberately so that it would have to be exceeded in actual practice. For every £1 issued in excess of the Fiduciary Issue, *a piece of gold to the value of £1 must be kept in the vaults of the Bank of England.*

The same rule obtains in France, in America, and every country where the gold standard exists. So that when gold is used by any country to square its trading account (that is to say, to pay for an excess of imports over export) a shrinkage of the amount of money in that country equal to the quantity of gold lost at once takes place. The effect may be indicated by quoting the comment of the man in the street: *There's less money about.*

How much less money there may be cannot, however, be understood unless and until the methods by which the Bank of England (for example) distributes money to the public are understood. Money reaches the public in three ways: as wages, as salaries, and as profits or dividends. Wages, salaries, and profits therefore make up, together, the whole buying-power of the country. They are demand. Beyond them no other effective demand for goods exists.

Consequently, by the law of supply and demand, the quantity of wages, salaries, and dividends or profits determines the prices of goods. The larger the demand (as may be seen at any auction sale) the higher the price so long as no more goods become available; conversely the smaller the demand the lower the price.

Now the great bulk of wages, salaries, and dividends or profits are paid by (earned by) producers of goods or services of one kind or another out of loans of money from banks. The reason is that production is usually a slow process. A farmer must plough before he can sow and sow before the can reap. Meanwhile he has rent and wages to pay. Consequently the size of the sum of money distributed as wages, salaries, and dividends or profits depends on the number and size of the loans made by banks to agriculture and industry. In other words, *demand*, or buying power, depends on the number and size of the loans made by banks to agriculture and industry.

But the loans made by banks are loans of money, and the amount of money in a country, as has been said, depends on the amount of gold in that country. *Consequently demand or buying power is made to depend on the amount of gold in the vaults of the Central Bank - for example, the Bank of England.* If gold leaves a country to pay for an excess of imports over exports, money will be reduced in amount; loans by banks will be reduced in amount; production will be reduced in amount; wages, salaries, and dividends or profits will be reduced in amount; buying- power or *demand* will be reduced in amount; and prices of goods will fall. As has been seen already, a fall in the prices of goods soon leads to further falls in wages and so to further loss of buying power.

In other words, it has been so contrived that when gold leaves a country prices of goods are reduced and wages fall. But this reduction in their price makes the goods of the country more attractive by reason of their cheapness. Consequently people in foreign countries buy them in larger amounts and the volume of exports increases. The exporting country now obtains what it could not obtain before, when the prices of its goods were higher - namely, a squaring of its account without any loss of gold - or better still, finds itself on the right side of the ledger and becomes, in its turn, entitled to receive gold.

The process, if left to itself, works of course both ways. When gold comes into a country the amount of money in circulation is increased; loans by banks to industry are increased; production is increased; wages, salaries, and dividends or profits are increased; buying power or demand is increased; and prices rise. That rise sooner or later necessitates a further rise of wages until a point is reached at which goods become too dear to compete in foreign markets.

And so, it is claimed, prices are kept uniform and stable throughout the World. But this, as can easily be shown, is not justified even when the game of gold standard is being played with all the matchless skills which was shown by the City of London during the latter part of the Nineteenth Century, when, in fact, the bulk of the world's gold was under the direct control of England.

England, in these days, had every year a big credit balance of exports over imports and continued, from year to year, to lend her balances, so that gold was spread over the world as widely as possible, and yet the value of gold in terms of goods in these years varied by as much as thirty per cent. In other words, there were times when owners of gold chose to withdraw it from use and so create a world-wide scarcity, and there were other times when fresh discoveries of gold gave rise to a world-wide abundance. The game of the gold standard does not provide against these contingencies. Further, it can be shown that, apart from these contingencies, gold itself is not *necessary* to the process of keeping prices uniform and stable. The Bank of England possesses the means, at any time, if it chooses, to increase or reduce the quantity of pounds, shillings and pence in this country, irrespective of the quantity of gold in its cellars. This has been made abundantly clear since England was forced off the gold standard. English prices have remained remarkably stable; in other words, the English currency has been *managed* with complete success. The same is true of the Swedish currency and indeed of most of the currencies which are at present *off* the gold standard. Meanwhile the currencies *on* the gold standard, the American and the French, have shown an inferior degree of stability. In the words of the British Reply to America on War Debts: "Sterling has remained more stable in terms of goods than the gold currencies."

It is evident, then, that the present anxiety of the world's bankers to restore the gold standard must be due to some reason other than a wish to obtain uniformity and stability of the prices of goods. Since no other reason has been disclosed, it is necessary to scrutinize the working of the gold standard with very great care. When this is done the important fact emerges that, though the standard appears, at a first glance, to work automatically as a regulator of prices, it is by no means automatic in actual practice, seeing that any large body of owners of gold can upset, and that most large bodies of owners of gold do when it suits them upset, its working. In other words, what are *economic laws* for the producers of goods (the borrowers) are matters of choice where the owners of gold (the leaders) are concerned.

These lenders of gold, as has been said, pretend that the gold standard acts as a kind of balance between them and their debtors so that a borrower will not have to pay back more than he has borrowed. If eggs fetch 1S. a dozen when the shilling is borrowed, for example, they will, according to the advocates of the gold standard, fetch no less when the debt is repaid a point of great importance to the egg farmer.

Those who argue in this way overlook the power of Central Banks to control prices without reference to gold, *while the gold standard is, apparently, functioning normally*. Suppose, for instance, that the Central Bank sells on the Stock Exchange a large quantity of Government securities which it happens to hold. These will be bought by the public and paid for by cheque drawn by the buyers upon their ordinary banks. The ordinary banks will therefore have to transfer money to the Central Bank and so will be compelled to call in loans from the public. This will reduce buying power and prices will fall. The egg farmer will consequently get less than a shilling for his dozen of eggs.

And all the time the amount of gold in the vaults of the Central Bank will have remained unchanged. The Central Bank, in other words, will have *managed* the price level that is to say, it will have tipped a balance which is constantly being advertised as immovable except under the influence of exports or imports of gold. This means, of course, that, as has been said, prices can be regulated perfectly without gold. But the owners of gold are not willing that such an idea should reach the public.

It follows that being *off* the gold standard means nothing so long as the Central Bank retains its power of *managing* the currency and so fixing the level of prices. If it can keep prices at any figure it chooses by its own methods and it can then producers are as much in its power when gold is not being used as when gold is being used. It is not inability to raise prices but reluctance, compounded of greed and fear, to separate finally from gold which is maintaining the present crisis. Thanks to hoarding by New York and Paris the gold-backing available for currencies has shrunk to one-quarter of its former amount. Consequently, from the point of view of Money, prices are much too high. If the relationship with gold is to be maintained, wages must fall and governments must reduce their expenses. This view takes no account of the fact that producers are all ruined. If they will only consent to further ruin the correct relationship between currency and gold may be restored.

Gold is wholly unnecessary to price stabilization; but its use by the world is very necessary to its owners, who would suffer if nobody wished, any longer, to borrow it. The gold standard, in other words, exists primarily to ensure that people shall wish to borrow gold and that, having borrowed it, they shall pay the highest possible rates of interest upon it. The gold standard is a money lender's lure.

For it is obvious that nobody will borrow gold unless and until he is persuaded of the advantage to himself of so doing. The world must be made as uncomfortable as possible for any country which abandons gold or shows in any way an inclination to impede the operations of the gold standard. So long, for example, as the paper money of the French Revolution (the Assignat) maintained its value it constituted a deadly threat to the owners of gold. What nation was going to borrow money at high rates of interest when it could print it? The French had financed fourteen armies on that paper money; why should not other nations do the same? Consequently, as has been seen, the Money power in every country of Europe exerted its utmost efforts to discredit the French paper money. Success was achieved by frightening the producers of food so that they refused to part with their bread and meat in exchange for Assignats, which consequently lost all their value. This is the method invariably made use of to *crash* a paper currency.

There are various ways of frightening the producers of food; by far the easiest is these days is to grant loans - and to go on granting loans - to industrialists who wish to build factories or install new plant, for by this means buying power in the shape of wages is increased more rapidly than supplies of food can be increased. The day must inevitably arrive - if the loans are made in large enough amount - when supply will not be adequate to an ever-growing demand brought about by an ever-increasing volume of wages. When that day comes, if more and still more loans are made to manufacturers, the prices of food will begin to rise - that is to say, the value of money will begin to fall. All that is now necessary is to keep on lending. The paper money is bound to lose the whole of is value if only you lend enough.

But who is it who does this lending? The Money power. The banks. The lending, as will be seen, costs nothing. (It amounts merely to a series of entries in a book.) It is, on the contrary, highly profitable seeing that each borrower has to deposit actual goods (houses, land, etc.) with the bank making the loan. As money begins to lose value these actual goods become, of course, more valuable. In other words, the Money power is in complete command of the situation. So long as it is permitted to lend and to go on lending, it can effect the ruin of any paper currency it chooses. It took a Robespierre to prevent the ruin of the Assignat. As soon as Robespierre was overthrown the Assignat perished.

Any nation, therefore, which defaults - that is to say, fails to pay across the counter of its Central Bank a fixed amount of gold to anybody presenting one of its notes - exposes itself to the danger that the Money power may destroy the whole value of its money by the simple process of lending and going on lending in the manner described until buying power far exceeds supply therefore (the owners of food refusing to part with it for the "worthless paper money"), famine stalks through the land.

It is the excessive lending for the production of non-consumable goods, of course, and not the paper money, which is the cause of the inflation. A Government which was able to exert an effective control of lending would have nothing whatever to fear from the use of paper money, and would the be under no necessity of borrowing gold from the Money power. It is this simple fact which accounts for the tireless efforts which Money expends to gain and to keep a stranglehold on government in every country in the world. Democracy is the chosen means to this end. For, as Napoleon said, there is no People, there are only parties, and the party with the most money behind it wins. When a party wins it has to reward is backers the people who supply the party funds. The Money power owns most of the world's resources. By means of the Freedom of the Press and its own resources for creating wealth out of nothing it can break its enemies.

By stark fear, therefore, supported by every conceivable kind of propaganda, the Money power compels the nations of the world to borrow its commodity - gold - and chastises with the scorpions of famine such of them as dare to resist its demands. It holds, too, in reserve minor punishments for any nation which tries to obtain its loans of gold too cheaplywhich tries, that is to say, to deliver, in payment for its loans, a smaller quantity of goods than its neighbours. Gold, as has been seen, *flows* into a country which is producing cheaply and *flows* out of a country where costs (wages) are rising. Loss of gold, thanks to various Acts of Parliament, is made to entail loss of buying power and so bankruptcy and unemployment. Gold, in short, is the slave driver's whip to punish the rascal who is not earning enough for his master; it is the bread of tribulation which men may eat only by the sweat of their brows, but, lacking which, they will be starved to death. It is - in the felicitous language of the Money power itself - *a food in small quantity but a poison in large.*

It is of the sap and marrow of this business of usury that there is not nearly enough gold to go around. For it is the scarcity of gold which enables its owners to demand such high prices for it and which inflicts such grievous distresses on those peoples who lose even quite small amounts of it. By the scarcity of gold usury is established and maintained and production, the world over, enslaved.

As has already been stated, the owner of gold (that is to say, the owner of money in a country on the gold standard) can invest his money where, when, and how he pleases. He can put his money to British farming or British industry, or French, or German, or American industry. He can lend his money to any Government he chooses. Finally, he can hoard his money in a bank or in a stocking, not using it himself and not allowing anybody else to use it. In all these activities he is absolutely free and unfettered, and yet from all these activities proceed effects of a serious kind upon the lives and enterprises of his neighbours both at home and abroad.

Suppose for example that the owner of £1,000 chooses to invest it in the Argentine Republic, and with this end in view subscribes to an Argentine loan. He has now removed £1,000 from English buying power. But there is standing *in a bank in England* a credit of £1,000 in favour of the Argentine. With this credit the Argentine will usually buy goods in England, and consequently English exports may rise by £1,000. The buying power apparently, has been restored to the home market.

But that rise of exports will not help to pay for any imports. Thanks to the loan it has received the Argentine has bought and paid for the goods already. It is certainly not going to pay for them again by means of goods sent into England - not at any rate until the day arrives when the loan itself must be paid back. Why borrow otherwise? Consequently these English goods which went out to the Argentine do not in any way relieve the burden of paying for imports by exports, but, on the contrary, add to that burden to the extent of £1,000 worth of goods. English producers of goods as a whole, in other words, must increase their exports by £1,000 worth of goods if the existing balance between imports and exports is not to be upset, and a loss of gold to pay for the excess of imports over exports is not to take place.

Generally speaking, exports of goods can only be increased in amount by lowering the prices of the goods, that is to say by lowering wages. So that the effect of the loan made to the Argentine (and this although, as has been seen, the money was spent in England) is a fall in the prices of goods (accompanied by a fall in wages) or, if English prices do not fall, a loss of gold by England. Loss of gold, as has been seen, is made, under the influence of the gold standard, to cause a fall in the prices of the goods of the country which has sustained the loss.

The reason why the investment in the Argentine was made now becomes clear. *Prices in England were higher than prices in the Argentine and consequently money bought more (earned a higher rate of interest) in Argentina than in this country.* The investment was therefore an illustration of the first rule of the owners of gold, that is to say of the Money power, that money must find its level.

But it might very well happen that the buyer of the Argentine security wished to enlarge his house in England and, for this purpose, handed over his

Argentine security to his bank in exchange for a loan of, say, £800. He has now put wages into English pockets, added to English buying-power and so brought about a rise of the prices of English goods to counteract to a large extent any fall of the prices of English goods occasioned by his Argentine investment. Has he thereby defeated the law that money must find its level where prices are lowest? Not at all. All he has done is to *hinder the fall in the prices of English goods which, had it occurred, would have prevented a loss of gold.* Loss of gold, therefore, takes place, money is withdrawn from circulation and loans - including possibly his own - are called up by bankers. The prices of English goods fall. Thus is the second law of the Money power - namely, that money which has been invested abroad must not be replaced - made effective. For in truth the man who lent £1,000 to the Argentine Republic was, in that capacity, a *lender* of gold, whereas when he deposited his security with his own bank, he became a borrower of it. As a lender of gold he was protected from loss by any conceivable action of borrowers, himself included.

And here is reached a secret of the virtue of the gold standard in the eyes of the Money power. The gold standard, while ineffective and unnecessary as a means of securing uniform and steady prices of goods throughout the world, is entirely effective as a means of preventing borrowers of gold from escaping out of the hands of lenders. The gold standard was invented by usurers. It is the Great Charter of Usury.

In order to understand this fully it is necessary to know how loans are made by banks and financial houses (including insurance companies and building societies) throughout the world. The case of the ordinary private loan from the ordinary bank will illustrate the process quite well and will, in addition, serve to show how the gold standard has been the means of depriving the borrower of any sort of defence against the demands of the lender.

The overwhelming bulk of the money in use in civilized countries today does not consist of currency (pounds, shillings and pence) but of credit (loans made by banks). Roughly speaking, every £1 of currency can be made to carry on its back £10 of loans (and even this gives but a feeble idea of the way in which loans of various kinds are built up on currency. The so-called *pyramid of credit* reaches to the skies).

A banker, it is true, when he gives a loan, professes himself as being ready, on demand, to supply pounds, shillings and pence to the borrower up to the full amount of the loan, and will supply them if asked to do so. A man, that is to say, who has obtained a loan of £1000 from his bank can, if he chooses, take it out in the form of 1,000 £1 notes (before the War he could get 1,000 golden sovereigns). And this, although *the quantity of bank loans outstanding is often ten times greater than the quantity of pounds in existence.*

How can a banker promise to pay pounds, shillings and pence which do not anywhere exist? The answer is that people who borrow from banks do not usually ask for more then one-tenth part of their loans in the form of pounds, shillings and pence. *They write cheques (or draw bills) for nine-tenth of their loans.* A cheque means, only, a book-entry in the ledgers of the banking system.

Experience extending over centuries has shown the banks that the proportions—one-tenth currency, nine-tenth cheques—are absolutely to be relied on in the case of the average borrower.

Bank loans, in other words, *only pretend to be loans of pounds, shillings and pence* If, by some chance, all borrowers asked for the whole of their loans in the form of pounds, shillings and pence, the pretence would instantly be made manifest. (This happened at the outbreak of the Great War; the Government had to declare a moratorium immediately.) Consequently it is true to say that what a bank really lends is money *invented by itself out of nothing*. On this invented money it charges interest, and against this invented money it demands and holds *securities possessing real worth* - for example, houses.

Now the only danger which threatens this engaging system is that lending may be carried so far as to leave the bank without enough pounds, shillings and pence to meet the demands of its customers. These demands, as has been seen, will not usually exceed one-tenth part of the total loans made by the bank. But occasions have arisen when banks have lent as much as £20 for every £1 in their possession and have, in consequence, found it very difficult to meet the needs of their customers for pounds, shillings and pence. As a bank is compelled by law to pay its customers pounds, shillings and pence if the customers ask for this kind of payment, failure to pay pounds, shillings and pence means bankruptcy.

But it will be objected that, if bankers lend even £10 for every £1 which they possess, they can never feel safe. For, although in the past only one-tenth of their loans has been asked for in the form of pounds, shillings and pence, *that is not, and cannot be, an absolute guarantee that, on some future occasion, a larger proportion of clients will not ask for pounds, shillings and pence* In truth bankers never ought to feel safe. It is obvious on the face of it that no bank in the world is ever in a position to pay all its clients all the pounds, shilling and pence which these clients have legal right to ask for. People who deal with banks do not always understand this.

They think that their banker possesses pound, shillings and pence to the full amount of his liabilities and would, perhaps, be horrified and alarmed if they realized that, on the contrary, his total stock of pounds, shillings and pence is only equal to one-tenth of his liabilities.

In other words, the banking system practises a form of illusion on the public. It is legally bound to give pounds, shillings and pence to any client who asks for them; it declares itself ready and willing to fulfil its legal obligation; and yet, as it knows very well, it will be wholly unable to do anything of the kind if even a quarter of its clients demand the legal right. Even a mild *run* on a bank (that is to say, a demand by large numbers of customers for payment in pounds, shillings and pence) is bound, if it continues for any length of time, to break that bank unless the Government or the Central Bank comes to the rescue with fresh funds or with securities which the bank's clients will accept instead of funds.

The process of making money out of nothing, therefore, is carried on *at the expense of the safety of the bank's clients*. This is true no matter how small the actual risk may be. But the process is legal and is so exceedingly profitable that bankers feel no scruples about employing it. It enables them to produce money as they choose; he who can produce money at will by merely writing figures in a book is evidently a lord of creation.

Indeed, far from feeling scruples, bankers exert themselves to prove to their clients that their methods are safe and sound beyond all possibility of improvement. *This is where the gold standard serves them so well.* For there is an idea in the public mind that behind the paper money which people carry in their pockets is a reserve of solid gold, a *backing,* a security. *Money*, says the man in the street, *must be backed by something. What better than gold?*

Now, as has been said, the pound notes which we carry in our pockets are in part at any rate backed by gold the gold in the cellars of the Bank of England. But that is where gold ends. Of the money we think *we have in the bank* only one-tenth part has a gold backing. Because we can ask for and obtain pounds, shillings and pence (which have a partial gold backing) when we go to our banks, we are kept in the pleasant illusion that there is gold behind every cheque we write and every cheque we receive - behind, generally speaking, all the banker's liabilities. There is not of course, as has been said, enough gold in the whole world to make a backing for even a small fraction of the liabilities of the world's banks. The *gold backing* idea, in consequence is pure illusion. Only £10 out of every £100 of bankers' liabilities at this moment are backed by gold - indeed, when the Fiduciary Issues are taken into account, the gold backing covers only about 6s. 8d. in every £10 of liabilities.

Gold backing, in short, are like chocolates which, being skilfully arranged in a box, give the impression that the box is full of chocolates and conceal the fact that what the box is really full of is paper. They are the top-dressing, a dummy, a smoke-screen, and the security afforded by them is no security at all. But the public must not be allowed to know this. If the public knew it would, sooner or later, find out that, behind this smoke-screen of gold, the bankers are at work making money out of nothing in order to charge substantial rate of interest on it. *Only so long as people think that a banker is lending them solid, glittering gold will they be willing to pay him five per cent. on his loans.* The moment they know to the contrary they will realize that they could do for themselves, and very much more cheaply, all that their bankers are in fact doing for them.

The borrower, it may be argued against this, gets what he wants - namely, the means to buy goods or pay his debts; such accommodation is clearly worth something to him. But that is not the point at issue. A man who lends £1 *which he has earned* or which somebody else has earned is evidently entitled to receive interest on his loan. He is lending real money. The banker, on the contrary, is lending unreal money, invented money, ghost money, money which has never been earned and which, in fact, does no exist. In other words, when a man offers his house to a bank as the security for a loan he is getting nothing from the bank and is being compelled to pay the bank a rent for his own house, this rent being disguised under the name of *interest on the loan*. If he does not pay his rent he will be turned out of his house. The banker, in short, has seized his house without payment.

But what, after all, does that matter if the loan made by the banker can be used to buy goods? In actual practice, surely, there is no difference between real (or earned) money and invented money? This argument is often advanced; it will not bear inspection. For in truth what is unreal is being traded for goods; the fact that goods are given in exchange for it does not and cannot affect or change its quality of unreality. Now it is forbidden to create unreal money, or indeed any money, for the power of issuing money belongs to the King. When unreal money (credit) is issued the King is mulcted and with the King *all his subjects*, including the borrower of the unreal money himself. The reason is that if the King had issued the loan the interest paid on it would have gone to defray national expenditure and so to reduce taxation.

A loan of real (earned) money by one private person to another inflicts no injury on the King. For this money is *not a fresh creation,* but merely a transfer from one hand to another of money already created, being, in that respect, on a footing with any ordinary transaction of buying or selling. It is the act of creation of money which constitutes the evil. If banks lent only money in their actual possession their operations would not be indictable on this count. The indictment rests on the fact that they *do not possess* the money which they lend.

The King, in short, is entitled to the interest on loans of *newly created* money since he alone is empowered to create money and since the creation of money, by adding to the amount of money in existence, imposes a loss, however small, on all owners of money (according to the rule that the more money there is in a country the less it will buy). Where the King takes interest on his loans he is thus restoring in some part the loss occasioned when money was created in order to make the loans. This does not apply to a private lender. For the private lender does not create money and does not therefore impose any loss on his fellows. His interest is merely a usufruct for a genuine loan of genuine money. If banks did not create credit, private lenders, in company with all the Kings's subjects, would enjoy - in form of reduced taxationthe benefit of the interest payments made to the King by the recipients of his loans (the equivalent of which interest is now going into the pockets of the bankers), and so (since interest paid to banks represents a relatively enormous sum each year) would be able to lend more cheaply. Thus the borrower would benefit twice over; in the first place as a subject of the King enjoying a remission of taxation himself, and secondly as a borrower from a subject of the King who also was enjoying a remission of taxation. The unreal money of the banks therefore costs more to borrow than true money would cost, whether that true money was created by the King or merely lent by private persons. In other words, the bankers are enabled, by reason of their creation of credit, to annex for their own advantage what belongs to the King and his people.

But this legal spoliation remains unsuspected because people think they are getting solid gold from the banker. The bankers therefore are desperately concerned to keep up the illusion of the *gold backing* - that is to say, to avoid being caught out, as would be apt to occur if they ran short of the indispensable *tenth part*, the pounds, schillings and pence which are likely to be asked for. Here is the reason for the frequent amalgamations of banks and for the tendency to concentrate the business of banking in fewer and fewer hands.

It is out of this tendency that the conception of a Central Bank or bankers' bank has grown. A chief function of a Central Bank is to prevent ordinary banks from inventing too much money (making too many loans) and so, perhaps, incurring liabilities in excess of their available pounds, shillings and pence, and so, by their default, exposing the hollowness of the gold standard sham. Ordinary banks are now compelled to keep some of their resources in the Central Bank. The power to prevent excessive lending serves, in addition, the purpose already discussed of withdrawing buying power from the country and so compelling producers to cut wages.

A Central Bank, as has been said, can perform all its functions in the absence of the gold standard. It, too, can and does invent money out of nothing by the simple process of writing cheques against itself. But it, too, is concerned to hide this operation behind a smoke-screen of gold lest nations should be tempted to adopt its methods for themselves. So long as nations believe that the loans advanced to them by Central

Banks are backed by solid gold, so long will they be willing to pay interest on these loans.

Consequently it was long ago secured by various Acts of Parliament that the Central Bank, the Bank of England, shall hold the gold stock of the country and, as has been said, shall only issue pounds, shillings and pence (above the limit of the Fiduciary Issue) against gold actually held by itself. No Government can create gold. Therefore under these Acts of Parliament no Government can issue any money and therefore no Government can invent any money in the manner of a banker making a loan. The owners of money consequently are in a position to compel all borrowers the world over (and that means all farmers, all producers, and all wage-earners) to produce as cheaply as possible and so to pay the highest possible rates of interest on loans, the question of security of course being taken into consideration. As has been seen, they are in a position to terrify Governments which show a disposition to become unprofitable debtors, whether by failure to balance their Budgets or otherwise. (In these circumstances the owners of gold demand it from the Central Bank in the form of bullion, with the result that the Central Bank must call up its loans and force the ordinary banks to do the same. Prices rush down and ruin and bankruptcy march through the land.)

It is the fact, let it be repeated, that pounds, shillings and pence are based on gold and that bank loans are based (in the proportion of 10 to 1) on pounds, shillings and pence which puts these powers into the hands of the owners of gold. They can act with an effect which is rendered the more devastating in that the withdrawal of gold from a country entails the withdrawal of ten times that quantity of bankers' loans from agriculture and industry (so that the proportion of £10 loan to £1 currency may be maintained). As has been said, the engines which operate the gold process are the Central Banks. The men who conduct these banks are, of course, persons of the highest honour and distinction, and usually of an extraordinary efficiency in the discharge of their work. But the system under which they labour dominates them. It is certainly true to say that, as a class, bankers are sincere believers in their system, which seems to have hypnotized them, just as it has hypnotized Governments. It is the few, not the many, who know what is going on. The Money power does not number a very great many individuals, nor are these individuals men of the same race.

Under this system both Governments and Central Banks are compelled, usually without their knowing it, to serve the ends of the owners of gold. The Money power always appears as an angel of light. Sometimes it is International Friendship, sometimes Disarmament, sometimes Cancellation of Reparations and War Debts, sometimes the Stability of Prices. Thus Central Banks, loaded with their chains of gold, become agents of what is essentially a foreign power in occupation of a conquered territory. The refusal of the owners of gold to lend it to countries which have not adopted the gold standard and set up a Central Bank affords a clear indication of the true state of affairs.

It is evident that if a *Central Bank of Central Banks* were to be established, the needs of nations, even of whole continents, would inevitably be subordinated, in the same way, to the movements of gold. There would be no appeal anywhere against the law as promulgated by such an institution.

But it must never be forgotten that any Central Bank can, by buying or selling on the Stock Exchange, prevent movements of gold from exerting their ordinary effects on the price level. Central Banks have the power to prevent money from finding its level and the power to replace it once it has been taken away. They have the power, therefore, even when the gold standard is in full operation, to prevent lenders of gold from inflicting punishments on the countries in which they operate.

Why do Central Banks so very seldom exercise this power? The answer can only be that the Parliaments which these Central Banks are supposed to serve are themselves so wholly under the influence of the prevailing monetary doctrine that they do not dream of questioning the will of the Money power. Parliaments have the right to compel Central Banks to keep the price level at any point decided upon, and Central Banks can obey such an order without the slightest difficulty no matter what the owners of gold may care to do with their commodity. The criticisms, therefore, which apply to Central Banks apply also, with even greater force, to Parliaments.

This is seen clearly when the present state of the world is considered. At this hour (December 1932) most of the owners of gold in the world are hoarding it. The removal of so great a quantity of pounds, shillings and pence has profoundly affected the quantity of bank loans based, in the proportion of 10 to 1, upon these pounds, shillings and pence (If, for example, it be true that a sum of £1,500,000,000 of the world's gold - three-quarter of the total stock - is hoarded at the present time, then loans to the value of £15,000,000,000 have been called in throughout the world.) A loss of buying power in the form of wages, salaries, and dividends of this colossal size has necessarily caused a catastrophic fall in prices. Though everyone is aware that, if the buying power could be replaced, prices would rise, agriculture and industry be stimulated, employment be provided, and the suffering and despair of millions of men and women be remedied, no Parliament on earth has lifted a finger to compel its Central Bank to raise prices.

The defence would be, of course, that if, for example, England raised her prices her exchange would fall and the cost of her imports would rise. How hollow is that contention is shown by the fact that Parliament has had no hesitation in imposing import taxes. The truth is that Members of Parliament cannot distinguish between gold and real wealth. They are fully persuaded that gold is wealth and tremble when they hear that it is leaving the country. Awful visions of ruin make them incapable of taking any strong line.

This attitude of bewilderment and anxiety is clearly displayed in the British Note to America on War Debts.

"The international monetary mechanism," said the Note, *"without which the modern world cannot effectively conduct its daily life, is being broken into pieces with all the manifold forms of privation and distress which this involves."*

The Note went on to describe in tones of ecstasy how -

"The market loans... raised during the last hundred years have converted whole territories from desolate swamps or uninhabited plains to flourishing provinces teeming with human life and producing great additions to the real wealth of the world."

So complete a misunderstanding of the aims of a Money power which invented out of nothing the greater part of these *market loans* in order handsomely to recoup itself with the real wealth which it had done nothing to create is indication enough of what mankind has to expect from the institution of Parliamentary Government.

The gold system was in operation in England immediately after Waterloo, though England was still, nominally, off the gold standard. Robert Owen, a most enlightened manufacturer, made at this time a tour of the industrial districts, taking his son, Robert Dale Owen, with him. This young lad wrote afterwards:

"As a preliminary measure we visited all the chief factories in Great Britain. The facts we collected seemed to me terrible almost beyond belief. Not in exceptional cases, but as a rule, we found children of ten years old worked regularly fourteen hours a day, with but half an hour's interval for the midday meal, which was eaten in the factory. In the fine-yarn cotton mills they were subjected to this labour in a temperature usually exceeding seventy-five degrees, and in all the cotton factories they breathed an atmosphere more or less injurious to the lungs, because of the dust and minute cotton fibres that pervaded it. In some cases we found that greed of gain had impelled the mill-owners to still greeter

extremes of inhumanity, utterly disgraceful, indeed, to a civilized nation. Their mills were run fifteen and, In exceptional cases, sixteen hours a day, with a single set of hands; and they did not scruple to employ children of both sexes from the age of eight. We actually found a considerable number under that age. It need not be said that such a system could not be maintained without corporal punishment.

Most of the overseers openly carried stout leather thongs, and we frequently saw even the youngest children severely beaten. We sought out the surgeons who were in the habit of attending these children, noting their names and the facts to which they testified. Their stories haunted my dreams. In some large factories from one-fourth to one-fifth of the children were either cripples or otherwise deformed, or permanently injured by excessive toil, sometimes by brutal abuse. The younger children seldom held out more than three or four years without serious illness, often ending in death. When we expressed surprise that parents should voluntarily condemn their sons and daughters to slavery so intolerable, the explanation seemed to be that many of the fathers were out of work themselves and so were, in a measure, driven to the sacrifice for want of bread; while others, imbruted by intemperance, saw with indifference an abuse of the infant faculties compared to which the infanticide of China may almost be termed humane."

It must be remembered, in fairness to the mill-owners, that spectacles of savage cruelty were very common a century ago, and that, in consequence, most people were hardened. Further, those mill-owners who had no independent access to capital were placed under the necessity of earning large profits if they wished to obtain credit from the bankers.

But Owen had proved, at his own mill at New Lanark, near Glasgow, that good conditions of work were not incompatible with profits. He approached the Government boldly, therefore, with demands that legislation should be introduced to prevent the horrors of which he had been witness. He got, at first, a favourable reception because the nobility was uneasy about what was going on in the new industrial towns, but the elder Sir Robert Peel, to whose care the *Factory Bill*, which embodied Owen's ideas, had been committed, soon began to waver. Peel was a manufacturer himself. In 1816 the House of Commons appointed a Committee to consider the Bill. In that same year Parliament decreed that gold coin should henceforth be the sole standard measure of value and should be legal tender for the payment of any amount. The sovereign made its appearance.

But the bank-notes remained side by side with the new sovereign in such quantity as to excite the lively distress of the financiers, who did not cease to agitate for the resumption of cash payments - that is to say, for a severe deflation of the currency. The Government, aware of the effect likely to be produced by a restriction of credit on the conditions of employment, hesitated to accede to these demands. Were the child-slaves to be driven yet more mercilessly? Owen expressed their feelings in his *Observations on the Effect of the Manufacturing System*.

"The poor," he wrote *"are at present in a situation infinitely more degraded and miserable than they were before the induction of those manufactures upon the success of which their bare subsistence now depends... The governing principle of trade*

manufactures is immediate pecuniary gain, to which, on the great scale, every other is made to give way. All are sedulously trained to buy cheap and sell dear; and to succeed in this art the parties must be trained to acquire strong powers of deception; and thus a spirit is generated through every class of traders destructive of that open, honest sincerity without which man cannot make others happy nor enjoy happiness himself.

"The effects of this principle of gain unrestrained are still more lamentable on the working classes, those who are employed in the operative part of the manufactures; for most of these branches are more or less unfavourable to the health and morals of adults. Yet parents do not hesitate to sacrifice the well-being of their children by putting them to occupations by which the constitution of their minds and bodies are rendered greatly inferior to what it might and ought to be under a system of common forethought and humanity...

"Thirty years ago the poorest peasants thought the age of fourteen sufficiently early for their children to commence regular labour, and they judged well... Under these circumstances the lower orders experienced not only a considerable degree of comfort, but they also had frequent opportunities for healthy, rational sports and amusements... Their services were willingly performed... Now the employer regards the employed as mere instruments of gain...

"Is it to be imagined that the British Government will ever put the chance of a trivial pecuniary gain of a few in competition with the solid welfare of so many millions of human beings?"

Owen was unaware that the God-system which King George III had vainly attempted to restore had now, with the fall of Napoleon, been wholly vanquished throughout Europe and replaced by the gain-system, whose god is money and whose weapons are greed and fear. He did not know that Kings had, everywhere, been cast down from their thrones in order that the usurper, Mammon, might reign as King of Kings. The people no longer possessed a father under God, but were to become, throughout Europe, the prey of parties each bidding desperately against the other for the favour of Money. But this enlightened man saw, very clearly, that the policy of cheapness which finance was imposing upon production was of no value either to the producers themselves or to the nation.

"No evil," he cried, *"ought to be more dreaded by a master manufacturer than the low wages of labour... There, in consequence of their numbers, are the greatest consumers of all articles; and it will always be found that when wages are high the country prospers; when they are low all classes suffer from the highest to the lowest, but more particularly the manufacturing interest... The real prosperity of any nation may be at all time accurately ascertained by the amount of wages, or the extent of the comforts which the productive classes can obtain in return for their labour."*

This was a re-statement of Napoleon's system. Like Napoleon, Owen saw the evil of placing foreign trade before home production.

"They (the manufacturers) *consider it to be the essence of wisdom,"* he wrote to the Prime Minister, Lord Liverpool, *"to expend millions of capital and years of extraordinary scientific application, as well as to sacrifice the health, morals, and comforts of the great mass of the subjects of a mighty empire, that they may uselessly improve the manufacture*

of, and increase the demand for, pins, needles, and threads; that they may have the singular satisfaction, after immense care, labour, and anxiety on their own parts, to destroy the real wealth and strength of their own country by gradually undermining the morals and physical vigour of its inhabitants, for the sole end of relieving other nations of their due share of this enviable process of pin, needle, and thread making..."

"We complain," he wrote to the manufacturers themselves *"that all markets are overstocked with our manufactures, and yet we compel our little children, and millions of adults, to labour almost day and night, to urge forward perpetually increasing mechanical powers that these markets may be still more overstocked."*

The explanation of the absurdity was hidden from Owen as it is hidden still from many of his fellow-countrymen. What was happening was that the masters of money were engaged in making their money more valuable in terms of goods, by refusing to lend it. Banks were restricting credit so that a larger quantity of goods had to be given in exchange for the money which remained. And this process was going on all over Europe in the countries which had been "rescued" from Napoleon's grasp. In order to pay the interests on their borrowings and earn a profit for themselves, manufacturers had to urge their workpeople to redoubled efforts, so that loss of price might be compensated for by increase of quantity. This remedy was effective only for a short time, for the restriction of credit reduced buying power throughout Europe and so also reduced the volume of sales. Sales could now be stimulated only by further reductions of price, and hence wages were mercilessly cut to the *subsistence level*

But these cuts reduced further the power of the workers to buy their masters' products, and so threw fresh masses of goods on to the foreign markets, which, being also deflated, could not absorb them.

This process of *healthy deflation* achieved its purpose. By July 1816, gold had fallen in value in terms of sterling (that is to say, of pounds, shillings and pence) from £4 an ounce to £3 19s. By October the price of gold was £3 18s. 6d. Sterling was rising in value; the exchanges moved in England's favour and gold flowed into the country. In November 1816, the Directors of the Bank of England announced that they proposed to give gold in exchange for all notes of less than £5 issued before the beginning of 1812. Five months later gold was paid for small notes issued before the beginning of 1816, and again, six months later, for small notes issued before the beginning of 1817.

But the severe distresses and afflictions which attended these operations spread dismay throughout the land. A great public meeting with the Duke of York in the chair was held. The Duke of York and the Duke of Kent devoted themselves to the work of alleviating distress, and so also did the leading churchmen. Nobody seemed to know what had happened, and, as the financiers offered no enlightenment, all kinds of incorrect explanations were offered - for example, that the war had effected a huge destruction of property and so taken the bread out of the mouths of the poor (this in face of a terrifying *overproduction* and piles of unsaleable goods), and that overpopulation was exhausting natural resources.

The financiers knew better, devoted their attention to the relationship between sterling and gold, and continued to agitate for *cash payments* - that is to say, for *stabilization* of the note issue on gold. But their cries happily were less urgent in the ears of the authorities than those of the starving children, and some additions were made to the available quantity of paper money. The gold value of the sterling notes fell in proportion to this increase in their quantity, and gold, therefore, became dearer in terms of sterling. The price of gold rose to £4 an ounce, then to £4 os. 6d. and £4 IS. The golden sovereign, in other words, had become worth more than the paper pound outside of Great Britain. Inside of Great Britain the law recognized no difference between gold and notes. Both bought exactly the same quantity of goods. The golden sovereign, therefore, was more valuable in, say, France than in England, for in France it was not placed on a level with the *"depreciated"* notes. Owners of sovereigns, therefore, at once began to melt them down - in defiance of the law - and ship them across the Channel.

"Gold," says Feavearyear, "began to leave the Bank, at first slowly, and then, in February 1818, when the price touched £4 2s. 6d., much more rapidly. The reserve (i.e., the Bank's reserve of gold) fell from over 11½ millions in August 1817 to less than 6½ millions in August 1818, and to little more than 4 millions in February 1819... In January 1819 gold went up to £4 3s... A new Parliament met and was faced at once with appeals and petitions from merchants and manufacturers all over the country against the resumption of cash payments (i.e. making the depreciated pound-notes again worth a golden sovereign). The House was not disposed even yet to face the real issue and decide whether the old standard should be restored, regardless of consequences, or whether some new gold unit of lower value should be introduced. The Government was prepared weakly to drift on... but there were... dissensions in the Bank parlour. Some at least of the Directors had begun to realize that, sooner or later, the Bank would have to justify itself in its failure to carry out the declared policy of the Government and resume cash payments.

"... Upon the motion of Vansittart the House at last appointed a Committee which included Castlereagh, Canning, Tierney, Huskisson, Vansittart himself, and Peel (the younger), the last-named being chairman, to inquire into the expediency of resuming cash payments."

Peel's Committee issued its first report on April 5, 1819, and its main report on May 6, 1819. It recommended a gradual return to the old gold standard (£3 17s. 10½d. per ounce of gold) to be completed by May 1, 1823. It further recommended that it should be lawful for any person to export the gold and silver coins of the realm to places overseas, and also to melt them and to manufacture, export or otherwise dispose of the bullion thereby produced, notwithstanding any provision to the contrary in any other Act.

To their great credit the Bank of England's Directors who seem to have foreseen the probable course of events protested to Parliament against these recommendations, which, as they knew, delivered the nation over to the mercy of the International Money

System. It was their business, they said, to look after the well-being of the commercial community, but the affairs of the nation were the concern of the King and his parliament. Their objection was brushed aside. Peel introduced the Bill to give effect to the report and it was passed without a division.

Thus were the financial bases of the God-system swept ruthlessly away and actions which formerly had been branded as felonies transformed into virtues. It was open now to Money to change the value of the King's currency according to its own will, to melt down that currency, to ship it out of England, and to plunge the English people into the grievous distresses of a lack of purchasing power. Money, with the unanimous consent of Parliament, had usurped one of the greatest prerogatives of the Throne. Money was seated on the throne. For he who can, at will, bestow plenty or inflict starvation holds a power that is like to God's. Until this time men had not been willing that such a power should be wielded except by Royal hands.

Here, in short, was a revolution greater by far in its scope and consequences than the French Revolution; the final break with the God-system upon which the civilization of Europe was built; the permanent enthronement of Mammon, the gain-system, in the place of Kings. Here was denial of the Christian doctrines of the fatherhood of God (and under God, of the King) and the brotherhood of men. Denial, too, of the nation and of the patriotism which binds men to their fatherland. Denial of duty, if duty should conflict with self-interest; of kindness, if kindness should add to costs; of mercy even, if mercy should entail the release of child labourers from bondage. Here was denial of faith, which is born of the service of God and men and of righteousness which exalteth a nation. *"The American economic system,"* said a City Note of *The Times* of August 8, 1932 *"is based on starvation"* That is the system which was established by the British Parliament on May 24, 1819.

It remains to ask how the high Tory, Robert Peel, and a Parliament based largely on the land owning classes were so easily persuaded by a power which in fact threatened them, and all they stood for, with destruction.

The answer is certainly to be found in the French Revolution and in the depreciation of the Assignat. No argument is more effective today, as a warning against inflation, than the depreciation of the German mark immediately after the Great War. It was the same in 1819. The Money power had only to recall how a national currency had fallen in utter ruin in a few months in order to terrify the Commons. The Assignat had been Robespierre's money; did they want to see the pound sterling fell into similar hands and be used to serve a similar purpose? Did they want to see it crash in similar ruins? Thanks to the deflation, riots were occurring in many parts of the country and the Commons were deeply uneasy. A financial panic, with which they were threatened, seemed to carry with it the dreadful threat, even the probability, of Revolution.

The Money power, in short, which had caused the Revolution in France and which, later, had destroyed the Assignat now made use of both these calamities to inspire terror in the minds of the English Government, which was persuaded that only the Money power could save it from ruin - an interesting example of economy of means.

The origin of these distresses was the belief of governments and peoples that gold gives money its value. That, on the contrary, *it is its use as money which gives gold its value*, will be obvious to anyone who asks himself what the value of gold would be if its use as money was suspended. It is only because very few people ever ask this question that the Money power is able to flourish, and is allowed to create (credit) unreal money. The Money power is therefore concerned to maintain the illusion that it has a gold backing behind all its liabilities and punishes severely any banker who, by unduly expanding his loans, threatens that illusion.

Chapter XII

MAMMON

ONE of Robert Owen's staunchest supporters was the Duke of Kent, the father of Queen Victoria. The Duke actually took the chair at a meeting addressed by Owen, and until the end of his life, in 1820, remained the mill-owner's friend.

For, if Parliament had enthroned money, the Royal Family of England remained to dispute that act of usurpation. All that can be said against King George IV, whether as Regent or Sovereign, has been said. It remains to add that he suffered, along with his brothers, in the affliction which now visited the English people, and that, like them, he desired ardently to rescue his subjects from these afflictions.

In this respect he resembled the other European Kings, Francis I of Austria, Frederick William of Prussia, Alexander I of Russia, and even Louis XVIII and Charles X France. All these Kings were being compelled to effect the "stabilization" of their paper money on pain of the refusal of further loans. The farmer everywhere had therefore to give more of his produce to secure the means of paying his debts; in consequence he had everywhere less to spend on manufactured goods. And so the manufacturers were compelled to cheapen production, to cut wages, and at last to dismiss their hands. They could not pay taxes; all the Budgets of Europe were unbalanced.

The cry of the out-of-work and the dispossessed ascended to Heaven. The Kings, who retained the bowels of mercy, tried to borrow money for schemes of relief, only to find that they had no credit. Those financiers who had been eager to discount their paper when the object was the destruction of Napoleon returned now insolent refusals or demanded rates of interest which were prohibitive. When Kings and nobles in bewilderment tried to resort to their ancient methods and to act with a high hand they were met by an opposition which caused them, instantly, to desist.

Necker's methods were in use once more. Necker, as has been seen, had destroyed King Louis XVI by allying himself to the nobles and had then destroyed the nobles with the Liberals' help. Thanks to the Revolution the Liberals were now both numerous and active in Europe. Finance made common cause with them. When Kings protested that their people were being destroyed, when nobles resisted the drain of young men and women from the countryside to the factories, they were met by shouts of execration about "privilege," "landlordism," and "feudal abuses." It was the fate which Napoleon had prophesied for them and they were powerless to resist it.

Money controlled the Press; Money was demanding already Parliaments purged of the "landed interest"; orators, agitators, and demagogues stumped all the countries declaring that the prevailing distresses were due to the greed of the "drones" who, in their castles, devoured the hard-won substance of the poor.

These Liberals were, of course, perfectly sincere men. They had imbibed the doctrine of finance as expounded by a number of brilliant writers, notably Adam Smith and Ricardo. They lay under a sense of horror not less lively than that which vexed the minds of Kings and nobles. Somebody they felt must be responsible for this shambles. Who more likely to be responsible than the reputed great ones of the earth? They declaimed therefore against "paper money," against "rotten boroughs," and against the laws prohibiting the free import of wheat, which, as they convinced themselves, existed solely in the interests of landlords.

It is only when these charges are examined in the light of the Money System that their real sources can be determined. It is of the essence of the Money System, as has been said, and must constantly be repeated, that it makes its loans in the most profitable areas and, in consequence - by means of forced exports - keeps the European countries in a condition of permanent deflation. There is never enough buying power in any European country to enable the inhabitants to absorb the goods produced by themselves. Consequently the export trade is always a matter of life and death for producers and manufacturers, and it is constantly being stimulated, in the manner described above, by new foreign investments. Goods must be sold at prices which will enable them to compete with the goods of other countries. Wages, therefore, must be kept down to the lowest possible level.

It is the price of bread which, everywhere in Europe, determines this lowest possible level. Cheaper bread means lower wages. When the Money power demanded the Repeal of the Corn Laws and the introduction of a system of free imports it was demanding, in fact, a general reduction of wages, or rather, since wages had already in many cases been forced down below reasonable subsistence level, a higher standard of nourishment - and therefore of working power - for the same wages. The chief obstacle to repeal was the existing House of Commons in which the interests of agriculture were predominant. The Money power, therefore, began to agitate vigorously for Parliamentary Reform and to subsidize the "Radicals."

In the first years after Waterloo the nation was split up into parties each one of which saw in the other a mortal enemy. The process of making the sterling notes worth more gold, which proceeded actually twice as quickly as had been intended, threw ten per cent. of the population, some 2,000,000 men, women, and children, out of work by causing a slump in prices and so making production unprofitable. These wretched creatures were compelled to seek parish relief or starve, and engaged in riots and other disturbances. Fear of them was abroad and they were quelled with cruel violence. Their former masters, the manufacturers, were by the same slump in prices brought in many cases to ruin, and large numbers of mills were closed. Master and man were, therefore, set in opposition to one another, because the men believed that their masters wished to enslave or starve them, and the masters saw in the demands of the men for wages on which they could live a deadly threat to their own power to compete in foreign markets - and so to their solvency.

Both masters and men, meanwhile, were persuaded that the farmers were their foes. For the farmers desired to retain the Corn Laws, which were their last shield against ruin Masters and men were not less hostile to the nobles and land-owners, and in this hostility had the support of the farmers, who could obtain only very low prices for their produce and yet were compelled to pay the same rents as they had paid when prices were high - when, that is to say, the pound was worth much less in terms of goods.

It was to these distracted and suffering people that the economists and radicals preached the doctrines of the Money power about human rights. Misery and starvation found the doctrines irresistible. A republican spirit began to manifest itself and hostility to the Royal House was openly shown. Noblemen were held up to execration and even the Duke of Wellington became an object of hate. In vain the nobles urged that her agriculture was England's soul. In vain they pleaded for the village as against the industrial town with its foul dens and its squalor. They were fighting for their privileges. Away with them.

The House of Commons became alarmed and set up a Committee on Agricultural Distress which reported in June 1821. This Committee expressed the view that some part of the fall in prices was due to the reduction in the quantity of buying power occasioned by the effort to make pounds, shillings and pence worth more gold at a time when so many other countries were doing the same thing and when, therefore, gold was scarce and dear. Similar depressions, it was pointed out, prevailed all over Europe. Though Charles Western, the Member for Essex, fought a stout battle for the farmers, Parliament, now subservient to its new sovereign in the City of London, refused to take any action. Ricardo was put up to defend the Money power.

But a year later the situation had become so desperate that a fresh "insurrection" broke out. The Government now actually dared, in opposition to the City of London, to allow some 500 country banks to issue unlimited quantities of £1 notes payable to bearer on demand, in gold. The Bank of England, at the same time, was urged to afford all the help in its power.

The Bank of England had not forgotten its protest against Sir Robert Peel's surrender to the Money power. The Directors of the Bank heartily disapproved of that surrender, refused to play the part of a Central Bank, and continued to look on themselves as the servants of King and people - that is to say, as the managers of the King's money for his Majesty's advantage. What could be more to the advantage of his Majesty than that the productive powers of his people should be used fully for his people's good? The withdrawal of buying power, consequent on the permission to melt and export the King's money, had paralyzed the national life. The Directors were ready, even eager, to restore buying power by making money more plentiful.

The effect exceeded every hope. Prices rose. The farmer was thus enabled to earn his living and to buy from the manufacturer, who, in turn, was enabled to employ labour. As labour was not too plentiful for the needs of a thriving industry, wages began to rise. So bright did the prospects seem that a great expansion of trade began and more than 600 new companies were formed within two years. It seemed, for a moment, as if the years of gloom had been, miraculously, dispelled for ever.

But only for a moment. For this making of money plentiful to meet the needs of the King and his people was an act of rebellion against Money of the most serious kind. Because money was plentiful prices were rising. Money therefore was losing some of its value; it bought less goods; the time had come to invest it in countries where its value was higher. Exports were forced up and prices began to fall, but the fall was not catastrophic enough to please the Money power.

The usual propaganda against "speculators" and "bubble flotations" now began in order to prepare the public mind for what was coming. Lord Liverpool, in March 1825, warned the "speculators" that gold was "leaving the country." The country banks remembered that (thanks to Peel) the duty of giving gold for their £1 notes had been laid upon them. Terrified, suddenly, they began to refuse to lend to their customers and a sharp restriction of buying power at once took place. Instantly prices began to fall really sharply. All the calculations which had been based on the idea that high prices would be maintained were falsified. The whole producing world feared bankruptcy. Holders of paper notes and persons with balances of money at their banks clamoured for *gold*. There was no gold, for, as has been seen, the Money power lends £10 for every £1 which it possesses on the assumption and in the hope that people will not ask for gold in any large amount.

The Government now submitted unconditionally to the sovereign in the City against whom it had dared to rebel by allowing money to be made plentiful. It actually promised to give no help of any kind to the "speculators," and *The Times* thus addressed its readers:

"As for relief from the King's Government, we can tell the speculating people and their great foster-mother in Threadneedle Street (the Bank of England) that they will meet with none - no, not a particle - of the species of relief which they look for. The King's ministers know very well the causes of the evil and the extent of it and its natural or appropriate remedy, and we may venture to forewarn the men of paper that no such help as they are seeking will be contributed by the State."

The "natural and appropriate remedy" was to make money scarce again and so to increase its value. This, of course, meant a fall in the prices of goods and so ruin for landowners, farmers, manufacturers and merchants, and the small country banks which had served their needs, and starvation for the entire working class. So violent was the crash produced that panic seized upon the whole country and troops had to be called out to protect the country banks. On Monday, December 12, 1825 ("Black Monday") the panic reached its height.

"To intensify the mental gloom of that Monday," says Feavearyear, "the city was wrapped in one of those blacknesses which only London can manufacture. Throughout the week every day brought news of a fresh crop of country failures. In three weeks sixty-one country banks and six important London houses ceased payment. The terrible despair and helplessness of everyone in the first week of panic in face of the complete refusal of both the Bank and the Government to render assistance were remembered for many years."

The Bank's refusal to help was, in fact, imposed on it by the Government. Throughout the week the Directors kept urging that help in the form of an increased amount of money should be given, for they had not, to their honour, accepted the view, now everywhere being dinned into the public, that the crash and the panic were a visitation in the form of "inexorable economic law" which had somehow been violated. The Bank of England, in other words, had not yet been wholly subjected to the Money power. The Directors found in their vaults a box of small notes dated 1818 which had never been issued and demanded of the Government the right to issue them. Because the ruin was so universal this was granted. The Directors now exerted their utmost efforts - by discounting doubtful paper and by every other known means of increasing buying power and raising prices - to rescue the nation. They succeeded; by the end of the year the financial crisis was over.

But the wreckage remained. The Money power, seated again on its throne, pointed to this wreckage as proof of the evil of making money plentiful and goods dear (whereas it had been caused solely by making money scarce and goods cheap), and demanded in menacing tones that the Bank of England must be brought at once into subjection and for ever rendered powerless to multiply and cheapen money in such fashion. Parliament met in February 1826 and immediately passed an Act (March 22, 1826) forbidding the issue in England and Wales of any more banknotes of smaller denomination than £5 and ordering the redemption of all existing notes within three years.

Meanwhile the suffering and tragedy which followed the collapse of prices of 1825 exceeded anything formerly known in England even in times of famine. Distress, however, has always furnished the Money power with fresh arguments against its opponents. As the agony of the working classes increased, the demands of the Radicals for Parliamentary Reform (as the necessary preliminary to the repeal of the Corn Laws) grew in violence. A nation frantic with suffering began to look forward to "Reform" as to the Millennium, and was encouraged in that attitude, every day, by those organs of the Press which expounded the doctrines of the Money power.

The Press in England, and throughout Europe, remained entirely faithful to Money. It owed its origin, at least in its modern form, to finance. Except for the years during which Napoleon had bent it to the uses of the service-system, it had served always the uses of the system of gain. Its complete freedom was therefore insisted upon as a first article of faith of Financial Liberalism. So much so, indeed, that when King Charles X of France, the last surviving brother of Louis XVI, who owed his throne to the conquerors of Napoleon, took pity on his oppressed and starving subjects and, in the Napoleonic manner, tried to muzzle the Paris newspapers as a preliminary to dealing with the Money power, the throne of the Bourbons was flung finally into the gutter.

The French peasantry, thus instructed about who their master was, cast longing eyes at Napoleon's son, the King of Rome, Metternich's prisoner in Vienna; but Money set Louis Philippe, the "bankers' King," upon the throne.

That the English Press would have effected a similar change, had any attempt to restrain it been made, is certain. As has been said, a strongly republican spirit was abroad; the sovereign in the City had no love of its rival at the Palace and would have attacked without compunction, for there lingers, unsleeping, in the mind of Mammon the fear of the King's grace. As it happened King George IV died in 1830 and was succeeded by his brother, King William IV, who enjoyed a very great popularity. Wellington, who was Prime Minister, was defeated and resigned, and Lord Grey succeeded him. Four months later Lord John Russell introduced his Reform Bill. It became law the following year, 1832. King William for a time refused to create enough Whig peers to force it through the House of Lords, but a sudden and threatening " run " on the Bank of England, which was deliberately organized by the supporters of the Bill, achieved its purpose of creating panic, and so alarmed the King that he gave way.

Nobody, during this period, questioned the right of the bankers to issue unreal (credit) money. The sole concern was to prevent action which might have the effect of shattering the illusion that bankers possess the means of meeting all their liabilities in gold. Obviously had bankers really possessed such means the crisis of 1825 could not have occurred. A series of financial panics extending over more than a century has not yet taught people that so long as banks are allowed to create money out of nothing - no matter in what proportion to the money held by them - the means of meeting all their liabilities must always be lacking.

Chapter XIII

"The Hungry Forties"

THE passage of the Reform Bill made Free Trade certain. For the only power which had an interest in maintaining English agriculture was now deprived of its political ascendancy. More and more the views of the leaders of finance and industry were bound to prevail.

The leaders of finance had two chief reasons for demanding Free Trade - namely, that they wished their foreign debtors to be able to pay in goods the interests on the loans made to them and that they wished to keep wages as low as possible in the home market. At the risk of repetition it must be insisted that the Money system is a system whereby human productiveness is made to yield advantage not to mankind as a whole but to the owners of gold. The owners of gold can obtain advantage only by lending their gold to producers and obtaining from producers interest upon it.

Now producers produce not gold, but goods of various kinds. It follows that, unless these goods can be sold for money, interest on loans cannot be paid in money. An Australian farmer who has borrowed 1,000 at 5 per cent., for example, must sell at least 50 worth of his products in order to be able to pay the interest on his loans. Farmers do not usually sell to farmers; they sell to people engaged in industry or business. Consequently when a man lends money to a farmer he wants to be assured that the farmer has a market in some industrial area. The greatest industrial area in the world, during the first half of the Nineteenth Century, was Great Britain.

It was therefore to the interest of every lender to agricultural countries that the British market should be open to farm produce of all sorts.

But the lender to agricultural countries, as has been shown, does not usually send money to those who borrow from him. What he does is to place a credit at the disposal of the borrowers. The borrowers, as farmers, use this credit to buy ploughs, reaping machines, and so on, in the lenders' home market and thus increase the total of exports from that market. It is obvious that the more ploughs and reaping machines they can get for their money the larger will be the profits they can earn *and the more desirable, therefore, they will be as borrowers*. The lender to these farmers is concerned consequently that industrial production shall be carried on as cheaply as possible.

Now industrial production cannot be carried on cheaply if wages are high. And wages cannot be lowered if food is dear. A free market therefore, in which every farmer must needs compete with every other farmer, secures the double advantage of enabling interest on loans to be paid and of placing the borrowers of these loans in a good position to pay them. It serves, further, as a check on these borrowers. For a farmer whose prices are too high, by reason, for example, of high wages, will not be able to sell his goods. Farmers no less than industrialists are compelled, in consequence, to keep wages as low as possible.

And what applies to lenders to farmers, applies with equal force to lenders to industrialists. Industrialists spend the loans made to them in buying machinery and raw materials and in paying wages. The lower the wages paid by them, the more cheaply can they sell in foreign markets and the more, therefore, can they export to the farmers who have obtained loans.

It will be seen that, in both these cases, there is laid upon the borrower (farmer or industrialist) the necessity not only of selling at a profit, but of *selling cheaply at a profit*. For if the industrialist does not maintain the balance of exports against imports gold will leave the country, as has already been explained, and if the farmer does not maintain his exports (which include the interest on the loans made to him) gold will leave his country also. The free market, as has been seen, pits farmer against farmer; it also pits industrialist against industrialist, seeing that foreign manufactured goods can be imported if home goods are not cheap enough.

In each instance the borrower, therefore, is forced to keep wages down to the lowest possible level and use every means to secure that wages never rise above this level. Thus the lender, usually a lender of unreal money, derives his advantage from the poverty and wretchedness of the working population, who are not permitted to share, except in so far as body and soul must be kept together, in the vast wealth they have helped to create.

Farmers have not, as a rule, been allowed to obtain much of this wealth for themselves, because they have fallen into the hands of middlemen equally concerned with the usurers to exploit them. But the great industrialists did certainly obtain immense profits as a result of working in the closest association with the Money power. Upon their shoulders, if to a less extent than upon the shoulders of Money, must rest the shame of the exploitation for gain of helpless men and women of their own blood and race.

Nevertheless the interests of producers and lenders, however closely these may work together at times, cannot permanently become identified. Although many of the leaders of industry have been, and still are, directors of banks and finance houses, a borrower and a lender become antagonists the moment the soundness of the borrower is in doubt. In the eyes of the Money power a borrower is unsound whenever his costs (wages) begin to rise. For this reason there is a constant ebb and flow of lending (the so-called "Credit Cycle"). Not only do the owners of gold change the incidence of their investments; at times, also, they cease to lend because their money seems unlikely to be safe or to earn enough interest. When this happens a world slump occurs. The conditions which prevail after a slump has continued for a time are very favourable, as will be shown later, to a resumption of lending on a substantial scale.

It is necessary to hold these facts in mind if the history of the booms and slumps which marked the first half of the Nineteenth Century is to be understood. And it is necessary above all to remember that the owners of gold were concerned, before everything else, to secure that money should never become divorced from their commodity. A rise of the prices of goods alarmed them therefore both as moneylenders and as gold-owners, for it was their constant fear that, if the rise was not checked, it might lead, through excessive borrowing by prosperous producers, to such a fall in the value of money as to drag the country off the gold standard. Their constant object was to obtain legislation compelling the Bank of England to make money scarcer the moment prices and wages showed any sign of rising. How they achieved this object is a story of much interest at the present time.

Naturally enough the producers of goods always offered resistance to attempts to lower the price of them. They favoured a plentiful supply of money. In periods of rising prices, before "costs" had begun to rise, they were usually favourably disposed to Finance; but in times of falling prices hostility tended to show itself until it was quenched by the lively fear of ruin.

During the years which immediately followed the passage of the Reform Act the leaders of industry were in evil case and therefore very humble; most of them had been so shaken and terrified by the crisis of 1825 that they had accepted the views of Money without reservation. They asked no longer for plentiful money and high prices of goods, but concentrated instead, as the economists advised them, on cheapness and the reduction of "costs" - *i.e.*, wages. Free imports, as has been said, promised lower wages and cheaper raw material. England might become the "workshop of the world," for nowhere else in Europe would money buy more.

The leaders of industry found their natural spokesman in Peel. Like him they were, for the most part, of conservative mind, deeply suspicious of the "Radicals," who had close affinities with the Whigs of the City of London, and, except in matters of finance, strongly imbued with nationalist feeling. It became Peel's business, therefore, after the passage of the Reform Bill, to change the old Tory party of the landlords into the modern Conservative party of the manufacturers, without, in the process, effecting any open rupture. The same kind of work was going on among the Whigs, where the landed interest was being superseded by the party of Financial Liberalism.

Thus differences which were purely political were replaced by differences which had an economic complexion.

Robert Owen, as has been said, saw the nature of these differences at a very early period. As he pointed out, it was in the interests of the manufacturer that his home market should be able to buy his goods. He had everything to gain by a flourishing agriculture and high wages. The interest of Money, on the contrary, was to hold down the price of goods and so increase its own value. Not the manufacturer, but the financier, as has been shown, has chief need of the export trade, and it is only when money has been made scarce in the home market, so that there is insufficient buying power, that the manufacturer becomes frantically concerned to cut wages, to "rationalize," to combine, and to find and develop foreign markets. If he could make a profit at home, he would not need to expend these exertions.

But in 1832, as has been said, the manufacturers were convinced that their best interests dictated humble duty to the City of London. They began, therefore, to agitate for the repeal of the Corn Laws and for Free Trade. Peel himself declared that he had been "converted" to Free Trade by Richard Cobden. The rump of the old Tory party naturally offered opposition to a policy which threatened what they believed to be the highest interest of the nation, but they stood no chance now that the representation of the Commons had been "reformed." Finance, indeed, was able to make of every protest which they uttered a fresh nail in their coffin. What, were they really in favour of unrepresentative government? Of privilege? Away with squire and parson politics. Those men who had no scruples about inflicting starvation on millions of their fellows actually appeared before the world as the champions of human right and of human happiness and spoke with unction of themselves as the "protectors of the people's food."

They were busy, in the year of reform, in "reforming" their enemy the Bank of England, which had now fallen into their clutches. A Parliamentary Committee on the Bank Charter (which Charter was due for renewal) was constituted and Jeremiah Harman, who had been Governor during the crisis of 1825, was called to explain his conduct. He stated that - "The first principle was attention to the security of the Bank itself, in which we considered the safety of the public, of course, very much involved; to render as much service as we could to the commercial community with propriety, always having reference to the means which we possessed of fulfilling our engagements."

His successor in the office of Governor, John Horsley Palmer, expressed different views. Palmer criticized the action of the Bank in supplying credit directly to commerce, saying:

"It is competition with private bankers and individuals in London which seems to me so objectionable."

The merchant, in other words, was in future to go to the Money market for loans and not to the Bank of England. The Bank of England was to become a Central Bank. If gold was leaving the country the Bank must raise its rate and so at once reduce buying power and bring down prices and wages; if, on the contrary, gold was coming in, the opposite process must be employed.

Palmer's views were soon incorporated in an Act which freed the Bank-rate from the operation of a Usury Law that forbade rates of interest above 5 per cent and turned the Bank itself into the chief agent of Money.

In 1835 large quantities of gold were shipped to America, where a high price was obtainable for the metal, and smaller quantities went to Ireland. The Bank of England obediently raised its rate from 4 to 4½ per cent. In September 1836 the rate was raised again to 5 per cent. This raising of the interest payable on loans happened to occur at a moment when a great number of railways were being built throughout England and Europe and when, in consequence, borrowing was active. A stout resistance was offered by the industrialists and they actually managed to compel their local banks to accommodate them. The Bank of England, in consequence, was forced to lend 1,300,000 to the Northern and Central Bank. It seemed for a moment as if industry had successfully defied finance.

In truth, however, the defiance was more apparent than real. It was made possible only by the accident of an influx of gold from the Continent which offset the efflux to America. The moment this influx stopped, in 1838, the Bank-rate was advanced again to 5 per cent.; then, in August 1838, to 6 per cent.; finally - the efflux to America continuing - the Bank of England was compelled to obtain a credit of £2,000,000 from the Bank of France to avoid being driven off gold. The prosperity which had returned to the industrial areas was destroyed by the fall in the prices of goods caused by the scarcity of money, and masters and men were plunged once more into gloom and despair. Further checks on borrowing and borrowers were now demanded by the Money power. These checks were supplied by the Bank Charter Act of 1844, the important clause of which was that which ordained that, *if gold left the country, pounds, shillings and pence to the value of the departing gold must be withdrawn from circulation.* Thus the danger that country banks dealing with industrialists might be tempted to make matters easy for their clients in defiance of the will of the Money power and to the detriment of the value of money was, it was supposed, finally removed.

But the demand for railways continued in spite of these measures, and the means of meeting the demand became available. Thanks to the fact that the demand for English goods outside of England was very great, employers were making profits on their exports. They began to invest their profits at home. The year 1844, therefore, saw a renewal of the "railway boom." It witnessed also a bad harvest which caused the price of wheat to rise. There was another bad harvest in 1845 and the Irish potato crop failed. Labour was in demand to build railways and was, therefore, relatively dear. Employers viewed with anxiety the possibility that it might become dearer still if the price of bread was advanced. They clamoured for the repeal of the Corn Laws, joining their voices to those of the financiers. Peel, now Prime Minister, gave them the Free Trade they desired.

The effect was to increase activity in every branch of industry, and this continued until all the capital available had been drawn into production. Prices and wages now rose and gold began to flow out. With the recollection of the panic of 1838 fresh in its mind the Bank of England hesitated to act, and proceeded so gently that nearly two years elapsed before the Bank-rate reached 5 per cent. When that happened, however, credit was everywhere restricted, prices fell, and failures began. In August 1847 the rate was raised again to 5½. Then on October 18, 1847, the Royal Bank of Liverpool closed its doors. The Government now ordered the Bank of

England to lend freely without regard to the Bank Charter Act and suggested 8 per cent. as the rate of interest. The panic passed and gloom once more descended.

It is probable that these "Hungry Forties," as their victims of the working class called them, would have been continued as "Hungry Fifties" had not the discovery in California and Australia of rich deposits of gold effected a sudden and dramatic change. The Californian gold began to arrive in 1849, the Australian in 1851. The owners of gold were now much more numerous.

There were more lenders than borrowers of a satisfactory type. Money became plentiful. Immediately prices throughout the world rose sharply and the dead weight of debt was everywhere lightened.

Chapter XIV

DISRAELI

BY the middle of the Nineteenth Century it had become apparent to a small number of people that the Money power was the most evil which had ever exerted oppression upon men and women. Among that small number was Benjamin Disraeli.

Disraeli earned fame by attacking Sir Robert Peel, and so, in effect, advancing the old Tory doctrine of the God-system against the doctrine of gain of the New Conservatism. With wisdom and justice he directed his early strictures against the condition of the workers, their wives and children throughout the land.

"When I hear," he told an audience in Shrewsbury, "a political economist or an anti-Corn-Law Leaguer, or some conceited Liberal reviewer, come forward and tell us, as a grand discovery of modern science, that 'Property has its duties as well as its rights,' my answer is that that is but a feeble plagiarism of the very principle of that Feudal System which you are always reviling. Let me next tell these gentlemen, who are so fond of telling us that property has its duties as well as its rights, that labour also has its rights as well as its duties; and when I see masses of property raised in this country which do not recognize that principle... when I hear of all this misery and all this suffering; when I know that evidence exists in our Parliament of a state of demoralization in the once happy population of this land which is not equalled in the most barbarous countries - cannot help suspecting that this has arisen because property has been permitted to be created and held without the performance of duties."

The same note was heard a few years later (August 1844).

"There is no subject," Disraeli told his constituents, "in which I have taken a deeper interest than the condition of the working classes... I had long been aware that there was something rotten in the core of our social system. I had seen that, while immense fortunes were accumulating, while wealth was increasing to a superabundance, and while Great Britain was cited throughout Europe as the most prosperous nation in the world, the working classes, the creators of wealth, were steeped in the most abject poverty and gradually sinking into the deepest degradation."

Disraeli had a shrewd idea of the nature of that "something rotten." He had founded a party called "Young England" and thus declared its mission:

"We want in the first place to impress upon society that there is such a thing as duty. We don't do that in any spirit of conceit or arrogance; we don't pretend that we are better than others, but we are anxious to do our duty and, if so, we think we have a right to call on others, whether rich or poor, to do theirs. If that principle of duty had not been lost sight of for the last fifty years you would never have heard of the classes into which England is divided...

"We see but little hope for this country so long as that spirit of faction is fostered and encouraged. We call it a spirit of faction, for the principles on which the parties who nominally divide this country were originally formed have worn out and ceased to exist; and an association of men, however powerful, without political principles is not a party but a faction. Of such a state of society the inevitable result is that public passions are excited for private ends..."

Disraeli, in other words, recognized the evils which subservience to the international system of Money had effected. He declared that the curse of money began with King William III, who had "introduced into England the system of Dutch finance":

"The principle (of Dutch finance) was to mortgage industry in order to protect property (money); abstractedly nothing can be conceived more unjust; its practice in England has been equally injurious. It has made debt a national habit; it has made credit the ruling power, not the exceptional auxiliary, of all transactions; it has introduced a loose, inexact, haphazard and dishonest spirit in the conduct of both public and private life; a spirit dazzling and yet dastardly; reckless of consequences and yet shrinking from responsibility. And in the end it has so overstimulated the energies of the population to maintain the material engagements of the State and of Society at large, that the moral condition of the people has been entirely lost sight of."

Never has the Money power been described with a more excellent justice, nor its responsibility for the destruction of the nations more clearly set forth. And Disraeli saw the remedy as clearly as Louis XIV, as Turgot, as Louis XVI, as George III, and as Napoleon had seen it:

"The tendency of advanced civilization is, in truth, to pure Monarchy. Monarchy is, indeed, a Government which requires a high degree of civilization for its full development. It needs the support of free laws and manners and of a widely diffused intelligence... In an enlightened age the Monarch on the throne, free from the vulgar prejudices and the corrupt interests of the subject, becomes again divine.

"Toryism still lives in the thought and sentiment and consecrated memory of the English nation. It has its origin in great principles and in noble instincts; it sympathises with the lowly; it looks up to the Most High... It is not dead, but sleepeth; and in an age of political materialism, of confused purposes and perplexed intelligence, that aspires only to wealth because it has faith in no other accomplishment, as men rifle cargoes on the verge of shipwreck, Toryism will yet rise from the tomb over which Bolingbroke shed his last tear, to bring back strength to the Crown, liberty to the subject, and to announce that power has only one duty; to secure the social welfare of the people."

Disraeli appeared, then, as the champion of the God-system, which "Dutch finance" had destroyed throughout Europe, and, consequently, as the enemy of the City of London. In this respect he was joined to his

Sovereign and her husband, both of whom beheld with horror and shame the destruction of the English people by the Money power, and agreed with the leader of the Young England party that this destruction was not primarily attributable to the leaders of industry.

"I beg to be understood," Disraeli had told his constituents, "that I do not join in the absurd cry against the manufacturing interest of the country. I respect the talents, the industry, the indomitable energy of that powerful class, and I acknowledge them as the primary source of our wealth and greatness; and although I am not blind to the fact that great distress, and perhaps tyranny, exists in the system... I fear, nay I am sure, that the condition of the agricultural labourers cannot be cited to the confusion of the manufacturing capitalists."

Nevertheless Disraeli was firmly convinced that agriculture is "the soul" (in Napoleonic phrase), and that therefore the "landed interest," which is neither more nor less than the leadership of agriculture, is essential to the national well-being. Disraeli saw in a restored and awakened "landed interest" the spearhead of the attack which it was now the purpose of his life to launch against "Dutch finance." He perceived, too, that a prosperity which depended chiefly upon the accident that England had possessed steam engines before other people was not likely to be of long duration. It was scarcely conceivable that the working people of England would be willing, for ever, to see their wives, while pregnant, compelled to toil in coal pits or to stand by - the men whose fathers had broken the Old Guard at Waterloo - while brutal overseers lashed the tender flesh of their children. Men would ask, one day, on whose behalf and for whose benefit were these abominations. They would learn, at last, that their employers, in spite of their wealth, were slaves like themselves, compelled to pursue courses hateful to most of their consciences and, in any case, harmful to all their pockets. In that day master and man, whether on the land or in the factory, would recognize their common enemy, that dreadful parasite which was consuming the blood of them both.

For this great Jew was under no illusions about the "services" which "Dutch finance" was supposed to be rendering to industry. He began to see this power as something great and sinister and terrible; without scruple and without mercy; ready, for its own interest, to hurl nation against nation, class against class, man against man. He gained knowledge about the sums spent by Money in subsidizing the economists and writers favourable to its claims and in maintaining a propagandist Press, and he soon reached the conclusion that Liberalism was but a pawn of the Money power. This was Queen Victoria's view also, and explains the deep and ineradicable dislike she felt for Mr. Gladstone.

Chapter XV

"Dutch Finance"

IT cannot be repeated too often that the reason why it was a criminal offence, before 1819, to export the King's money was that, when money leaves a country, no matter in what fashion, prices in that country fall. (This, as has been seen, is true today, although any Central Bank can prevent a fall of prices if it chooses to do so.)

By acquiring the power to export gold, therefore, its owners acquired the right to change the level of price of goods both in the country from which the gold was taken and in the country into which they chose to send it.

Generally speaking, they were guided by the simple rule that money must be removed at once from any country in which its safety or its power of earning a high rate of interest is threatened. High prices, as has been said, are an indication for the removal of money. On the other hand, social unrest, occasioned by very low prices, may also be an occasion, since, in the absence of a strong Government, it may lead to revolution and the repudiation of debt.

These considerations, as Disraeli saw, bear no relationship either to human welfare or to the power of producing goods. The Money power has acquired the right of creating demand and also of abolishing it at its pleasure, and so, in effect, has set itself in the place of humanity as well as in the place of Kings. When it wills that production shall take place it expands credit; when it wills that production shall cease, credit is restricted. Thus boom and slump may be made to follow each other in endless succession.

These considerations were present to Disraeli's mind. He saw that a free British market was an essential part of the scheme of "Dutch finance," not only as enabling wages in England to be kept down, but also as securing a dumping-ground for goods sent in payment of the interest on foreign loans and for goods which the deflated markets of Germany and France and America were unable to absorb. The free British market was the corner-stone of the whole edifice of boom and slump, of the feverish stimulation of production and the equally violent sabotage of goods and plant which always followed, of the inflations and deflations, of the hopes and despairs, above all of the destruction of national life and national credit in that most precious of its forms, the spiritual and moral well-being of the people.

Why not cut adrift from this hideous system and make of England a separate economic unit? Why not, by new Corn Laws, encourage the production of food at home and to keep upon the soil the matchless youth of England? Why not take away from Money the power to change at its will the value of the Queen's currency?

Suddenly a larger vision broke upon the statesman's mind. He saw, instead of England, the British Empire, rescued at last from "Dutch finance" - one Throne, one nation, with its agriculture and its manufactures established on the old basis of need and set free, for ever, from the bondage of Finance.

This was not a Free Trade area which he beheld, but a Nation; not an economic union, but a living organism. The British Empire should express the "God-thought" and the "King-thought"; it should find in the mystical power of the Throne its focus and its meaning. Then Money would return to its ancient servitude and be suffered no longer to usurp Crown and Sceptre. The leaders of agriculture and the leaders of industry would be the nobility of Empire, inspired by a lively sense of duty to their Sovereign and to their fellows, asking only the right to render a more excellent service.

The statesman unfolded his vision to the Queen and discovered that it was her vision also. For she, too, as has been said, grew sick at the spectacle of the bloody sacrifice of England which was being wrought. They entered into a fellowship of service, the first objects of which were to establish the Throne more firmly in the people's love, to awaken patriotism, and to re-make the nation, and to use this power ceaselessly to improve the lot of the workers so that, at every turn, the oppressor might find himself thwarted. Neither Queen nor statesman under-estimated the difficulties which lay ahead of them. For the moment the policy of the Money power was dominant and the doctrine of the Money power, in consequence, hard to refute. **The whole world spoke and thought in terms of gain, of**

foreign investment, of exports, of favourable balances of trade, of cheapness, of the movements of gold, of credit facilities. Money was proclaimed as the "life-blood of industry." But already, in glutted markets and falling profits, the signs of a change were being revealed. The day could not be very far distant when men would turn in weariness and disillusion from a system which no longer offered any recompense for the loss of faith and hope and charity.

Chapter XVI

Empress of India

DISRAELI did not exercise effective power in England until he had reached the age of seventy years. When he became Prime Minister in 1874, he found the country recovered from a financial crisis which had reached its height in 1866, but threatened already with a new crisis. The Franco-Prussian War had just been fought and Germany hat arrived at the position of a great Empire. She was adopting a gold, standard. Norway, Sweden, and Denmark had also (1872) adopted gold. In 1873 Holland had suspended the free coinage of silver. And meanwhile the stream of new gold from California and elsewhere was drying up. There was, therefore, a world-wide lack of gold, and consequently a tendency everywhere for prices to fall, seeing that money was held bound to gold with "hoops of steel."

"The fall of values," says R.G. Hawtrey (Sauerbeck's index number measuring prices in England fell from 111 in 1873 to 102 in 1874), "combined with the sudden subsidence of the stream of capital which had flowed from Europe to America, led to a violent crisis (in America) in September and October 1873."

The fall of prices was of world-wide extent, and consequently nobody could sell to anybody. The state of mind produced by such a calamity is the same everywhere and at all times.

Producers turn from the god gold, which has betrayed and deserted them, and busy themselves with devising methods of escape from their distresses which, in fact, represent approaches to the old order of service. The masters of Money have not, as a rule, been greatly alarmed, for experience has shown them that they have only to open their purses in order to recall the worshippers. But Disraeli saw his opportunity. Just before he took office he delivered a speech in which the keynote of his policy was sounded:

"No minister in this country," he declared, "will do his duty who neglects any opportunity of reconstructing as much as possible our colonial empire and of responding to those distant sympathies which may become the source of incalculable strength and happiness to this island."

After he had been in office for two years he bought the Suez Canal shares owned by the Khedive of Egypt, and secured to England control of the way to India. There followed the greatest act of statesmanship of the Nineteenth Century. Disraeli, almost alone of his countrymen, knew the virtue and value of the Throne. He knew that, under God, it is the Sovereign who makes the nation and that without Kingship nationhood is delivered over to Money. He conceived the idea not only of bringing India into the British Empire - that had already been accomplished - but of establishing for her a direct relationship with the Queen of England, so that the peoples of India might become a nation within the spiritual body of the British Empire. A Bill was introduced into Parliament by which the title Empress of India was conferred upon Queen Victoria.

Perhaps the only person who fully appreciated the service thus rendered to Britain and to India was the Queen herself. Then the Prime Minister set himself to discharge his duty to the workers of England. He had urged before taking office that one of the planks of his platform must be:

"SANITAS SANITORUM OMNIA SANITAS... Liberals call this a 'policy of sewage.' It is a policy of life and death... It involves the state of the dwellings of the people, the moral consequences of which are not less considerable than the physical. It involves the enjoyment of some of the chief elements of Nature - air, light, and water. It involves the regulation of their industry, the inspection of their toil. It involves the purity of their provisions, and it touches upon all the means by which you may wean them from the habits of excess and of brutality."

The magnificent work which was performed in the realms of public health, of factory life, and of peasant life by Disraeli laid the foundations of a better world. For the rest, Disraeli's term of office was spent chiefly in upholding the greatness of England in the face of Europe. This he considered to be a duty of the very highest importance. For, like Louis XIV and Napoleon, he understood that Nationhood and its emotion, patriotism, constitute a value in human affairs the importance of which is surpassed only by religion.

"Nationality," he said early in his career, "is the miracle of political independence. Race is the principle of physical analogy."

That distinction between the nation and the tribe comes with all the greater force from the lips of one of the most illustrious members of the Jewish race. It is fundamental to an understanding of the history of Europe. In his last days the old man, in his retreat at Hughenden, restated his principles and emphasized again the mystical relationship existing between God, King, and Nation. He seems to have felt that, just as Monarchy must be progressive and evolutionary, so must religion be, since man's knowledge of God cannot stand still.

"To have secured," he said in 1872, "a national profession of faith with the unlimited enjoyment of private judgment in matters spiritual is the solution of the most difficult problem and one of the triumphs of civilization."

Disraeli had no opportunity to carry farther his plans for a return to the God-system, and, indeed, knew that much time must pass before the system of gain was wholly discredited. But there was anxiety in the courts of Money. It was during his premiership that the Bank of England assumed control - still against the will of some of its Directors - of the entire gold reserve of the country, and so finally established an iron discipline over the banks with which the leaders of agriculture and industry had their dealings.

Chapter XVII

CHAMBERLAIN

DISRAELI's approach to the Empire had been that of a man deeply persuaded of its spiritual foundation, and impregnated with that highest form of romance to which the term Classicism is usually applied. He believed in God; he believed also in man. But in man as the servant of God, dimly aware of the Divine purpose and, by reason of that noble bewilderment, bound the more firmly to duty. The romanticism which finds its sanctions in passion was remote from his understanding. The idea, announced by Madame de Staël, that "love prepares the soul for virtue" was wholly repugnant to him, for he held that it is virtue which prepares the soul for love - love of God, of country, and of one's fellows. Whereas Madame de Staël was the prophetess of financial liberalism, as well as the founder of the French Romantic movement, Disraeli found his comfort in the sternest tradition of the aristocracy, *Noblesse oblige*, and wished to see that tradition brought splendidly into the fields and the market-places.

It is a matter of much interest and importance to turn from the study of this excellent statesman to the man, once his opponent, who, more than any other, entered into his mind and assumed his responsibility.

Joseph Chamberlain came to politics from industry and, in his youth, was a whole-hearted supporter of those doctrines which constitute the creed of the Money power and of which the Liberal party has usually been the vehicle. This creed, which exalted *laissez-faire* into a moral principle, proclaimed that nationalism is a survival from a barbarous past and must be replaced by an international outlook. The word nationalism indeed, was used only as a term of opprobrium, and was taken to mean a peculiarly objectionable form of insularity. To nationalism and "economic nationalism" were imputed wars and armaments; and it was argued that Free Trade promoted friendly feeling and banished suspicion. The worst form of nationalism, it was held, was that which is called Imperialism, because Imperialism led to plans for "Empire trade," and so threatened to restrict the entry of foreign goods into British markets throughout the world.

The fact of England's exclusive possession of steam-driven machinery gave much attractiveness, as has been said, to this creed, for the demand for English plant and English-manufactured goods was at one time very great. But, with the growth of manufacturing in Germany, France, and America, things began to wear a different complexion. It was found that, though fortunes had been made by producers, the poverty of the mass of the workers was unrelieved; many leaders of industry began to see that unless a lower standard of living was accepted by the working-class, profits, even modest profits, could no longer be hoped for. In these circumstances men of large hearts and lively patriotism began to experience doubts. Why had prosperity refused so obstinately and mysteriously to spread itself out over the whole population? Unlike Disraeli, these masters did not think of questioning the financial system under which they lived, and of which the extraordinary merits were dinned daily into their ears. Instead, they cast hostile eyes at the "Tory landlords," against whom the Money power had for long been directing their suspicions. This was both natural and inevitable. For the middle class held the upper class in jealousy, and there seemed to be no other enemy of progress and prosperity in sight. Henry George's famous book, *Progress and Poverty*, in which the landlord is indicated as the villain of the piece, became the bible of the new crusade. On August 12, 1881, Mr. Chamberlain, as President of the Board of Trade in Mr. Gladstone's Government, expounded the pure doctrine of Money to the House of Commons:

"Foreign countries," he said, "must continue to pay their debts. Not being able to pay in goods (if tariffs were imposed), they would have for the time to pay in bullion and specie; there would be an accumulation of the precious metal in this country, and that would speedily bring about a rise in the price of all other articles. When that rise had been established our power to export would be diminished..."

The speaker clearly under-estimated the skill of the financiers in preventing gold from reaching the home markets. Being challenged to explain the depression of trade then prevailing, which had revived the idea of protecting home industries, he delivered himself (on January 5, 1885) of a speech on "the doctrine of Ransom."

"There is," he said, "a doctrine in many men's mouths and in few men's practice, that (landed) property has obligations as well as rights... What are the rights of property? Is it a right of property which permits a foreign speculator to come to this country and lay waste two hundred miles of territory in Scotland for the gratification of his love of sport, and to chase from the lands which their fathers tilled, long before this intruder was ever heard of, the wretched peasants who have committed the crime of keeping a pet lamb within the sacred precincts of a deer forest?

Are the game laws a right of property?... Is it an essential condition of private ownership in land that the agricultural labourers in this country, alone of civilized countries, should be entirely divorced from the soil, that they should be driven into towns to compete with you for work and to lower the rate of wages, and that, alike in town and in country, the labouring population should be huddled into dwellings unfit for man or beast where the conditions of common decency are impossible and where they lead directly to disease, intemperance, and crime?"

A month later, on January 29, at Birmingham, the idea was cast in a new form.

"The present system," he said, "has been described as a system under which the landlord and the farmer combine to take everything out of the land and put nothing in. It has broken down.

Farmers have no capital; landlords declare they are penniless. Then the land must pass into other hands, and we must consider the advisability of creating and of preparing the way for a return to the old conditions when English agriculture was prosperous and the Poor Law was unknown."

But Mr. Chamberlain's mind was not satisfied with his villain, because, later in his speech, he referred to the excellent example set by "Lord Tollemache, who is, I am told, a very bitter Tory," in creating small farms. Who then was the villain? The picture of great wealth and great poverty side by side continued to disturb him.

"It is perfectly true," he told the Eighty Club on April 28, 1885, "that political economy has every reason to be satisfied with itself. The aggregate wealth of the country has increased in a degree and proportion for which the most sanguine of our predecessors was not in the slightest degree prepared. The accumulation of capital has been enormous. The progress of science and invention has multiplied our comforts and has increased our business. Trade has advanced in giant strides out of all proportion to our population.

"That is one side of the picture. But continuously and concurrently with that there are always one million, or very nearly a million, of persons in receipt of parish relief. There are more than one million others on the verge of pauperism, who, in times of depression like these, and at any moment of bad trade, are subject to the most desperate privations. The whole class of the agricultural labourers of this country is never able to do more than make both ends meet, and they have to look forward in the time of illness, or on the approach of old age, to the workhouse as the one inevitable refuge against starvation. Tens of thousands of households do not know the luxury of milk. Children are stunted in their growth and dulled in their intellects for want of proper nourishment and proper food... the ordinary conditions of life among a large proportion of the population are such that common decency is absolutely impossible; and all this goes on in sight of the mansions of the rich, where undoubtedly there are people who would gladly remedy it if they could."

August 5, 1885, at Hull: "I believe that the great evil with which we have to deal is the excessive inequality in the distribution of riches."

This was not agreeable doctrine in the ears of financial Liberalism, and Mr. Chamberlain began to earn frowns in his own party. But he was far too deeply disturbed to turn back.

"Gentlemen, believe me," he urged his audience in Hull, "the questions of the poor labourer cannot be put aside. Our ideal, I think, should be that, in this rich country where everything seems to be in profusion, **an honest, a decent, and an industrious man should be able to earn a livelihood for himself and his family, should have access to some means of self-improvement and enjoyment, and should be able to lay aside something for sickness and old age**. Is that unreasonable? Is it impossible?... It exists in England on the estates of Lord Tollemache and of some other great and generous landlords...

"The English farmer pursues a will-o'-the-wisp in the shape of Protection... Well, he must be a very foolish person to imagine that the people of this country will ever again submit to the terrors of the small loaf..."

Glasgow, September 15, 1885: "All the resources that vast accumulated capital can bring, all that the inventions and discoveries of science can bring to aid in the production of industry or the relief of labour, have done nothing to improve the condition of the most numerous and the most industrious portion of the population. Professor Rogers says: 'There is collected a population in our large towns which equals in amount the whole of those who lived in England and Wales six centuries ago, but whose condition is more destitute, whose homes are more squalid, whose means are more uncertain, whose prospects are more hopeless than those of the poorest serfs of the Middle Ages and the meanest drudges of the medieval cities."

A fortnight later he was dating the rise of pauperism in the United Kingdom from the disappearance of the yeoman class. Mr. Gladstone's first Home Rule Bill brought this phase of his lieutenant's career to an end. Mr. Chamberlain was certainly not satisfied that he had found his villain.

Chapter XVIII

Imperial Patriotism

HIS attitude to Home Rule turned Mr. Chamberlain's thoughts in the direction in which Disraeli's thoughts had moved. Thus, on his return from Canada and America in 1888, he declared:

"I am willing to submit to the charge of being a sentimentalist when I say that I will never willingly admit of any policy that will tend to weaken the ties between the different branches of the Anglo-Saxon race which form the British Empire and the vast dominion of the Queen."

In 1895 he became Secretary of State for the Colonies in Lord Salisbury's Government. A year later he quoted in a public speech Tennyson's lines:

> Britain's myriad voices call,
> Sons, be welded each and all
> Into one Imperial whole,
> One with Britain, heart and soul!
> One life, one flag, one fleet, one Throne!

On June 9, 1896, he spoke at the Congress of Chambers of Commerce of the Empire in favour of –

"a British Zollverein or Customs Union which would establish at once practically free trade throughout the British Empire, but would leave the separate contracting parties free to make their own arrangements with regard to duties on foreign goods, except that this is an essential condition on of the proposal - that Great Britain shall consent to place moderate duties upon certain articles which are of large production in the colonies... These articles would comprise corn, meat, wool, and sugar, and perhaps other articles of enormous consumption in this country, which are at present largely produced in the colonies, and which might, under such an arrangement, be wholly produced in the colonies and wholly produced by British labour. On the other hand, as I have said, the colonies, while maintaining their duties on foreign importations, would agree to a free interchange of commodities with the rest of the Empire and would cease to plan protective duties on any products of British labour. That is the principle of the German Zollverein, that is the principle which underlies the federation of the United States of America; and I do not doubt for a moment that if it were adopted it would be the strongest bond of union between the British race throughout the world."

There was no suggestion in this of protecting the British home market. But it was evident that this was likely to follow if trade declined. Such evidence as is available does not suggest that Mr. Chamberlain had any idea, when he made his suggestion, that he was about to draw his villain, or that, when the villain was drawn, he recognized him. But about the drawing itself there is no doubt. The Money power, as has been said, had for long been aware that the free British market and the comparatively free markets of the British Empire were essential to the maintenance of the free market for gold which is the foundation of its power.

The idea of a British Zollverein therefore had a bad reception, and Mr. Chamberlain saw the banner of Free Trade raised aggressively by the devoted hands of Financial Liberalism. "What!" they cried. "Tax the people's food?" He had not meant to attack Free Trade, certainly not to attack the "Dutch system" (no man probably had a higher opinion than he of the excellence of British finance), and the stir he had caused surprised him. The war with the Boers in South Africa intervened. It revealed the extreme degree of animosity against England and Mr. Chamberlain which was cherished in many European countries, notably in Germany, France, and Holland. The incident of the Kaiser's telegram to President Kruger and Queen Victoria's rebuke to her nephew further exasperated feelings. But Mr. Chamberlain had no cause to complain of the people whom he served, of their patriotism, of their patience, of their capacity for sacrifice. Nor did he fail to render justice to the great lady, the Queen of England, to whose example and devotion the spirit of service bore such eloquent testimony. Queen Victoria, in her long reign, had raised the Throne of England from a position of weakness to a pinnacle of influence and strength. She had reasserted Kingship, in its Divine as well as in its political aspect, before the world and in the sight of all her subjects. She had insisted upon the ancient law of service, and so far as she was a free agent had bestowed honour only upon those who obeyed that law. Republicanism was dead;

men believed once more in Monarchy as the essential foundation of the nation and of the Empire.

In the public schools the sons of the new-rich had been taught the law of service and made to understand that what a man is and does is of more importance than what he has. This teaching began to make itself manifest in the factories and workshops. Thus the feudal spirit of responsibility to God was revived and became again the common heritage of noble and master and man.

When it is recalled that Queen Victoria's reign began soon after the Money power and its "Dutch system" had been established in her capital city, so that London was the metropolis of international finance, the magnitude of her achievement is made plain. All were for cheapness, for quick returns, for gain; she upheld the ideals of the England that was supposed to be passing away, sorrowing in the afflictions of the poor, labouring ceaselessly to rescue them from the calamity which had come upon them, and looking forward always to the day of deliverance. The Great Nation was her care, and with a fine courage she upheld its honour in face of the world, rebuking those of her ministers who faltered and sustaining those of whose patriotism she felt sure. Nationalism, with her, was the will of God; not a violent or truculent spirit, but love of fatherland deepened and quickened by every sacrifice and resolute to face every emergency.

Peace at any price had no more place in her heart than vainglorious war. She was a woman whose mind was set upon that God Who, as she believed, had called her to reign over His people and would certainly hold her responsible for her actions. It was by the Grace of God that she reigned, and that, at the last, was the deep conviction of all her subjects.

Chapter XIX

Germany

THE end of the Nineteenth Century and the beginning of the Twentieth witnessed a movement to which the name "Social Reform" is commonly applied. It is well to understand clearly what is meant by this term. Until the reign of Money began it was believed by all men that advantage, spiritual and moral as well as material, attaches to the exercise by the individual of certain functions and responsibilities. **A man**, it was held, **ought to be enabled to earn his own and his family's livelihood and ought to make provision for his children, in sickness and in health**. The conception of a wage was a quantity of money or of goods which, in the words of the Pope, secured "those sacred rights of the working man which proceed from his dignity as a man and as a Christian."

But the Money power's conception of wages as "costs" put an end to this idea. If the object is not to enable men to sustain their dignity before God and their fellows, but only to keep them alive in such a condition that they can work, then any consideration of spiritual or moral values is beside the mark. Wages, as Disraeli and Chamberlain saw, being subject to the overriding law of cheapness, could never rise above subsistence level, no matter how great might be the productiveness of industry. Wages could never, therefore, sustain continuously such burdens as medical attendance of a really adequate kind and education.

Social Reform was therefore a sop. Money dared not, in the latter part of the Nineteenth Century, shock the consciences of men too far by restoring the conditions against which Robert Owen had protested. But it would not for a moment tolerate the idea that a wage level which had to compete with that of half-civilized or wholly uncivilized peoples should be raised by an avoidable penny. The way out of the difficulty was found in allowing the politicians of Liberal sympathy, so useful otherwise in upholding Free Trade, to vest in the State the whole office of manhood and parenthood. The State would be fairy godfather to the "poor." Having robbed them of their dignity as men and Christians, by handing them over to the mercy of Money, it would educate their children, provide them with doctors, and, if Money no longer needed them, even go so far as to fill their empty bellies. This was the British Parliament's answer to Mammon, and it was an immoral answer.

Social Reform possessed the supreme advantage, from the point of view of Money, that, in its beginnings, it exerted no effect on costs. London was so incredibly rich in those days that it was possible to institute a large number of social services without laying the Money power under any contribution big enough to frighten it. Money, on the contrary, blessed the "reforms," beamed upon them, and spoke of the advantages, in the form of a more efficient type of "labour," which was likely to flow from them.

The insincerity of this attitude may be understood by reference to the present-day attitude of Money towards the social services. Meanwhile it cannot be too fiercely insisted that Social Reform, far from being a blessing to anybody, was a betrayal by Parliament of the nation. It represented the price paid by the Money power for the right to rob the King's Englishmen not only of the fruits of their labour, but also of their dignity as men and Christians, of their office as fathers and husbands, and of their qualities of independence and courage which are the real wealth and credit of this Kingdom.But to say this is not to agree that, as things stand today, "economy" should be exercised at the expense of the social services. Far from it. So long as the Money power remains, the social services ought to be defended by every opponent of that power, since, happily, they have come thanks to the ruin of the world wrought by the Money power itself to constitute a serious hindrance to the operations of International Finance.

England at the beginning of the present Century was no longer the secure citadel of the Money power. That power had been alarmed by the revival of nationalism brought about by the increased influence of the Throne. It had been alarmed, too, by the swift extension of the policies of Social Reform upon which, as has been said, it had looked favourably at the beginning. Education, housing, public health, and factory inspection were now, in changed conditions, adding to costs and so preventing "wholesome measures of deflation," and equally (though unavowed) "wholesome measures of inflation."Booms could no longer be trusted to mount so high, nor slumps to sink so deep.And it is on the extent of the difference between mountain and abyss that "Dutch finance depends for its greatest profits." But much more than all these, the demand for Imperial Unity and Empire Free Trade was growing more insistent every day. Above every other menace was the menace of Chamberlain.

Another question exercised the minds of financiers: Was England safe in the military sense? The Germans did not think so. They declared openly that the experiences in the Boer War were without value for European warfare on the scale on which they meant to wage it. "The invincible army," said the Kaiser, "cannot be beaten." The faith of the German naval leaders was not less secure. The command of the seas, they boasted, would very soon be wrested from England.

There was witnessed, in the early years of the present Century, a remarkable propaganda in favour of Germany to which a great number of patriotic Englishmen fell victim. This propaganda declared that Germany's intentions were wholly pacific, that she was without designs upon any of her neighbours, and that those who spoke or even made suggestions to the contrary were guilty of the crime of inciting to war. This was the attitude of the greater part of the Liberal party, which preached, quite sincerely, "a better understanding with Germany" and disarmament and which based its hopes on trade relations fostered by the free British market. Another kind of propaganda was conducted at the same time namely, that war was impossible because no nation could afford to wage it. This was an argument advanced with perfect sincerity and favoured by many Liberals. It afforded to large numbers of honest citizens an unwarranted sense of security.

It was into this bewildered world that Mr. Chamberlain launched his policy of Tariff Reform. That part of the British people which had found in Rudyard Kipling an evangelist of Empire and a messenger of hope received gladly the new doctrine; but the mass of the people, lying still in abject poverty, was unprepared. The campaign was launched in Birmingham on May 15, 1903, at a meeting of Unionists called to welcome their member on the conclusion of his tour in South Africa. Mr. Chamberlain said:

"The Empire is not old. The Empire is new. The Empire is in its infancy... Now what is the meaning of an Empire? What does it mean to us? We have had a little experience. We have had a war (the Boer War) a war in which the majority of our children abroad had no apparent direct interest. We had no hold over them, no agreement with them of any kind, and yet, at one time during this war, by their voluntary decision, at least 50,000 colonial soldiers were standing shoulder to shoulder with British troops, displaying a gallantry equal to their own and the keenest intelligence. It is something for a beginning; and if this country were in danger I mean if we were, as our forefathers were, face to face some day, which Heaven forfend, with some great coalition of hostile nations, when we had, with our backs to the wall, to struggle for our very lives it is my firm conviction that there is nothing within the power of these self-governing colonies that they would not do to come to our aid...

"Now I suppose that you and I are agreed that the British Empire is one and indivisible. You and I are agreed that we absolutely refuse to look upon any of the States that form the British Empire as in any way excluded from any advantage or privilege to which the British Empire is entitled. We may well, therefore, have supposed that an agreement... by which Canada does a kindness to us (in the matter of preferential treatment in her markets) was a matter of family arrangement, concerning nobody else. But, unfortunately, Germany thinks otherwise. There is a German Empire. The German Empire is divided into States. Bavaria and, let us say, Hanover, Saxony, and Würtemberg may deal between themselves in any way they please. But in this case of Canada, Germany insists upon treating Canada as though it were a separate country. It refuses to recognize it as a part of our Empire entitled to claim the privileges of that Empire. It regards this as being something more than a domestic agreement, and it has penalized Canada by placing upon Canadian goods an additional duty.

"Now the reason for this is clear. The German newspapers very frankly explain that this is a policy of reprisal and that it is intended to deter other colonies from giving to us the same advantage. Therefore it is not merely punishment inflicted by Germany upon Canada, but it is a threat to South Africa, to Australia, and to New Zealand. This policy, a policy of dictation and interference, is justified by the belief that we are so wedded to our fiscal system that we cannot interfere and that we cannot defend our colonies, and that, in fact, any one of them that attempts to establish any kind of special relations with us does so at its own risk and must be left to bear the brunt of foreign hostility. To my mind, that is putting us in rather a humiliating position I do not like it at all. I know what will follow if we allow it to prevail; it is easy to predict the consequences. How do you think that under such circumstances we can approach our colonies with appeals to aid us in promoting the union of the Empire or ask them to bear a share of the common burdens? Are we to say to them: 'This is your Empire, take pride in it, share its privileges'? They will say, 'What are its privileges? The privileges appear to be that if we trust you as relations and friends, if we show you kindness, if we give you preference, you, who benefit by our action, can only leave us alone to fight our own battles against those who are offended by our action?' Now is that Free Trade?... No, it is absolutely a new situation; there has been nothing like it in our history.

The vigour of the reaction against his Tariff Reform policy surprised Mr. Chamberlain himself. It was not confined to Britain; it extended throughout Europe and America. The Money power became threatening and every conceivable agency of which use could be made was brought into the field against the author of the "outrage." The Conservative party was split; Mr. Chamberlain himself resigned his office in order to "go in front of the army as a pioneer." From one end to the other the country rang with challenges and counter-challenges about the food of the people and the attack which "landlordism" was supposed to be making upon it. Mr. Chamberlain continued his campaign and advanced in understanding of the evil which, still unbeknown to him, he was attacking. Thus:

"Take the capitalist the man living upon his income... He can invest his money in foreign countries and live upon the interest; and then, in the returns of the prosperity of the country, it will be said that the country is growing richer because he is growing richer. But what about the working man?... This is the state of things against which I am protesting."

He went on to speak of a director of the American Steel Trust who, foreseeing a slump, was preparing to "invade foreign markets" when his own market was deflated by "financial difficulties."

"Remember," Mr. Chamberlain said, "it may not be easy... to invade the German market or the French market or the Russian market, because in every case they will find a tariff which, if necessary, can be raised against them. They will go to the only free market; they will come to this country...

"Since 1882 the total imports of foreign manufacturers (into Great Britain) have increased by £65,000,000."

Liverpool, October 27, 1903: "Dumping takes place when the country which adopts it has a production which is larger than its own demand. Not being able to dispose of its surplus at home, it dumps it somewhere else. Now the United Kingdom is the only country where this process can be carried on successfully, because we are the only country which keeps open ports.

"Now a curious thing which Mr. Asquith does not seem to appreciate a curious thing to him, but not to us is that 'dumping' only takes place seriously when the country that has recourse to it is in a state of depression."

This was a sword thrust into the enemy's vitals. Mr. Chamberlain's real foe was certainly hidden from him; nevertheless he had wounded him, for, as has been seen, it is when a market is being deflated by the restriction of credit, so that, for want of the means of exchanging them, goods are tumbling down in price, that producers are compelled to rush their goods into foreign markets that is to say, into the British market.

Mr. Chamberlain, meanwhile, was approaching more and more closely to the position of Disraeli. He expressed regret that his policy imposed so little sacrifice, saying that he felt the importance of sacrifice as part of a life of service. His vision was set upon an Empire in which men and women would receive the fruits of their toil and be rescued from the horrors of those periods of slump when the poor are stripped of their possessions and turned adrift to starve in the middle of plenty.

His appeal failed. In 1906 the Liberals were returned with an overwhelming majority, while soon afterwards Mr. Chamberlain himself was stricken by a fatal illness. His work, however, was not suffered to diminish. In those years after 1906 men's minds in England remained disturbed by the grievous poverty of the "richest land on earth," and the Radical wing of the Liberal party that a to say, the wing farthest removed from Finance under the leadership of Mr. Lloyd George introduced a fresh instalment of Social Reform in the shape of the principle of State Insurance against unemployment and ill-health and instituted the Old Age Pensions.

These measures of course met with a strenuous opposition by the Money power, which, in return, was attacked by Mr. Lloyd George, who spoke scathingly of "that area, a mile square, which calls itself the City." The Conservatives, meanwhile kept alive the demand for Protection for the Home Market and Empire Free Trade. England emphatically was becoming unsafe for "Dutch finance" and its twin daughters dumping and starvation.

In these years came the Entente with France and the understanding with Russia. The argument that Germany would be compelled to fight if her goods were excluded from Great Britain and the British Empire was employed by the Money power, which had been glad to coquette with Prussianism and to use the "German bogey" as a means of frightening the English people away from Protection and Empire Free Trade. Having originated and intensified by every conceivable means the scramble for foreign markets, which was one of the causes of the World War, Money began to preach peace and good-will and urge that, even if France should be attacked, England ought to remain outside of the struggle, propaganda very useful to Germany.

Chapter XX

King and Parliament

UNDER the Feudal System, the King as God's steward remained in tenancy of all the land over which he ruled and land could not be alienated from his tenancy. He appointed men, ennobled by himself, to administer his land that is to say, to promote and protect production so that each of his subjects might be enabled to perform his duty to God and to his fellows; at the same time he appointed Bishops to secure to his subjects the necessary knowledge of God and the benefits of religion.

Private property in land, in the sense in which that term is understood today, did not and could not exist. While a man might dispose freely of his crops and products he could not dispose of his land. Individual enterprise, in other words, was looked upon as the most productive and effective and for this reason encouraged; the land was God's possession invested in the sacred person of the King by God for the benefit of men. The King was responsible to God for the use of the land, which was the essential basis of men's power to serve God and enjoy Him, and to make provision for themselves and their families.

Side by side with the prohibition to alienate land stood the prohibition to alienate the King's that is to say, God's money. The use of money, in Feudal times, was to serve as a means of distributing products and so ensuring their consumption. It was held that the power of the issue of money was scarcely less important than the ownership of land, and ought therefore to be withheld from private hands which might conceivably apply it to their own uses.

As has been said, the goldsmiths, at a comparatively early date, set themselves up in business by clipping, melting, and exporting the King's money, and so discovered for themselves the powers which can be wielded by anyone who is able to increase or diminish the quantity of money in a country. As time went on the system of credit largely replaced that of currency, but the methods of the bankers remained substantially the same. They managed to secure as a right what they had formerly secured by stealth, and became, therefore, entitled to create money and to abstract it at their pleasure. This gave them the further right to make the King himself and all his subjects pay them in goods and services for the money thus created. Consequently the chief powers of the Crown were transferred to them and they assumed a virtual control of the kingdom and all its riches, and speedily brought the God-system to an end. At the present time the King must go to the financiers for money, must incur a debt for the money he receives, and must pay such interest as the financiers choose to charge him. And what the King is compelled to do, every one of his subjects must do also. More extraordinary still, the Money power, as has been seen, persuaded Parliament to enact that that form of money still deriving ostensibly from the King namely, the currency should be subject rigidly to the movements of gold, so that his Majesty might be severely restricted in any financial operation he might dare to initiate of himself, whereas the form deriving from itself namely, loans (credit) should be left free of restrictions other than those which it might choose itself to impose. The "game of the gold-standard" to use the bankers' phrase served primarily the purpose of preventing the King from performing his most ancient and most undoubted duty to God and to his people. He was tied to gold by men whose chief fear it was that he might do that which it has ever been his office to do namely, supply his subjects directly with the means of exchanging their goods; that is to say, with the means of living. By basing its own money (issues of credit) upon gold, in the ratio of £10 credit to 1 currency, the Money power secured further, as has been seen, that the effect of every movement of gold into or out of the country would be intensified tenfold. The King could not therefore use his own currency to make purchases outside of his realm without instantly bringing about a severe reduction in the means of exchange of his people and so a fall in prices. For that reason increased importation of goods in time of scarcity led necessarily, when the goods were paid for in gold, to decreased production at home as a consequence of the resulting fall in prices. In other words, it was no longer open to the King to relieve his people in their want or conversely to help them to exchange their superabundance.

It cannot be realized too clearly that the defence of the Money power is based on the assumption that it has the *right to create credit* and (having produced it by an entry in a ledger) to *lend it at interest* that is to say, to exchange it for goods and services. If this right is granted it follows, of course, that, if the created money (credit) is being employed unprofitably, the loan will be called in. **But the title of the Money power to create money out of nothing and exchange it for goods and services is exactly what is in dispute** though legally, of course, the right exists. There is no essential difference between this claim and a claim to be entitled to increase the number of the King's coins by minting them. In both instances what has cost nothing is traded for real goods, seeing that book entries of credit are costless and that consumable goods are costly. It may not be literally true that banks are private mints; it is true that their creations of credit money out of nothing have the same effect as private mints would have. Thus it would seem that the English people has lost immeasurably by the change which took power from the King and gave it to the Parliament. Parliament today borrows humbly from Finance what belongs only to God, King, and people.

It was, as has been said, one of Napoleon's beliefs that men have found no answer to usury except a King by God's Grace. The history of England in the Nineteenth Century goes a long way towards confirming that view. England, by the special mercy of God, retained her Throne; but she saw the Throne shorn of power in favour of the Parliament. Under her Kings England suffered many trials; but, upon the witness of all unprejudiced observers, her case was better then, in days of scarcity and limited production, than it is now, when productive power has reached its present overwhelming proportions. Where was poverty like the poverty of the great industrial towns of England when Disraeli and Chamberlain dared to challenge the rule of Mammon and when, by efforts that ought for ever to bind this race to its Royal House, Queen Victoria raised high the ideal of duty in the hearts of her people?

Parliament failed England by delivering her over to "Dutch finance," and by that failure made it clear that Liberalism is impotent except in a Monarchy where the King is possessed of real power. It was not the Government but King Edward who took the first vital steps to bring England and France together in those days when the fate of this country depended upon that alliance. **Parliament has not known how to abolish abject poverty in the middle of overflowing plenty**, how to refute the doctrine of gain, how to curb the insolence of Money, how to save agriculture and industry from the intolerable burden of usury. But it may be that the fault does not rest with Parliament, but rather with those who supposed that such an instrument can discharge the office of the King, failing to understand that it is the Grace of God, by which he reigns, that arms the King against the power of Money by arming him against the greed and the fear on which that power is founded. That British Governments and Parliaments are actuated by the highest motives and composed of men and women whose sole aim it is to do service to their fellows is, of course, beyond dispute. It is not the men but the system that is at fault. This applies also to bankers. As has been said, faith in God has given place to faith in gold so that gold has become a god. Even the Money power itself probably believes to some extent in the virtue, as opposed to the profitable nature, of its commodity.

Chapter XXI

Credit

WHEN war against Germany began the Bank Act was suspended and a moratorium declared. Had this not been done default must immediately have taken place because there was a run on the banks. The great question arose: Shall the King resume his office as the fountain of Money?

It was a perfectly simple question. All that had to be done, supposing that the Royal office was exercised once more, was to issue Treasury notes for such national expenses a had to be met in pounds, shillings and pence and to open State credits with producers after the fashion of the bankers upon agreed terms. But the moment it recovered from its first panic the Money power rushed to prevent a course which would have destroyed its foundations. Parliament, greatly alarmed, agreed to issue the Treasury notes through the banks and to borrow in order to pay for the War.

In other words, the King was prevented from exercising his office of issuing money to his people and was forced to pay the banks and their clients high rates of interest upon book entries. The King was forced, that is to say, to pledge the products and labour of his people for generations in exchange for that which belonged properly to himself and at a moment when the bankers' inability to pay in gold had just been revealed.

What was the credit behind these loans from the banks? Only the Treasury notes. And what was the credit behind the Treasury notes? The nation, King and people, the courage and heroism of those about to die, the will to victory of the men and women at home, the influence of the Royal House, the patriotism of the humble subject, and added to these the leadership of the masters of agriculture and industry, the skill of British craftsmen, the machinery and plant bought by service, the stock of goods produced by work, the land, England herself. It was this credit of which a free gift was made to the Money power in order that that power might lend it back again to its owners at immense profit. Does anyone suppose that the fact that the national credit was given to Money and lent by Money to the nation at interest increased its worth? Can it be contended that if the nation itself had acted as its own banker its notes would have been accepted with less alacrity, or that the effort to arm and feed the nation would have been weakened?

"The general conviction certainly was," wrote Lord Milner " and it was strongest on the part of men versed in economic studies that if nothing else brought the War to an early close the impossibility of financing it must do so. In view of the enormous costliness of modern warfare, it was argued, and reasonably argued, that no great civilized country could long endure the financial strain. If anyone had suggested in 1914 that our own country, for instance, could by any possibility raise £10,000,000,000, or even half, or even a quarter of that sum, in order to carry on the War, he would have been regarded as a madman. Yet not only did we raise that amount and more over £3,000,000,000 out of revenue and over £7,000,000,000 by loan but we were prepared to go on raising money. I can speak from personal experience in this matter, for I was in the centre of affairs at that time...

"It had become evident from experience that mere financial embarrassments were never going to put a stop to the War. It might indeed be terminated as to a certain extent it was terminated by an absolute shortage of indispensable things, food in the first place, but also coals and various materials necessary for the manufacture of munitions. But as long as the things themselves could be produced in adequate quantities, the counters for dealing with them would always be forthcoming."

These counters for dealing with them, as Lord Milner saw, are counters. It is production, that only, which gives the counters value. They are the King's counters offered to his people as payment for service on the one hand and as the means of exchange of goods on the other. Why force the King to pay interest upon them, as if bankers by their mere motion had created the guns and shells and food instead of creating only an entry in a book?

No answer has ever been given to these questions. Nor is it denied anywhere that at least seventy per cent. of the War Loans was "created" in the sense that bankers afforded credits of non-existent money for taking them up. The book-entry part of the War Loans has earned exactly the same interest as the much smaller part composed of the savings of patriotic citizens who were lending money earned in the production of goods or services and not merely written figures. The huge burden of debt, which is called the War Loans, is chiefly a debt by the King to the Money power not for goods or services received, but for the exercise by that power of the King's own prerogative. The King, in short, is buying back his own Kingship. It is the Mother of Parliaments in its ignorance which has made this legal, the children of this Mother have followed her example in every country where they have obtained power. Wherever there is Parliamentary Government, the Money power rules. Consequently Parliamentary Government, foul slums, abject poverty, and flaunting wealth are always found together. Kings in the past have been compelled to go to moneylenders when goods and services were used up; but no King unfettered by a Parliament has at any time pleaded humbly to be allowed to borrow that which evidently belonged to his office at a moment when both goods and services were available in the greatest abundance.

"If (a country) is at war," says R.G. Hawtrey, "success must be a matter of life and death; there is no halfway house between a whole-hearted prosecution of the War and an immediate peace... It is possible to stave off a want of funds by temporary borrowing. Temporary borrowing has this advantage or this danger that the money to be borrowed *need not exist*. Directly or indirectly the lender is a banker; what he lends is a credit his own obligation. This obligation he can himself create...

"It is only in so far as the credits (issued by banks) give command over wealth which can be applied to the purposes for which it is needed, over labour, over supplies of food, over weapons and ships and rolling stock, over the services of soldiers and sailors, over the use of suitable fixed capital, that they are more than a mere financial conjuring trick..."

The "obligations" created and lent by the bankers to the nation during the War were made valuable, in short, by the nation itself and not by the bankers. The question therefore arises why the bankers should be allowed to count obligations or credits given in future as money belonging to themselves and therefore, when lent, repayable to them by the public with interest. For, in truth, every creation of money by a banker imposes a tax on the community in the sense that, there being, after the act of creation, more buying power in existence, each unit of buying power existing, before the creation, has lost something of its value. As has been said, Parliament has conferred upon the Money power the right to change the value of the King's money at its will (by expanding or contracting credit). Thus, that power of Parliament about which the greatest boast has always been made namely, the right to impose taxation, the "power of the Purse" has followed the Royal prerogative into the hands of the financiers. The rule, "No taxation without representation," does not apply when bankers are expanding credit.

It is an illusion to suppose that the making over of these great powers to the bankers has conferred any benefit of safety upon the King or his subjects. Bankers never tire of uttering warnings against the dangers of inflation; but inflation, as has been seen, is one of their own everyday methods.

"The only effective method of controlling the issue of paper money," says R.G. Hawtrey, "is to control the creating of credit, for the demand for legal-tender money for circulation is consequential upon the supply of credit. It is their (the banks') action and not the note issue which directly affects the value of the monetary unit."

It is well to bear these facts in mind when considering the warnings against inflation which the Money power began to utter during the War and has been uttering ever since. The public is vaguely aware that by inflation is meant the payment by the King of his debts in "worthless paper." The debts of Government are largely debts to bankers for credits which the bankers have created *out of nothing*. It is the concern of the bankers to prevent Government repaying nothing with nothing, which would happen if the Government *borrowed in excess of the productive capacity of a country*.

Chapter XXII

MILNER

THAT every belligerent country was suffering from some degree of real inflation at the end of the War is not open to doubt. Every country had put forth its utmost effort, and its utmost effort had scarcely sufficed to keep the people fed and the armies supplied. The spur of more and still more issues of credit had been applied even after the peak of possible production had been reached.

But the end of the War brought a complete transformation. If consumable goods were still scarce, the means of producing them had now been multiplied a thousandfold, for no further supplies of guns and shells and the like were needed for the armies. The Money power, therefore, encouraged production, which would have the effect of replenishing stocks and so restoring value to the credits issued in such profusion during the War. The result was the "boom" of 1919 and 1920, during which industry displayed an immense power of recuperation. The fields were now grown white towards the harvest. It remained only to restrict credit (make money scarce) in order to bring down the prices of the newly created goods and so to restore to Money the whole, and more, of its lost purchasing power.

"In the first year of peace," wrote Lord Milner, "there was a general clamour for intensified production. All those engaged in production work, capitalists and workmen alike, were incessantly exhorted to redouble their efforts, in order to make good 'the losses of the War.'

"And, as a matter of fact, fresh capital was freely poured into some branches of manufacturing industry, which were already more than sufficiently equipped to deal with a considerable increase of demand. But presently the demand fell off, first in one trade and then in another...

"I am weary of the endless jeremiads of the Press, and the solemn lectures of so many public men about our alleged poverty as a nation the huge destruction of wealth caused by the War, the immense burden of debt, the danger of national bankruptcy, and the necessity of drawing in our horns in every direction, of painfully husbanding our diminished resources and of no longer 'throwing a sprat,' even in the hope of 'catching a herring. '... Not contraction but expansion should be the watchword; not mere economy but the development of new sources of wealth."

Had Lord Milner been alive today he might have read these words in the British Reply to America on War Debts:

"But Reparations and War Debts represent expenditure on destruction. Fertile fields were rendered barren and populous cities a shattered ruin. Such expenditure, instead of producing a slow and steady accumulation of wealth, destroyed in a few hours the stored-up riches of the past. Like the shells on which they were largely spent, these loans were blown to pieces. They have produced nothing to repay them..."

This is all excellent example of the confusion of thought which is so widely prevalent today. The truth, of course, is that the War Loans were distributed, as all loans must be, in the form of wages, salaries, dividends, or profits. The Government bought the products of this enterprise and consumed them in defending this country against the greatest danger by which it has ever been threatened. It would be too much, certainly, to expect of International Money that it should detect any special value in the salvation of England; but Englishmen might, perhaps, have supposed that His Majesty's Government would display a higher understanding. If a loan is made for the growing of tobacco the product will go up in smoke, like the shells. Why has no Government expressed its regret at this "unproductive" expenditure?

Lord Milner had played a chief part in that leadership which enabled Britain and her allies to win the War. He was at a loss to understand why a people fresh from immortal victory should hesitate to show courage in the ways of peace. He was to learn that the English people is not a free agent. The excellent merit of his writing lies in the fact that he was situated in the centre of affairs and was able, therefore, to take informed views.

"The reason commonly given," he wrote, "to justify the descent from such high hopes to such paltry achievement is the great dissipation of national resources due to the War. The War, so runs the argument, left this country greatly impoverished. It is true that, immediately after its conclusion, there was a great boom in trade, that wages and profits continued high, and that there was a keen demand for labour. But this apparent prosperity was really delusive. It was due to 'inflation,' concealing the true state of affairs. Sooner or later the losses of the War were bound to make themselves felt. We had been wasting our capital, and though this waste might be temporarily concealed by the great rise in prices which made our national wealth, though really diminished, look larger it was certain in the end to restrict enterprise and diminish employment.

"By those who hold this view the present depression (1922) is regarded as inevitable... This is the popularly accepted theory, blessed too by 'orthodox' economists. Another theory is that depression and unemployment in Great Britain are due to the failure of effective demand for British goods in certain foreign countries with which, before the War, we did a considerable trade.

"It is evident that (these theories) weaken rather than support one another. For if it be the case that we are unable to reach our former level of production for want of capital, it matters less that the demand for our products is also in some measure reduced."

Lord Milner might have added that the idea that the loans made by bankers (that is to say, the money they create) are provided out of savings was finally killed by the War, when the credits provided exceeded the total savings of mankind. The Money power continues to talk as if savings provided it with the money which it lends, but this is merely to hide the fact that it itself creates that money *out of nothing*. In the first Addendum to the MacMillan Report on Finance it is stated:

"The theory that there is in any sense a fixed loan fund available to finance investment which is in all circumstances fully employed, or that the amount of the savings of the public always exactly corresponds to the volume of the new investment, is, we think, mistaken... We gathered from the evidence of Sir R. Hopkins that it would be a mistake to attribute this view to the Treasury at the present time."

The real object of the Money power, as has been said, was to reap, in the usual way, the harvest created by the boom namely, by a slump. And this object was achieved so successfully that in 1922 as in 1822prosperity had vanished and producers were flinging their goods on the market below cost-price or rushing them into foreign markets. Bankruptcy marched through the land hand in hand with unemployment. The confusion wrought in the public mind is thus described by Lord Milner:

"Let us try to picture the impression which his experiences are likely to have left on the mind of any fairly intelligent workman a man, say, good at his own job, but with only so much information about the general affairs of the world as he could gather from the steady perusal of his daily paper.

"For months and months after the close of the War, he had it dinned into his ears that the world was suffering from a shortage of goods, and he was overwhelmed with exhortations to him and the men of his class not to spare themselves, but to work with intensified energy to make up the deficiency. There, he was vehemently assured, was their duty to their country and the world and at the same time the one sure road to the improvement of their own condition. Such was the unanimous appeal made to him by all the highest authorities in the world of industry and finance. And he obeyed it to the best of his ability, but only to find, a year or two later, that the warehouses of his employers were choked with goods which they could not sell and that his services were no longer required.

"And then, when, stung by disappointment, he began to probe for himself into the causes of this strange contradiction, he was told that there had, unfortunately, been a mistake, that the activity to which he had been so fervently exhorted to contribute was 'feverish,' that he ought to have known, we ought all to have known, that after the War there was bound to be a big slump because 'the pool of Capital had been depleted,' and we had no money for making things and nobody else had any money for buying them. And yet, at the same time, he read in his paper that in Germany, where presumably the 'pool of Capital' was equally depleted, there was still intense industrial activity and next to no unemployment.

"More than that, he knew that the Germans were still sending their wares into this country, which despite its lamentable impoverishment was apparently still rich enough to afford the best market in the world for every kind of foreign goods. But then the Germans, so he was assured, were only able to do this owing to their wicked and idiotic action in debasing their currency, which enabled them to under-sell us not only in our own country but everywhere else. This manuvre of theirs might, however, possibly still be defeated if he and his fellows would only accept, for an indefinite period, such a reduction of wages as would enable the British manufacturer once more to compete with the German on something like equal terms. And this very depressing prospect certainly grew no brighter when he came to look at the figures for himself, for he could not help seeing that even if his wages were cut down almost to zero, it was still not evident that British goods could be produced as cheaply as German.

"And yet he was assured that any other remedy was unthinkable. And this he mournfully accepted, for had he not been taught from his childhood, and were not all the best-educated of his fellows agreed, that it was a sign of mental imbecility and almost of moral depravity not always to 'buy in the cheapest market,' or to do anything which could by any possibility give the slightest advantage to the British producer in his competition with the foreigner? That position, I say, he accepted, and yet it seemed to him rather hard that, as the price of victory, the victors should be condemned to perpetual indigence..."

In 1922 the Coalition Government, which in its bewilderment and anxiety at the spectacle of ruin had submitted humbly to the policy of deflation, and the consequent sabotage of all its vaunted schemes of "Reconstruction," including the "Homes for Heroes," was replaced by a Conservative Government under Mr.

Bonar Law. The new Government was favourable to Tariff Reform and Empire Free Trade. The Liberal Party, broken during the War, was hastily reconstituted in order to fight the "threat to Free Trade." The result was the defeat of Mr. Baldwin who had succeeded Mr. Bonar Law in 1923, and the first Labour Government under Mr. Ramsay MacDonald. Liberalism had saved Free Trade, but had not succeeded in saving itself. The Money power had to set against a Socialist Party flushed with triumph and committed irrevocably to the "dole" and Social Reform, respite from the horror of a protected British market.

Of Socialism, as such, Money was not afraid. Financiers prefer Governments with unlimited resources to private borrowers who may conceivably default, and have always therefore been partial to the idea of State enterprise and trading provided that they can exert control over it. The experience of Russia, where a whole nation has been enslaved in order to pay very high rates to the financiers who are supplying the material of the Five-Year Plan, has amply proved that Money has little to fear from the destruction of the Capitalist System of individual production. (The Capitalist System, on the contrary, as has been seen, is usually an enemy of the Money power.) Bolshevism having destroyed Monarchy and loyalty in Russia, was compelled to rely, like Robespierre, on greed on the one hand and naked fear on the other these being the only alternatives to the law of love. The Socialistic idea of the Commonwealth would probably lead to a similar result, tempered no doubt by the character of the people concerned.

For when gain is avowed as the object, fear is already on the threshold, even though many years may elapse before that threshold is actually crossed. Money has been militant in the past and may easily assume a military form in the days that lie ahead.

The fall of the first Labour Government and the return to office of Mr. Baldwin effected very little change. But Mr. Baldwin was now pledged to refrain from touching Free Trade and was, in addition, subject to criticisms which had not formerly been passed on him. These were advanced by the left wing of his party, become exceedingly strong. In 1925 the Government decided to return to the gold standard at the old parity. It was a move of very great importance, because the French, Belgian, and Italian currencies were not yet "stabilized" on gold, while in Germany the "stability" of the new gold currency, which replaced the debased mark, had only been maintained by a drastic rationing of credit by the Central Bank in 1924. The future of Indian exchange was not yet determined, and the Federal Reserve System of America had only recently begun to develop in a deliberate way its system of open-market operations. The situation in America from this time onwards is the key to the policy of Money.

"America had freed herself from indebtedness to Europe during the War," says the MacMillan Report; "and thereafter it appeared that the tide had definitely turned and that the United States, having undergone the transition from a largely agricultural to a predominantly manufacturing country, was about to repeat the history of Great Britain and to emerge as an exporter of capital upon a vast scale. For some years after the end of the

War, indeed, the growth of American capital exports was the indispensable means of recovery of economic conditions in the rest of the world. Issues of long-period securities in the United States reached their maximum in the four years 1925-1928, during which period the net amount offered on long-period account aggregated $4,789,000,000 or nearly 1,000,000,000 an amount twice as large as the volume of long-period capital issues (£482,000,000) floated in London during the same period... (American investments) had striking effects upon the areas Central and South America and Central Europe where the investments were chiefly made."

In other words, an immense power of lending had become vested in the hands of Americans at a moment when the conditions in America were very far indeed from being favourable to the operations of lenders. Lenders, as has been shown above, demand the power to invest their money wherever they choose and also the power to prevent the money which, by their investments abroad, they have taken from the home market, being restored to that market by anybody else. In effect, as has been seen, these are demands for the strict operation of the gold standard by a powerful Central Bank and for Free Trade. For to repeat if trade is not free the recipients of loans cannot pay in goods the interest due on them, while, on the other hand, tariffs afford such protection to the home market that manufacturers are able to keep the prices of their goods well above world prices and so to defy the efforts of Money to compel them to produce as cheaply as their neighbours in other countries.

The Money power in America, therefore, was forced to conduct its operations through London, where a free market for goods existed and where, therefore, debtors could sell their goods for gold, preparatory to forwarding the gold so received to New York.

The objection to this system is that the quantity of gold is limited. That objection was increased enormously in weight by the fact that War Debts had to be paid to America in gold. There was not enough gold in the world to pay both War Debts and the interests on ordinary debts unless America kept sending out gold as fast as she received it unless, that is to say, she put gold at the disposal of foreign Governments. As has been seen, she adopted this course.

But even so, payment of interests on these loans to foreign Governments, added to payment of interests on commercial loans, added to payment of War Debt interests, so swelled the tide of gold flowing towards New York as to threaten the rest of the world with a gold famine. The Money power therefore began to agitate for a reduction of tariffs so that foreign goods might be received into American ports. At once the powerful American manufacturers took fright. They exerted their influence and there occurred a clash between finance and production that is to say, between lenders and borrowers.

This is the real cause of the world slump, and deserves therefore the closest possible attention. As has been said, it is the aim of the Money power to lend always at the highest possible rate of interest consistent with security. In order to accomplish this the Money power must be free to move its commodity, gold, about the world when and how it chooses. The sin of the American producers in the eyes of Money was that they were preventing gold from being moved out of America (or, in the language of finance, from being "redistributed" throughout the world). In other words and this is the important point *they were preventing gold (very large quantities of it, too) from earning interest for its owners.*

An owner of gold will not lend it to a market where prices are high and money therefore is cheap when he can lend it to a market where prices are low and money is dear; he likes, so to speak, to get the best value for his money. American prices were exceptionally high and consequently American owners of gold did not want to invest in the American market. They wanted to invest outside of America in foreign countries.

But an owner of gold will not lend it to a foreign country unless he is sure that that foreign country can pay him interest either in gold or with goods. If there is so little gold left in foreign countries that their power to pay in gold the interest on loans made to them no longer exists and if, at the same time, goods are being refused entry into the country where the lender is situated, then, sooner or later, lending will cease.

If lending ceases the owners of gold lose their usury. Not only so, but if the amount of gold thus immobilized or rendered sterile is very large, the smooth operation of the gold standard in other countries is seriously hampered. The Money power likes gold to be scarce; it does not like gold to be so very scarce that the prices of all goods fall below the cost of production, with the result that every Government becomes bankrupt because nobody can earn a profit on which to pay taxes. A gold famine of that sort is apt to lead to awkward questions about the necessity for gold and to inquiries about ways of doing without it.

Because of the tremendous flow of gold into America occasioned by the payments of War Debts and because of America's refusal (expressed in her tariff) to admit foreign goods, half the gold of the world was earning much less (merely bankers' interest) than it might have earned, while the gold standard was falling into disrepute in every other country in the world because every other country was suffering from gold starvation.

The Money power therefore throughout the whole world set itself the task of fighting the battle of the American owners of gold that is to say, the task of breaking the power of the American producers of goods as the necessary preliminary to getting the American tariff wall lowered. It was worldwide Usury against the American industrial "bosses."

It soon became clear that the American industrial "bosses" and their workpeople would offer a much stouter resistance to the Money power than that power was accustomed to encounter in any European country. The idea, for example, that the policy of protection should be abandoned in order to allow the debtors of American finance to pay in goods the interest on their loans was rejected with violence by American manufacturers, who asked if it was proposed to ruin them and their work people by forcing them to compete with cheap European labour.

That, of course, was exactly what the Money power did propose. American manufacturers, on the other hand, were not averse from an expansion of foreign lending by American owners of money, because loans, as has been seen, are usually taken out by those receiving them in the form of goods. The pressure thus exerted on industry to export more at cheaper rates in order to maintain the ordinary balance of trade between imports and exports was not so welcome. (As has been pointed out above, goods exported by a country, and paid for out of loans raised in that country, do not pay for imports into that country. They constitute, as it were, a free gift. Consequently if imports are to be paid for with exports, the total of exports has to be increased by the amount of the goods bought by the borrowing countries with the loans made to them, and this usually entails a considerable reduction in the prices of the goods.)

The American manufacturers were willing and anxious to export as much as possible, but they were not willing to lower the buying power of the home market (by cutting wages) in order to do so. They were asked by the Money power how they proposed, if they refused to reduce wages, to export cheaply enough both to supply the demands for goods of the foreign recipients of loans and to pay with goods for the goods being imported into America. "If you refuse to produce more cheaply," the argument ran, " you will be unable to sell abroad enough goods to square the balance between imports and exports, and it will consequently be necessary to export gold in order to square the account. The effect of an export of gold will be a reduction of money and loans that is to say, of buying power in the home market."

This, as has been seen, is the old demand of the Money power *that money which has been invested abroad shall not be replaced in the home market*. It was a demand for price reductions and wage reductions in America and so for a reduction of American buying power. It was further a demand for the reduction of tariffs, for if wages and prices fall very far, the demand for freer imports becomes more insistent. Thus the way would be opened to the borrowers of American money to pay in goods the interests on their loans. This is the old demand *that money shall be free to find its level*.

The American manufacturers, however, were not at all willing to listen to the voice of Money. They exerted the utmost possible pressure on their Government to maintain the tariff walls; behind these walls they contrived to keep the prices of their goods at such a level that they could recover their costs in the home market and so be free to "dump" goods at prices even below the world prices. The immense quantities of goods required to meet these demands were supplied by intensive methods of mass production, by schemes of "rationalization," and by amalgamations of so formidable a character that the banking system could not easily resist them. The buying power of the home market was, further, raised by such devices as the hire-purchase system.

This was a direct and dangerous challenge of usury by borrowers. It meant, as has been emphasized, that lending abroad must cease, seeing that no foreign borrower could pay in goods across the tariff wall the interest on the loans made to him. It meant, therefore, that money, being no longer free to find its level, would inevitably be invested in the home market.

Meanwhile, as has been seen, the tide of gold flowed ever faster and faster towards New York. Gold began to heap up in the Central Banks. The Money power did not know how to lend it abroad, but was as determined as ever, if possible, to avoid lending it at home and so further increasing prices in the home market. The gold therefore remained in the bank's vaults. That is to say, it was hoarded as if it had never been taken from the bowels of the earth.

This was a deliberate policy, approved in the special circumstances by the Money power of the whole world. The Money power was well aware that America is a great agricultural country and that American farmers depend on their sales abroad of wheat, cotton, tobacco, and other products. A fall in world prices would necessarily, it was seen, hit these farmers hard and so reduce their power to buy from the manufacturers, who, in turn, would be compelled to reduce their prices and cut their wages. The policy of hoarding, in other words, was directed to the same object as had been the policy of lending to foreign countries. It was designed to compel American producers to produce more cheaply (that is to say, to compel American borrowers to pay higher rates of interest on the advances made to them), so that the power of these producers might be diminished and their resistance therefore to tariff reductions broken. In this way it was hoped that the American owners of gold would be enabled to lend abroad with the assurance that their debtors would be able to pay interest in the only way open to them namely, by sending their goods to the American market.

The policy of hoarding succeeded very well. As gold was withdrawn from the Central Banks of Europe to pay debts to America, these Central Banks (in accordance with the rules of their offices withdrew money from circulation. As money was withdrawn from circulation bank loans to agriculture and industry were called up in the proportion of $10 loan to $1 money. Country after country was emptied of buying power, prices fell and wages were cut.

The American farmer felt the force of this hurricane, for he was far less well protected than the American manufacturer. He, too, had to cut his prices in order to sell his goods. Wheat fell; cotton fell. The farmers ceased to be able to buy on the old scale from the manufacturers and the manufacturers in their turn began to suffer.

This was the position in 1927. At that time, however the American farmers and manufacturers were still an exceedingly powerful and influential body. They brought such pressure to bear on the Government and the Banking System that the policy of hoarding had to be abandoned and, in spite of all the objections to it, a new policy of lending abroad embarked upon.

It was a conspicuous victory of production over usury. The Money power found itself once more in the position it had occupied in England so often in the Nineteenth Century before its powers of resistance had been sufficiently well organized to render both agriculture and industry defenceless against its demands.

"Broadly speaking," says the MacMillan Report in language of admirable restraint, "the United States continued throughout the post-War period to gain gold until by the middle of May 1927 the gold stock of theU.S.A. reached its maximum figure of $4,700,000,000. It had been the avowed policy of the Federal Reserve Authorities to regard this gold stock as a trust fund... the policy of gold sterilization was the objective expression of this point of view. In 1927 the moment seemed to have arrived when the exigencies of the local credit situation coincided with the necessities of the outside world. In the autumn of 1927 the Reserve System encouraged low money rates in the New York market and thereby stimulated a boom in international securities.

"Gold flowed out, and by June 1928 the United States had lost $600,000,000 of gold... Easy credit conditions... had generated a period of world prosperity which *inter alia* enabled Great Britain to recover to some extent from the direct effects of the return to the gold standard and the industrial troubles which had followed upon it."

The resistance offered by the American producers had naturally caused great anxiety to the Money power throughout the rest of the world, by whom its true significance as a deadly threat and challenge was clearly understood. London, for instance, had not lacked profit from the position thrust upon her of broker between American lenders and Central European and South American debtors, but she was far from approving of the manner in which many of the American loans had been made and foresaw endless difficulties with debtors who had been enabled to obtain money too easily and in too large amount.

London meanwhile was suffering severely from the fall in prices.

"The return to gold in 1925," says the MacMillan Report, "required the reduction of sterling prices and consequently of money costs of production (*i.e.*, wages) to an extent which is variously estimated. At any rate the actual situation which was disclosed in the years following the return to gold marks that step as the beginning of a new series of difficulties for our trade and industry. Whatever the disequilibrium between costs and prices which still existed in 1924, it was seriously accentuated by the adjustment of sterling prices to gold prices. If gold prices had continued to rise, as they had been rising just previously, these difficulties would have largely vanished; as it was gold prices fell and the hopes then entertained in that respect were disappointed."

Among the penalties paid by Englishmen had been the General Strike and the Coal Stoppage. Happily, as has been said, the victory of the American manufacturers over the policy of hoarding brought some relief to the world's, and so to English, agriculture and industry.

The American manufacturers now for the time being had everything their own way. Their farmers began to buy from them again, as foreign lending was still difficult in view of the tariff and as hoarding had been put out of court, the owners of money were more or less compelled to invest in the home market. The American home market therefore became suddenly possessed of so great a volume of buying power as had not before been witnessed in human history. Prices and wages leaped up and the fruits of labour and science became suddenly available to millions of men and women. The rest of the world, writhing in the strong grip of Usury and beginning to suffer again from lack of gold, could scarcely believe its eyes. Here was the "golden age" about which men had dreamed from the beginning of time. The event is thus described in the MacMillan Report.

"The credit situation in the United States was now to change, and to change disastrously in its reactions upon the rest of the world. In the first place cheap money in the United States strengthened the tendency, already present in spite of a relative ebb of business in 1927, to a rise in the price of common stocks. From 1925 to1928 building and other construction in the United States was on an unprecedented scale, reaching the colossal aggregate of $38,000,000,000 for the four years together (or about 100,000,000 a month), which was double the value of the construction in the four years 1919 to 1922. The putting into circulation of this enormous volume of purchasing power, which was not directly associated with any corresponding increase in the production of immediately consumable goods, caused a huge growth of business profits which culminated in 1928 and 1929.

"At the same time the market-value of securities increased in an even greater proportion than profits, the process of the appreciation of securities being greatly assisted, apart altogether from the influence exerted by cheap money and business prosperity, by the belief that a 'new era' had dawned in the United States due to mass production and rising money wages. The difficulty of determining what was a reasonable basis for capitalizing the yield of securities made it possible for securities to sell at thirty to forty years' purchase, or even more, without upsetting public opinion, and they did in fact sell at such values.

"With such glittering chances of stock appreciation before their eyes, it is not surprising that it began to be more and more difficult to float international loans in New York or to sell bonds to American investors, nor that the prices of already existing bond issues should decline. To the bullish bond market of 1924-1927 had succeeded the bullish stock-market of 1928-1929."

Now, normally, of course, this tremendous increase of buying power in the home market ought by the rules of the gold standard to have caused the complete destruction of the American export trade and an outflow of gold to pay for imports. But, as has been seen, the American manufacturer thanks to his tariff had found a way of recovering his costs in the home market and so of being able to dump his goods abroad at competitive prices. The export trade, therefore, remained intact, while lending abroad was as difficult as ever. In these circumstances, far from gold being lost, gold was gained. The prizes being won daily on Wall Street were so tempting that foreign owners of gold began to gamble on a great scale in American shares.

As soon as these people bought shares, of course, they ceased to be owners of gold. Their gold went to America, nevertheless, to swell the tide of gold flowing to that country. Thus the Money power in the rest of the world saw its commodity disappearing in larger and still larger quantities behind the American tariff wall, where it was earning all too little (it was cheap money which began and sustained the boom). The Money power therefore redoubled its efforts to inflict defeat on the industrial "bosses" and their "new era."

There was one fatal weakness in that "new era" namely, the fact that the gold standard had been reestablished throughout Europe and the world. In its effect on the rest of the world the American boom was, as has been seen, a huge hoarding of gold. The rest of the world experienced, once again, restriction of credit (occasioned by lack of gold) and falling prices.

Seeing that the buying power of American farmers is essential to the prosperity of American manufacturers, and that American farmers have to sell at world prices, the boom was bound to bring about its own destruction as soon as the world prices of wheat and cotton fell far enough to rob the American farmer of his buying power.

This fall occurred in the summer of 1929 while the boom was still going on. It occurred, therefore, in spite of the increased American demand, occasioned by the boom, which increased demand naturally affected the rest of the world to some extent. As soon as world prices of agricultural products began to fall the pressure everywhere being exerted by the Money power to bring the American producers to heel began to become effective.

"From the very beginning of the more spectacular stage of the boom," says the MacMillan Report, "the Federal Reserve Authorities watched the situation with misgiving. By three successive stages in 1928 the New York Reserve rate was raised from three and a half per cent., to which figure it had been reduced in August1927, to five per cent. in July 1928 and, at the same time, in an effort to get control of the market, securities held by the Reserve System were sold upon a large scale... These (and other) actions of the Reserve Bank operations prevented credit from expanding by more than the amount required to offset gold movements, but could not cope with other elements in the situation... There was... drawn into the vortex of American speculation a mass of short money, not only from non-banking agencies in the United States but from European countries as well... Between June 23, 1928, and January 11, 1929, the gold stock rose by $7,000,000; between that date and October 25, 1929, it increased by a further $282,000,000...

"The effort to stop the boom in the United States... led everywhere to a policy of dear money, almost at the moment when economic conditions were becoming ripe for a policy of cheaper money."

The American producers now found themselves face to face with a shrinking buying power and began, of necessity, to cut their prices. As they cut, profits shrank and the visions of the "new era" were dissipated. In the autumn of 1929 the great crash on Wall Street announced to the world that the Money power had inflicted a heavy defeat upon its enemies.

The defeat was not, however, from Money's point of view, nearly heavy enough. Not the ruin of speculators and stockbrokers was the object, but the final breaking of the power of the industrialists and the destruction of their tariff wall that stubborn obstacle to the free movements of gold. In spite of the crash and the terror and disillusionment which followed it, the producers in America were still strong enough to offer an effective resistance to any tampering with their tariff.

That they did well to resist none who realizes what they were fighting for can doubt. Many hard things have been spoken (usually by the friends of Money) against the leaders of American industry. But these men, after all, are the captains of the production by which their fellow countrymen live. If they are unable to distribute their goods, the life of America necessarily comes to a standstill; factories must be closed, millions of humble men and women must be flung to the wolves of destitution. The cause of the industrialists was the cause of humanity.

Had they possessed a leader of clear sight the demand would instantly have been formulated by them for a degree of protection for farmers equal to the degree of protection given to themselves. Farm products would then have been sold at a profit once more and the farmer would have regained his buying power.

Unhappily the industrialists were not less solidly wedded to the gain-system than their enemies the bankers. They were anxious to see the farmers regain their buying power; but they were not willing that buying power should be regained at their expense. They did not want the price of food to rise any higher, because that must have meant a corresponding rise of the wages paid by themselves. There was, therefore, no support by industrialists for the farmers' demand for a high tariff wall. The Money power was relieved of the dreadful anxiety that America might escape out of its clutches by a policy of economic nationalism.

After the crash on Wall Street there was nothing for the Money power in America to do but to begin hoarding again, for in the disturbed state of the world nobody had the slightest wish to make any more loans. Gold, therefore, continued to flow to New York, and prices throughout the world continued to fall, with the result that manufacturers were compelled to reduce wages, discharge employees and even, in many cases, go out of business. Everywhere profits disappeared as unemployment increased. Taxes could not be paid and national budgets failed to balance.

But the spectacle of this universal ruin did not deflect the Money power from its object of effecting a release of the gold held imprisoned in America. American and European owners of gold were of one mind on this subject. French owners of gold who, in their own country, were passing through a similar experience, were very specially concerned.

France, thanks to the policy of M. Poincaré, had erected high tariff walls to protect her industries and agriculture and had in consequence and by reason of Reparation payments, like America, gained large quantities of gold, no less an amount, indeed, than a quarter of the world's supply (£500,000,000). French farmers and industrialists, like their American brethren, were determined that protection should not be taken away from them and, in this, had the support of their Government, which, for national reasons, was glad to see a substantial stock of gold held in Paris. The French Money power, like the American Money power, was averse from lending to a ruined world and consequently hoarded its gold, in the manner of the American Money power.

French prices in the world's markets were very low because M. Poincaré had taken the precaution, when France returned to gold, to link the franc to a quantity of gold of lower buying power than the actual buying power of the franc itself. (For example, whereas one franc bought a dozen eggs in France, the owner of that franc could only change it for an amount of gold capable of buying nine eggs in the world's markets. A Frenchman could therefore afford to sell twelve eggs in the world's markets as against, say, an Englishman's nine eggs.) Consequently the French export trade was less affected at first by the fall in world prices than the export trade of any other country. But a large part of the French export trade consists of articles of luxury for example, wines, silk, women's dresses, perfumes and face-powders, and the tourist traffic. The increasing poverty of the world naturally hit these luxury trades very hard and robbed the people conducting them of their buying power. The continued fall in world prices, again, gradually deprived the French of the advantage given to them by M. Poincaré. (The value of gold, due to its scarcity, had increased so much that the amount of gold represented by one franc now bought twelve instead of nine eggs and seemed likely soon to be able to buy many more.) France, therefore, saw the buying power of her home market threatened as seriously as the buying power of the American home market was being threatened. Like the American producers, the French producers in these circumstances clung with desperation to their tariffs.

Meanwhile the French Government viewed the course of events with the liveliest anxiety. It was concerned chiefly with the security of France against Germany, which, as it believed, depended on the French army, navy and air force. If France became involved in the universal ruin how could she hope to maintain her fighting forces? In these circumstances Reparations, the financial penalties imposed on Germany by the Peace Treaties, assumed paramount importance in French eyes.

But the Money power, as was well known in Paris, was anxious to get rid of the Reparations and War

Debts which had played a chief part in bringing about the flow of gold into Paris and New York. The French Government therefore adopted a hostile attitude towards the policy of the Money power, which it accused of being pro-German. The French Government at the same time complained bitterly about the financial support which, in its view, Berlin had received from New York and London. What, it was asked, was to happen to France if the financial blizzard struck her at the moment when Germany was actually being helped on to her feet again?

Thus into the strife between usury and production was imported the strife between nations. The French attitude towards England became exceedingly disturbing and the anxiety occasioned by it spread far beyond the confines of the City of London.

This is the explanation of much in the history of the second Labour administration which, otherwise, is inexplicable. Labour became associated with Liberalism. It declared itself in favour of Free Trade and turned a deaf ear to the demands of the more extreme groups among its own members. At the same time it used its utmost endeavours to save the system of Unemployment Insurance. The Conservatives lent support to these endeavours while, at the same time, attacking Free Trade and urging the importance of Empire Preference.

London, meanwhile, was struggling to counteract the effects upon itself of the stubborn resistance of the American manufacturers and French Nationalists to the demands of the Money power. It was obvious that the abandonment of the gold standard by England offered the surest and quickest way of escape from a position which, even in 1930, was daily growing more difficult, for, by abandoning gold, England would release herself from the strangulation of falling gold prices and would, at the same time, rid herself and her producers of the added burden of debts and costs imposed on her by these falling prices.

But against these evident advantages of the abandonment of gold was the glaring disadvantage, from the point of view of Money, that the gold standard would be greatly discredited in the world's eyes at a moment when quite enough discredit was falling upon it. If London abandoned gold, would anybody adhere to it? Usury was haunted by frightful visions of a world getting along very well without its gold of a world, that is, in which men would be able to exchange their products and enjoy the fruits of their labour. Again, what would be the effect on the minds of the large number of foreigners who had lent money on short-term to the London market if they lost, say, a quarter of their possessions by the deliberate act of the borrowers? Add to this a general belief that gold was necessary to salvation.

All idea of abandoning gold was put away, and as every mind the writer's not excepted was befogged by the accepted monetary doctrine, British producers continued to feel the full force of the hurricane. Production slowed town, since prices had fallen well below costs of production; unemployment and bankruptcy increased; receipts from taxes fell. And this was the experience of every country in the world because, everywhere, prices continued to be reckoned in the swiftly vanishing gold. By the middle of 1931 America was again in possession of nearly half of the total gold stock of the universe (£1,000,000,000), while France's stock, as has been said, represented half of the remainder (£500,000,000). A world glutted with goods was left to rub along with one quarter of its accustomed means of exchanging and so of consuming them.

Country after country now began to abandon the gold standard that is to say, to break the rule that gold of fixed amount must be given in exchange for currency upon demand. It became apparent to many observers that if all countries were to adopt this course and then boldly to supply themselves (by printing it) with the amounts of money necessary to the exchange of their goods, the crisis would immediately determine. But so constant and clamorous was the propaganda maintained by the Money power in favour of its commodity, gold, that the mass of mankind remained convinced that such a course must lead straight to ruin. Consequently the march to ruin continued with ever-increasing speed. Debtor nations sank to destitution under the weight of their debts, and the great creditor nations England, America, and France saw their industries and their agriculture fall and beheld their cities thronged with unemployed men and women, figures of tragedy and despair.

These great creditor nations are all governed by Parliaments. But none of their Governments understood what was happening clearly enough to dare seriously to challenge the Money power in the name of the men, women, and children on whom it was laying afflictions of the heaviest kind. Government, on the contrary, in each case adopted, quite sincerely, an attitude which suggested that humanity was face to face with some natural calamity, a visitation of God against which no effort of man could possibly avail. A suffering world was told that its afflictions proved how impossible it was for any nation to live to itself (this, of course, is tragically true where the gold standard operates) and how necessary, therefore, it had become to place international before national considerations. The word *inflation* was freely made use of to describe the period in America (the boom) when a free exchange of goods had brought comfort and happiness to the whole people. This period, it was now suggested, was a time of riotous living, a time in consequence of which America ought to feel ashamed. Americans, it was added, might properly rejoice that they had been delivered from such "fictitious prosperity" and set once more on the sure foundations of poverty and unemployment.

Nor did the American producers themselves venture to challenge this doctrine of Usury. Their world was falling about their ears and they seem to have felt that nobody was to blame. If they clung desperately to their tariffs, that was in obedience to an instinct which they scarcely tried to justify. Not one of them questioned the advantage of the gold standard or of that "sound finance" which was the sole cause of their ruin. It does not seem to have occurred to one of them that had the gold standard not existed, and had ordinary common sense been exercised in the issue of loans, there would have been no "slump" either in America itself or in the world outside of America, *for the simple reason that an increase of American buying power would not, in that case, have entailed a contraction of the buying power of the rest of the world.* The men, indeed, who were fighting so stubbornly to retain the tariff, which protected their industries and their workpeople, were showing an equal determination in demanding payment in gold of War Debts. Such is the confusion wrought in men's minds by the gain-system.

The Money power alone in this confusion knew what it wanted and understood what had happened. It abated nothing of its demands and remained in implacable hostility both to the American tariff and to the Treaty of Versailles. Without in the least sympathizing with Germany, it espoused her cause for the reason that her cause had become that of the gold standard and of Usury. Without hating France, it abused and misrepresented her because her well-founded fears of Germany threatened to hinder the speedy accomplishment of its own purpose to redistribute the gold stock of the world and so make secure once more its stranglehold on production.

It is only when this object is clearly understood that it is possible to account for the movements of popular feeling in many lands against America and France, but especially against France, which characterized the early months of 1931. These movements were the result of an intensive propaganda which was designed to represent the Money power as the champion of a world being devoured by the American Shylock and of a Germany doomed to writhe for ever under the iron heel of France. Englishmen and Americans were invited to hate the French; Englishmen and Frenchmen to hate the Americans. It was represented that while the miser in New York glutted himself with gold, the Moloch in Paris was opening his jaws to devour the helpless German people.

The plan as is now quite clear was to arouse enough sympathy for Germany in America to touch President Hoover's heart and so induce him to declare a moratorium of debt, and to excite enough fear of Germany in France to cause the French Government to acquiesce in that moratorium. For, as it was argued, once the flow of gold to New York, which the payments of War Debts occasioned, was stopped, the relatively high prices of goods still prevailing in America might hinder her from exporting her goods and so compel her to pay for her imports with her gold. Thus, in spite of her tariffs, gold would begin to flow out. Sooner or later the outflow of gold would compel manufacturers to lower their prices to the world level.

This plan of the Money power very nearly succeeded. So eloquent and moving were the appeals made on behalf of Germany that President Hoover duly declared his moratorium. But the French Government was less easily persuaded. France haggled over the Hoover moratorium. At the same time she made it clear that if British policy was not kept in line with her own policy, she would call up immediately the large stocks of gold which she held in the Bank of England.

That threat was terrible in the ears of Englishmen, for the world slump had dried up all England's resources by making nearly all her debtors bankrupt.

Was England about to be driven off the gold standard by a "run" on the Bank?

The whole population of this country viewed the possibility with dismay. So great a calamity, it was resolved by the country as a whole, must at all costs be avoided even at the cast of appearing to submit British foreign policy to the dictates of France by asking for a loan of gold. Credits were arranged with France and America.

Chapter XXIII

The King's Grace

IT is habitual with the Money power to lay the blame for the ruin which it causes upon the shoulders of other people. A remarkable illustration of this was afforded when the storm blowing from Paris broke over London. At that moment, as has been seen, the world was bereft of about three-quarters of its accustomed buying power because about three-quarters of its stock of gold was being hoarded. Prices of goods everywhere had fallen to exceptionally low levels, and consequently producers were going out of business, dismissing their workpeople, and ceasing to pay income tax. In these circumstances every national Budget in the world was unbalanced and every country in the world was faced with the prospect of a falling export trade.

But these facts did not deter the International Money power from declaring in loud and most threatening tones that the financial crisis in London was due in large measure to the profligate extravagance of the British Labour Government. The Government, it was stated, was allowing the country to drift into bankruptcy. It was living above its means by reason of borrowings on behalf of the Unemployment Fund. Its expenditure on the Social Services was threatening the safety of the nation.

It is eloquent testimony to the dominance over every mind which Mammon, in these days, is able to exercise that charges so evidently untrue and preposterous were admitted almost without question even by those against whom they were brought. The British Labour Cabinet stood humbly in the dock while the greedy architects of a universal ruin, posing unctuously as the Saviours of Society, overwhelmed it with abuse and contumely. His Majesty's ministers, for the most part, confessed their error and promised miserably to mend their ways. They would cut down expenditure; they would balance the Budget; they would live in future within their means.

This surrender naturally aroused protests on the part of the people who were destined to suffer for it. It was then made clear that the Cabinet, though apparently well persuaded of the justice of the accusations preferred against it and of the necessity of a change of policy, was afraid to offend its political supporters.

The utmost alarm was immediately manifested in the country, and this alarm quickened when it became known that the credits from France and America were exhausted and that, if new credits were not immediately obtained, "ruin" must follow. In these circumstances the tottering and demoralized Government went rapidly to pieces and was shipwrecked.

It is well that the English people should hold that dissolution in mind. The real reason why the slump began in England before it began elsewhere was the overvaluation of the pound in 1925 when this country returned to gold. The cause of the world slump itself lay far beyond the borders of this country. Yet both these catastrophes were laid at the door of the King's ministers and ascribed to a profligacy the sole object of which, in any case, was the preservation of the British people from hardship and distress.

Parliament was paying the price of its surrender a century before to the Money power. Never was spectacle more pitiable. For here was the governing authority of a people which, on a hundred battlefields, had just upheld its title to worship, hat in hand to foreign countries.

Suppose these countries refused to lend any more money?

Suppose the pound "crashed"? Would it be possible then to feed the millions in the great cities? So befogged had every mind become by the propaganda of Money that the credit of one of the bravest, most enterprising, and most able races on earth was felt to be doubtful.

Meanwhile His Majesty the King left Balmoral and travelled back to London. Mr. MacDonald tendered his resignation, and there was joyous anticipation in financial circles of a speedy disappearance of Labour from office and of a ruthless cutting down of "doles" and Social Services. It rested with the King, however, to choose the new Prime Minister. His Majesty requested Mr. MacDonald to retain his post and to form a National Government.

That was a Royal promise to the British people and to the world that such sacrifices as might be made would be imposed equally upon all, and that the safeguards of the weak and the poor would not be diminished. It is certain that, in the future, men will see in this choice of the leader of the Labour party to be the leader of the nation an act of Kingship of decisive importance. When all fainted, the King remained trustful of the courage, the self-sacrifice, and the high patriotism of his people. When all were disposed to yield to the bullyings and threatenings of the Money power, and make an end of everything to which that power took exception, the King chose the man who, as leader of the fallen Government, had been most bitterly attacked by Money.

It is well to set that kingly gesture against the blustering pusillanimity of Money. A ruined world and a universal panic bore witness to Money's rule. The ugly god sat, livid with fear, on his throne, screeching that all must be delivered to destruction so that "credit" might be restored. Only a King had dared to ignore these bellowings. In the hour of destiny the Pretender was made manifest; he who possessed the King-thought, which is the Grace of God, came to the rescue of his people.

Chapter XXIV

Counter-Attack

NOW the King's faith in his people was justified is fresh in every man's memory. Britain was driven off gold; the patriotism, the courage and the discipline of the British people made that event an occasion of joy rather than of calamity. In the belief that they were helping their country the well-to-do imposed upon themselves new and crushing burdens of taxation; the unemployed, on the very day on which the cuts in their meagre allowances became effective, voted for the men who had made these cuts. An astonished world was instructed that a nation's credit resides in the hearts of men and women, in their loyalty and devotion and sense of service.

But it would be an error, nevertheless, to suppose that these manifestations of the love which Englishmen bear to their King and country were not immediately turned to account by the International Money power. Englishmen had agreed to balance the national Budget because they believed that this action would uphold England's honour before the world. How many of them knew that the merit of a balanced Budget in the eyes of Money resides in the fact that it removes the necessity, which might otherwise arise, of raising the prices of goods? If a nation refuses to be taxed further in order to balance its Budget, the process of balancing can only be carried out by creating more taxpayers that is to say, by increasing buying power and raising prices so that more people are enabled to earn profits.

The sole object of the Money power, to which crisis or no crisis it continued stubbornly to adhere, was to extract the gold lying hoarded in New York and Paris, and so restore the gold standard to full activity. That object, as has been seen, demanded the cessation of the flow of gold towards these centres. It demanded, therefore, the wiping out of Reparations and War Debts and the reduction of the American and French tariffs. America had to be persuaded of her splendid destiny as the Peacemaker of the World and the Friend of Humanity; France had to be persuaded that the only way to security was by means of the forgiveness of debt and the reduction of armaments.

Now it is evident that the ideals of disarmament, of forgiveness of debt, and of brotherly love between peoples must make immediate appeal to men of sympathy and kindly feelings in every country in the world. That is being proved anew daily. How surprised, then, the good people who, up and down Europe, are pleading for reductions of debts and armaments, for equal status for Germany, for a strengthening of the power of the League of Nations and of the various peace pacts and agreements would be if they knew that they are acting exactly as the Money power desires that they should act, and are therefore probably the enemies rather than the friends of the causes which they advocate. For it is the will of the Money power to fasten again upon the world that system of ruinous competition for foreign markets which is the gold standard and which, as a true law of the jungle, is a chief cause of strife and battle between nations.

Not less surprised than these, probably, would be the members of the Conservative party if they understood that the policy of Protection and Empire Trade is, at the moment, serving well the ends of International Money. It has been stated again and again in these pages that a free British market is essential to the satisfactory functioning of the Money System, and this statement remains true as the Conservative party may one day discover. The point is that the Money System is not, at present, functioning satisfactorily because of the impossibility of getting the hoarded gold out of New York and Paris. It was pointed out above that, when the American and French Governments raised their tariff walls so high as to prevent debtors from paying in goods the interests on the loans made to them, these debtors made use of the open markets of England. They sold their goods in England for gold (thus increasing unemployment in this country) and sent the gold to New York and Paris. Seeing that the most immediate object of the Money power is to put a stop to this one-way traffic in gold, the closure of the British market is for the moment a step agreeable to its wishes. Further the tariff, by excluding imports, helps to redress the balance of trade and so to prevent an outflow of gold, which outflow would inevitably set in the directions of New York or Paris.

But the propagandists of the Money power never suffer it to be forgotten that their final object is not protection, but Free Trade with all the world. The

British tariff and the Ottawa agreements, it is a safe guess, will, if the chief object of International Money namely, the redistribution of gold is effected, be made the objects of violent attack and bitter criticism by the Money power throughout the world. If London is to remain the financial centre of the world the London market must be free. The Conservative party, therefore, which, in its bewilderment, is allowing British agriculture to drift to hopeless ruin and is making of itself the mouthpiece of the campaign for lower wages and salaries, ought to seek speedy enlightenment. It may be true that a rise in the price of meat would inflict hardship on the wage-earners of the North of England, but so, certainly, and to a much greater extent, will the loss of wages occasioned by campaigns for economy. Economy campaigns, undertaken at a moment when the world is sinking under the weight of its unsold products, are apt to inflict injury on those who conduct them. Is the Conservative party sure that its unpopularity, when the time arrives to return to Free Trade, would be a matter of regret to the International Money power? Conservatism is weak because it has too long turned its back on Toryism. Let it recall Disraeli's words: Toryism has its origins in great principles; it sympathises with the lowly; it looks up to the Most High. It is not dead but sleepeth.

That the International Money power wishes to see England return to the gold standard is, of course, absolutely certain. But this does not mean that there was much lamentation among financiers when the break with gold took place in September 1931. The Money power certainly would, for the reasons already stated, have liked to avoid that break; but it has wasted no time on idle regrets. Meanwhile English producers have received some small advantage. This is easily understood when it is recalled that, by simply allowing the pound to drop in terms of the dollar and the franc, the prices of English goods can be reduced in foreign markets without the necessity of effecting any diminution of buying power that is to say, of wages in England itself. The lower the prices of English goods fall in the world's markets, the more difficult does it become for French goods and American goods, to compete with them, because French and American producers, being still on gold, can reduce their prices only by making direct cuts in wages that is to say, by diminishing the buying power of their home markets, and this buying power is now too low to allow of costs being recovered in the home markets, Dumping consequently is, for the present, out of the question.

The Money power of the world, however, is using the opportunity afforded by the suspension of the gold standard in England not, as is popularly supposed, to try to raise the world prices of goods, but to drive prices down to still lower levels. The truth is that whereas producers look on the existing prices as ruinously low, the Money power looks on them as ruinously high.

For the Money power measures prices only in terms of gold. As there is very little free gold available now to the world, and as the world's buying power is still rigidly limited by this small quantity of gold, prices, according to the view of Money, ought to be considerably lower than they are and wages ought to be severely cut in order to enable prices to be reduced.

On this theory, as will be obvious, a total disappearance of free gold, which may possibly occur if America insists on being paid the uttermost farthing, should reduce both prices and wages to zero and bring human activity and human life to an end, no matter how large may be the productive power of men. In other words, food is not food unless and until there is gold to endow it with the quality of food. This is a mystical rather than an economic doctrine and suggests that the Powers of Darkness are more real than many people in these days are disposed to believe.

There are competent observers who believe that the long and fearful struggle for lower and still lower prices which is the economic expression of the struggle between Usury on the one side and the American industrialists and the French Nationalists on the other will be determined in the not very remote future in favour of Usury. In other words, the gold hoarded in New York and Paris will be invested once more at high rates throughout the world. This view is based on the facts already mentioned namely, that the English Budget has been balanced, and that, unlike France and America, England possesses a currency which is not at present tied to gold.

Both the American and French Budgets are hopelessly unbalanced. They can be balanced only by further drastic cuts in Government expenditure and by further heavy taxation *or by raising the internal price-levels*. Further cuts and further taxation are held to be impossible. Higher prices, it is contended, must therefore come in both countries.

But higher prices in the existing demoralization of the home markets of America and France mean failure to compete against England in the world's markets. (English producers, with a balanced Budget and a free currency, can reduce prices still farther if need be without reducing wages.) England therefore, it is argued, will capture the export trade of the world and so draw to herself, in payment of her exports, much of the gold now lying hoarded in New York and Paris, though it may reasonably be objected that this is likely to prove a slow process in view of the American monopoly of cotton, Virginian tobacco, and (partially) petroleum, and that, in any case, America *may* return to the policy of dumping. There can be no doubt that all the elements in the economic situation which favour the International Money power have been made use of by that power with great skill and daring. But it would be a mistake to suppose that American industrialism and French Nationalism have not continued to offer a stout resistance.

It is generally assumed in England that since September 1931 the French and American Governments have been following policies sharply opposed to each other. This is not necessary so. Neither the American nor the French Government doubts the supreme value of gold, but both these Governments have special claims resting upon them. The American Government, as has been said, is pledged to tariffs; the French Government to the Treaty of Versailles. And the Money power is implacably opposed to both tariffs and Treaty.

It would be surprising, in these circumstances, if bonds of sympathy did not somewhere exist between the American industrialists and the French Nationalists. After the visit of M. Laval, the French Prime Minister, to Washington, it was represented in England that America had been bullied into abandoning her support of Germany by threats of heavy withdrawals of French gold. There were heavy withdrawals of gold, but these continued after American interest in Germany seemed to have evaporated.

It seems more likely that the outbursts of anger against France, which occur from time to time in America, proceed from the owners of gold, and that the real key to American policy in 1931 is the attitude of the American industrialists towards the Hoover moratorium. The American industrialists before M. Laval's visit had persuaded themselves that the moratorium was a first step in the long journey towards reduction of the American tariff. They saw how welcome the moratorium had been to all their rivals throughout the world and argued, no doubt, that it boded them no good.

The American industrialists therefore criticized the moratorium so bitterly that President Hoover had no option but to refrain from further action in European affairs. M. Laval's visit approved this attitude, which was later imposed upon the President formally by Congress, just as, at an earlier date, non-intervention in European affairs had been imposed on President Wilson.

At the beginning of 1932, therefore, the Money power was as far as ever from its object. There seemed to be no prospect of getting the gold out of America or out of France. But as the year advanced new hope was awakened. Germany announced flatly that she would pay no more, and her attitude occasioned lively anxiety in Paris, where, as in America, the effects of the slump were beginning to exert their full and fatal influence. Both America and France showed signs of exhaustion; fear was abroad in every city; the atmosphere was becoming favourable for a deal.

In these circumstances the American Government displayed a new interest in European affairs and notably in the efforts of the League of Nations to cope with the Sino-Japanese quarrel, and the French Government adopted a milder tone. Optimistic people declared that if France and her former allies could be induced to forego Reparations, and if disarmament could be carried to a point at which President Hoover might claim it as a victory of the American spirit in world affairs, the American people would be won over to agreeing to a cancellation of War Debts.

Discussions began to this end in many European centres. It was suggested that the claims against Germany should be waived at a preliminary conference to be held contemporaneously with the Disarmament Conference at Geneva, and the hope was expressed that a gesture from America might indicate to the Disarmament Conference, during its sittings, the kind of agreement which would be most pleasing to the American people and their elected representatives. Every effort, meanwhile, which the wit of man could devise would be made to influence French opinion in favour of a more unbending attitude and American opinion in favour of freer trade.

The Ottawa Conference was not welcomed by International Money. Its dangerous character, on the contrary, was clearly recognized. It was likely to exasperate American opinion, and it might easily afford a platform to those Empire statesmen who wished to discuss the gold standard and its supersession by a managed sterling currency. Ottawa, in the view of Money, was a liability, but it was unavoidable.

For a time the hopes of a settlement achieved a large measure of fulfilment. In France the Nationalist Government of M. Laval fell and was replaced by the Liberal Government of M. Herriot. Germany moved to the right and presented the world, and especially France, with the prospect of a return to Prussianism a sufficiently terrifying spectacle. The force of the economic blizzard wrought upon both France and America so effectively as to induce a condition of mind described by one observer as chronic panic. At Ottawa, too, discussion of the financial question was left over to a World Economic Conference at which America was to be represented. It is worthy of note, however, that America made it clear that she would not, at this World Conference, discuss either War Debts or tariffs the subjects which the Money power was implacably determined that she should discuss.

Meanwhile Americans manifested, in most gratifying fashion, the satisfaction they felt at the result of the Lausanne Conference a satisfaction which the whole world shared. Reparations were out of the way at last; could War Debts continue to flourish? The belief that even the hard heart of Congress must be touched was widely expressed and widely accepted. Men of goodwill everywhere opened a campaign for European disarmament, on the lines duly suggested by President Hoover to the Disarmament Conference.

Suddenly Germany became troublesome. It was obvious to Berlin that every hope of her former enemies was set upon Disarmament as a means of persuading America to cancel War Debts.

Here was the opportunity to demand and obtain equality of status with France. The German representatives were instructed by their Government to withdraw from the Disarmament Conference.

So heavy a blow threw both Europe and America into a condition of lively anxiety. If the Disarmament Conference failed hopes of persuading Congress to wipe out the War Debt might be abandoned. These anxieties were not relieved by the failure of the Powers to induce Germany to come to a Conference in London or elsewhere. The Germans, when they saw the dismay occasioned by their demand for equal status, immediately put up their price. France reacted. America drew back once more from a Europe which, as her industrialists assured her, is a hotbed of war.

But hope revived once more when the French displayed a more accommodating spirit towards Germany. Interest in the Disarmament Conference, which had almost evaporated, was quickened. The result of the American Presidential Election came to give added comfort, seeing that the Democratic party in America is Liberal in sentiment and has never been very friendly to high tariffs.

In this atmosphere the Notes of the European Governments to Washington asking for a cancellation or postponement of War Debts were despatched. At the moment of writing (December 1932) the answer of America is before the world. A further large consignment of gold is gravitating towards the vaults in New York and the American parties are once more affirming their faith in tariffs on the one had and in gold on the other. The American industrialists are still in the saddle, and even though the horse is making heavy going they look like staying there. In the circumstances the World Economic Conference presents a less hopeful aspect.

But though nations are depressed, he is sanguine who believes that Money has wholly abandoned hope. Money never abandons hope. So long as Governments and peoples remain incapable of distinguishing between real wealth and gold, and so fear exceedingly loss of gold, new plans will be made and new expedients devised. And so perhaps we shall one day return to the Money System in its old ruthless form, to slumps and booms, to slums and Social Reform (with, however, a smaller dole), to starvation and over-productionin short, to that inexorable economic law which, as is now being seen, is a law designed to **sacrifice the whole universe in order to make the universe safe for Usury.**

Even if such a return should take place it is unlikely to be wholly satisfactory to Money. For the smoke-screen of gold is less dense than formerly. What the Americans are doing in demanding payment of War Debts in gold corresponds exactly on a world scale to a run on an ordinary bank. It is being made clear even for the dullest to see that the Financial System of the world does not possess a gold backing for a tithe of its liabilities. The Financial System is therefore in the greatest danger, unless the American industrialists and French Nationalists can be converted in time, of having to close its doors and default.

This is the nightmare which is haunting the dreams of every international financier. Because the odds are that, after the last shipload of gold has crossed the Atlantic, Europe will rub along well enough on paper money. Will the illusion of gold then be shattered for ever? One is reminded irresistibly of Rostand's hero, the barnyard cock which, every morning, amid profound silence, ascended a little hill and crowed. At the sound of the cock-crow the sun rose and all the other inhabitants of the farmyard believed that they saw a miracle. Where would they be if Chanticleer did not bestow on them the blessing of light? But one morning Chanticleer slept in and the sun rose without awaiting his summons.

Why is nobody insisting today that British agriculture and British coal-mining are valuable quite apart from their powers of earning profits? Or that a thriving agriculture would afford the best of all markets the home market for a thriving industry? The only obstacle which stands in the way of such a development of the home and imperial market is the Money power and its gold standard. If British and Empire agriculture could buy the products of British and Empire industry so that producers could obtain their livelihood within the Empire, the whole fabric of Dutch finance would be destroyed, for it would no longer be possible to empty this country of money in favour of some foreign country and so to compel sellers to seek buyers in the ends of the earth. For the doctrine of cheapness we should then have the older and better doctrine of service. The Money power and its gold god would cease to exert the power of life and death over producers and, through them, over the whole people, and we should be spared the impending horror of a world bank.

Doubtless if the financial system breaks it will be patched up again. But will the Money power really succeed? Against it, today, stands the spirit of service which, in 1931, rescued the terrified lords of Mammon from the ruin they had compassed. If it is England's calamity that she has been chosen as the citadel of Money, it is her glory that her people retain, more perhaps than any other people, the ideals of Christian Feudalism. There is no sacrifice which Englishmen are not ready to make for England. If the Money power is really to triumph, therefore, it must convince this people and must keep them convinced that its patriotism is not inferior to their patriotism and that, in serving its ends, they will be serving the ends of their country. All the engines of a vast publicity belong to Money; but it is doubtful, nevertheless, if the propaganda which succeeded so well in the Nineteenth Century will be equally effective in the Twentieth.

One reason for this is the power which man has acquired over the forces of Nature. Until this moment buying power, as has been seen, has invariably been distributed to the people in the form of salaries, wages, dividends, and profits; but man power is being displaced by machine power so quickly that even now *since machines do not earn wages* enough buying power to enable the output of production to be consumed is not being issued. It is certain that, under the Money System, this state of affairs will be greatly intensified. Even at the height of the American boom there were 2,000,000 unemployed persons in the United States who had been thrown out of work because machines were doing that work. A recent calculation suggests that at least a quarter of the 12,000,000 persons now unemployed in America can never again be employed under the present system perhaps under any conceivable system.

How then, as salaries and wages disappear, is buying power to be distributed? Here is a new battle-field for Money which will resist to the utmost the idea that, as human labour becomes more productive, larger quantities of money will be needed to exchange the products of that labour. The question, Are men to be given money for nothing? is bound to be asked by those whose office it is and has always been to give money, invented by themselves out of nothing, in exchange for the largest possible quantities of goods and services.

It is no part of the writer's intention to enter into the question of the distribution of buying power in a world in which the power to produce is being increased almost from hour to hour. (The reader is referred to the illuminating works of Major Douglas.) But it may be pointed out that enlarged opportunities of rest and recreation were not, under the God System, looked upon as an evil. It depends on what you believe to be the object of man's life. If that object is work, as Money understands the word, then every human invention, including the spade, is an evil, since it reduces the amount of work. If, on the contrary, the object the service and enjoyment of God and of one's fellows, then there is no evil.

Men have, until now, enjoyed few opportunities of that kind of spiritual development which is associated with the contemplative life.

The conditions of social and economic life, the Pope stated in his recent Encyclical, are such that vast multitudes of men can only with great difficulty pay attention to that one thing necessary namely, their eternal salvation.

It was the belief of the architects of the God System that the Christian revelation of God is of so infinite a richness that its wealth will not fully have been explored at the world's end. These architects would not certainly have regarded as an evil discoveries which, when the power of Money has been broken, will release men and women throughout the world and so enable more men and more women to achieve a deeper enjoyment of God and therefore a nobler service of their fellows.

It may be argued that prosperity and leisure constitute great temptations. But it is well attested by experience that poverty and misery are the fruitful mothers of vice. Every man today sees before his eyes a world overflowing with goods, but crowded with paupers. So far all the eloquence of Finance has not sufficed to explain away that strange and grim spectacle. On the contrary, such incidents as the advice of the Federal Farm Board to the growers of cotton to plough up every third row remain engraved on the public memory. The Money power must reckon now with the fact that it has shocked the conscience of humanity. Knowledge is coming to the common people; it was by the support of the common people, as has been shown, that, under God, Kingship originally was made effective and the nation established. Englishmen owe it to Queen Victoria and her descendants that the ideals of duty and service have not been suffered to fade in a world in which greed of gain achieved an almost universal sanction.

Chapter XXV

Stewardship

THE Feudal System, let it be repeated, was based upon the belief that "the earth is the Lord's and the fullness thereof." Even the King's ownership of the land over which he reigned was a tenancy under God, the real Owner. The meanest vassal, therefore, was associated in that universal service of God which was the sole office of Kings and nobles and priests.

There is no place in such a system for ownership without responsibility. There is, equally, no place for the socialistic conception of the "State" as a mutual-benefit trust. Mutual benefit implies the possession of rights; Feudalism recognized only duties towards God and, under God, towards men.

A little consideration will show that the God System is, in fact, the only substitute for the Money System. Any other system is bound sooner or later, from its nature, to lead back to Money. It follows that the distresses of the world cannot be cured by any device, however subtle, but only by a return to faith upon which, in the beginning, European civilization was built. If men have really ceased to believe in God, they will remain the victims of Mammon, and no method of currency control or State economy will save them.

Napoleon did not err when he declared that religion is the basis of Society.

It was the scepticism of the Eighteenth Century which prepared the way for the coming of the Money power. But that scepticism was no more than the revolt of honest minds against an abuse of privilege by both the spiritual and temporal authority. The trouble was not Feudalism, but the want of it. Had the Church remained in all things true to her Master, had the Kings and their nobles adhered to the rule *Noblesse oblige*, there would have been no occasion of doubt. A Church advancing ever in knowledge of God and His purpose, Thrones in which all men saw the pledge of service, would have suffered nothing from criticism or ribaldry. That the Throne in England possesses today the deepening confidence of men and women is a matter, therefore, of sincere rejoicing. Little by little the idea of individual ownership without responsibility - and also the idea of a common ownership without responsibility - is giving place to the idea of a stewardship. The mass of the people, in other words, remains true to the old ideals - as was shown during the War and again in 1931 - and lacks nothing but knowledge of the Money System to make an end of it. The best service, therefore, which a man can render his fellows is to instruct them about the Money power and urge them to use their votes.

True Internationalism, let it be added, is friendship between nations, not a return to tribalism under the overlordship of International Finance. In its essence, it is the recognition by one nation of the God-thought of another nation and so an extension of man's knowledge of God. It is a meeting of two systems of service whereby God is recognized as the object of both, and men, in consequence, discover a common duty and a common brotherhood in duty. True Internationalism, therefore, like Nationalism, is a system of service deriving from Heaven and opposed wholly to the system of gain. The Money power can no more achieve such a union than it can achieve the welfare of any individual nation.

For the nation is a society the basis of which is spiritual and not material. A nation is not a commonwealth in which every citizen possesses an equal share, it is not a "State" the people of which enjoy the same rights; the idea of natural right or birthright is foreign to its constitution. In its essence it is a lieutenancy of God, a part of His universe entrusted to one of His captains and existing solely for His good pleasure. The subjects of the King, like the King himself, have no right save that of obedience to the Divine Will, and can possess nothing except in so far as possession may be necessary to the performance of duty. If it is objected that such an idea partakes of the grotesque in this modern world, the answer may properly be made that it is not more, but less grotesque than the spectacle now presented by the Kingdoms of Mammon, wherein every new exhibition of man's power to make use of the resources of God is attended by fresh calamity and ruin, and where each addition to the wealth of humanity adds inevitably to the number of the destitute.

PREFACE TO THE SECOND EDITION (OF MONARCHY OR MONEY POWER)

EVENTS have moved very quickly since the first edition of this book was published last year. I have accordingly added to the present edition, in the form of "Book I," an account of these events and a discussion of their bearing on the views which I hold. I make no apology for setting in the forefront of that outline the religious aspect of the great struggle which is now proceeding in every corner of the world; for I believe that that struggle is essentially of a religious character. Elsewhere I have attempted to show that the worship of Mammon partakes also of the nature of religion.

The literature of this subject is, of course, the most extensive in the world, ranging as it does from the Bible to the latest monograph on economic science. A life-long study of the French Revolution and of Napoleon's reign is the basis of the chapters dealing with these events, but I wish to make special mention of *A King's Lessons in Statecraft,* by Louis XIV, edited by Jean Longnon and translated by Herbert Wilson (Unwin); of *The Life and Writings of Turgot,* by Walker Stephens (Longmans); of *The Assignats,* by S.E. Harris (Harvard Economic Studies Cambridge University Press); and *Currency and Credit,* by R.G. Hawtrey. These four books, though I disagree cordially with many of the opinions expressed in them, seem to me to be essential to a proper understanding of the nature and finances of the French Monarchy and of the French Revolution.

The state of Great Britain after the close of the Napoleonic Wars is best understood by reference to the files of *The Times* and to contemporary speeches, but I wish to acknowledge indebtedness to *The Life of Robert Owen*, by G.D.H. Cole (Macmillan). I owe a debt also to A.E. Feavearvear for his excellent work *The Pound Sterling* (Oxford University Press). The Reports of the Inspectors of Factories should be consulted for an account of industrial conditions, and a study ought to be made of Marx's *Das Kapital*. The speeches of Peel, Disraeli, and Chamberlain have been freely drawn upon, and also the writings of Disraeli and the *Biography of Disraeli*, by Buckle and Monypenny. Keynes' and Hawtrey's works afford great help in studying the more recent developments of currency and credit. The *Stabilization of the Mark*, by Dr. Schacht, even if the views expressed are not accepted, is a valuable book. It need scarcely be added that the "Macmillan Report" (and its addenda) is indispensable to a proper understanding of the existing situation. I wish in conclusion to acknowledge my debt to the late Lord Milner for his expression, "The Money Power," and for his book, *Questions of the Hour*, and to Major C.H. Douglas for his writings upon the monopoly of credit. My sincere thanks are due to my friend Douglas Woodruff for his most valuable help, to my friend W.F. Casey for his kindness in reading the proofs, to my friend Douglas Jerrold for his sympathy and understanding, and to my friend the Rev. Samuel Ford, Vicar of All Souls', Loudoun Road, London, for the inspiration of his preaching.

R. MCNAIR WILSON.
LONDON, March, 1934

Introduction to
the Second Edition

It is, naturally, a joy to me that the first edition of this book has been sold out within a period of months, for I believe that the opinions expressed in the book are of importance to my own and other countries at the present time.

I can hold this view without vanity or self-congratulation because these opinions, far from being new, are as old as European history. At no time in that history have they lacked some advocate. It is with the most profound happiness that I see, across the Atlantic, a new champion of these opinions rising who is worthy to be their exponent alike by reason of his Christianity, his statesmanship, his knowledge, his political sagacity and his courage. I mean President Roosevelt.

Public comment upon President Roosevelt's administration has already made it plain that in the minds of the majority of men and women it represents what may be called a halfway house between democracy and dictatorship, and there is further implied in these comments the idea that democracy and dictatorship are the only methods of government available to men, and that all forms of government, however apparently varied, can be placed in one or other of these great classes.

It is the purpose of this book to combat that idea and to urge that a third choice exists - namely,

Christian Monarchy. Emphasis has been laid upon the word "Christian" because Christian Monarchy possesses qualities peculiar to itself which derive directly from the Christian faith. In my submission all forms of human society are based on religious ideas and express relationships of one kind or another to the supernatural. I take the view, for example, that the dictatorships now in being in many European countries are based upon the same religious ideas as underlie the so-called democracies which these dictatorships have replaced. It is outside the scope of this work to trace the origins and history of the religion whose modern expression is financial democracy, but I wish to emphasise my belief that it is a real religion, of respectable antiquity. I am disposed to think that Buddhism is one of its earliest manifestations, and I feel convinced that Platonism and Neo-Platonism, Stoicism and Cynicism, have all made contribution to its growth. Spinoza certainly deserves mention if only as the precursor of Rousseau, and so also do Voltaire, Montesquieu and many other philosophers of the Eighteenth Century. The French Revolutionaries were all imbued with this faith, as they showed in various more or less crude ways; for instance, the worship of Reason as god or goddess, the insistence, upon Rights as opposed to duties, and the praise offered to Beauty both as abstraction and as woman.

Robespierre's "acknowledgment of the Supreme Being" was a belated attempt to reconcile this pagan faith with what remained to the French people of Christian thought. In the Nineteenth Century that reconciliation was effected so that millions who called themselves Christians lived, on the contrary, in accordance with ideas which are opposed to Christianity, without finding out that a deception had been practised upon them. The decline of Christianity in the Nineteenth Century is due, in my opinion, chiefly to this cause.

I wish my reader to form some idea of the "pagan faith" about which I am speaking, because, if he fails to do this, he will fail to understand the strength and the tenacity of the Money Power which constitutes, to-day, a kind of priesthood of the pagan god. The essence of the pagan faith was its rational character. It separated the intellect of men from all other faculties and exalted it above all other faculties. The appeal was ever to Reason against superstition, to Right against privilege, and to Beauty against ugliness. The conclusion was inevitable that the most intellectual ought to rule and direct. That, however, was a conclusion at variance with the idea of universal human right - namely, that every man ought to govern himself. Reconciliation was effected by allowing "the people" to choose "enlightened" representatives who, having been chosen, would become leaders. The party system secured that choice at elections should lie between persons of substantial wisdom. This was the avowed basis of parliamentary democracy. The real, unavowed basis was money, because parties had to meet heavy expenses and could only do so if rich men were prepared to finance them. It was easy, as it happened, to fit the rich man into the political structure of this paganism, for none but men of intelligence could acquire great wealth, and in fact most of the great bankers were men of high intellectual attainment. Soon, therefore, the attributes of the pagan god were enlarged to include wealth. When this had been accomplished it was an irresistible conclusion that he had made bankers in his own image.

Consequently the business of usury, which in the Age of Faith had been viewed with horror and loathing, came to be honoured above all other businesses and to acquire a peculiar, almost sacred, character. Bankers were called pillars of the state and even of the Churches, and none hesitated for a moment to bestow the name of Christian upon their activities. God, it was felt, had given largely to recipients so worthy of his bounty. Thus governments or politicians who opposed the bankers or called down their wrath were held to be immoral, dishonest, and even unpatriotic or irreligious. The power which Parliaments had taken from Kings was handed over to bankers, and the representatives of the people were warned that in no circumstances must they dare to interfere with Money. This was another way of saying that popular representatives were necessarily less honest than usurers.

Thus the pagan faith found expression in a dictatorship which required no bayonets, apparently, to maintain it. Men could have votes; they could have free speech and free writing. Their rights were secure and their destiny belonged to their own intelligence. What they did not see was that one thing was lacking to this freedom - namely, food. The power to give or to withhold the means of livelihood had passed wholly into the bankers' hands because, as the sole fountain of money, the banker was able to give or to take away the means of exchanging the products of labour.

We see to-day that, if the banker's power is seriously challenged in any country, so-called democracy is transformed overnight into crude dictatorship. What we are apt not to see is that such dictatorship differs very little from the democracy which preceded it. Still the foundation is the "pagan faith," and the source of power, starvation. Financial democracy and dictatorship are always, and necessarily, interchangeable, because they are based on the same philosophical and religious ideas.

It is of importance that the difference between this pagan religion and Christianity should be understood. Christianity is a revelation of God proceeding from God Himself. It is also the means of Salvation by which men may achieve the object of their existence - namely, eternal life: "And this is life eternal, that ye may know the Lord your God, and, Jesus Christ Whom He has sent." Christian policy was, and is, based upon the belief that the kingdoms of this world are part of, and preliminary to, the Kingdom of Heaven. The commands of Our Lord that the Christian must love God and his neighbour were interpreted as establishing, in the sphere of temporal government, what the Pope has called his "dignity as a man and a Christian." There was no question of any intellectual merit or monetary power; on the contrary, the Lord Jesus Christ expressly thanked God that He had chosen to hide His Truth from the wise and prudent and to reveal It to babes. The poor, the humble, the weak and the afflicted were declared to be nearer to the Kingdom of Heaven than men and women more happily situated, whether by reason of intellectual gifts or of worldly possessions.

In accordance with this teaching Christian policy was based upon the individual. Its object was to secure to the individual the opportunity of worship and the means of service, which necessarily included the means of living. Thus, human right was identified with, and was derived from, duty. Duty itself expressed man's relationship to God; its mainspring, therefore, was love or loyalty, a willing and reasonable service. This loyalty was the cement of the social order, which, in consequence, stood in need neither of inducement nor of fear to maintain it.

Leadership was, thus, conditioned by objects which were apprehended and understood of all; it was guaranteed by a supreme sovereignty, the Christian Monarchy, through which the people made its will effective. King and People were one. Because of the religious faith which united them they were irresistible, so that no private claim to right or privilege could be sustained against them. Christianity, in other words, was the legitimacy of kingship; Christianity, at the same time, was the charter of democracy. It sustained the throne; it upheld the poor man's roof; it made the weak strong and the strong weak. Even money was held in subjection as a means to an end. God's image was not the powerful sovereign, nor the baron, nor the merchant prince, nor the moneylender, but "one of the least of these my little ones." "He that is greatest among you, let him be your servant." All were servants, ministers, vehicles of love; and rank itself was measured in degrees of service, not of man only or chiefly, but of God. The Christian state was not a commonwealth in the sense that all its citizens were shareholders for their worldly benefit. The idea of worldly gain was wholly foreign to its conception. The object of Christian government was not to exploit natural resources for the advantage of men and women, but to secure to men and women the means of eternal life, their highest advantage. Every other consideration yielded place to this supreme necessity. While, therefore, Christian Monarchy can properly be described as government by the people for the people, such a description is wholly inadequate. In its pure form it was government of Christians according to the will of Christ which each one of the governed acknowledged to be binding upon him. Such questions as private ownership of property, investment and financial policy were decided in the light of the Christian revelation, and every decision had reference to the poor, the needy, and the afflicted.

R. McNair Wilson.

Re-Dedication "God is Marching On" – President Roosevelt

I beg my readers' indulgence for an attempt to bring into focus the events described in the Conclusion of the book, which was written in December 1932. At that time the history of England at the beginning of the Nineteenth Century was being repeated in America at the beginning of the Twentieth. The Napoleonic Wars left England the creditor of Europe, and placed in the possession of London and firms connected with her most of the gold in the world. This wealth was concentrated in a relatively small number of hands. In Book II my reader may see for himself how, in spite of attempts to maintain freedom, first the nobility and the squires and then the industrialists were brought into subjection. This process of subjugation was attended by grievous affliction of the English people, whose sufferings are on record in a series of Blue books, to which later generations cannot turn without dismay. Briefly stated, the avowed object of the financial authorities was a stable price-level, a benefit easily understood by everyone. In fact, however, it was not the stability of the price-level but the control of it which really interested the financiers. Those who know anything about the credit system know that the one thing which it cannot possibly produce and which it never has produced at any time is a stable price-level. Hundreds of economists have exerted themselves to explain what is called the "credit cycle" or "trade cycle" - namely, the upward and downward movement of prices which continued right through the Nineteenth

Century. None, so far, has offered any real hope that the cycle can be avoided under a system of credit.

What is a credit system? Without trespassing too far on the explanations which follow, it may be described, briefly, as a system in which promises-to-pay money take the place of money itself. Real money, under this system it is true, is issued by the Government; but it is very strictly limited in amount. "Credit" consists of promises-to-pay this real money, which promises are lent to producers and industrialists by bankers and, in time, reach the public as wages, salaries, dividends or profits. Money is never issued except as loans of these promises-to-pay, and consequently the amount of money in the hands of the public corresponds to the amount of the bankers' loans. Thus the bankers control buying power absolutely.

Most people believe that bankers possess real money to the full amount of all the promises-to-pay issued by them, and consequently the promises of bankers are always readily accepted. In fact, however, this belief is erroneous. Bankers possess only one-tenth of the money they promise to pay. Further, and contrary to general belief, bankers never lend the money deposited with them by their clients. Ordinary banking practice the world over consists in lending promises-to-pay ten times the amount of real money in the banker's possession. The fact that this is so is proved by the behaviour of the bankers themselves. Every banker stops lending promises when the amount of his promises on loan exceeds by ten times his holding of real money. It is true that bankers demand security for their loans, and it is also true that some bankers try to maintain that their promises-to-pay are based do the value of these securities.

But this cannot be so because, if it were so, no need would exist to stop lending when loans had reached ten times the holding of cash. Still less would need exist to cut down loans at once if the cash holding happened to be reduced in amount.

It is of the utmost importance to grasp and understand this practice, because in this practice lies the explanation of the series of booms and slumps which have always attended the operations of the credit system. Obviously, if private promises-to-pay money (I.O.U.s) have been allowed to replace real money as the medium of exchange and if a strict limit is set to the amount of these promises which can be issued, every boom in trade must end when all the promises that can be lent have been lent. If the banker, the promise lender, is limited in his operations to ten times his holding of cash, he will be compelled to refuse further loans often at the very moment when markets are overloaded with goods. The effect of this refusal must be a fall in prices, seeing that the surplus goods cannot be bought at existing price levels - the means of buying them being withheld. For money is buying-power. And, as has been said, money reaches the public only in the form of loans by bankers of their promises-to-pay money. Such a fall in prices always tends to be sharp and is always, necessarily, attended by a fall in wages.

Thus business languishes and the desire to borrow dies away. In these circumstances the lender of promises uses the promises he cannot lend (that is to say, the promises which have been paid back to him by producers who are no longer able to manufacture on the old scale) to buy Government securities and buying power, consequently, oozes away from the commodity markets. But reduced production, in the long run, leads to depletion of stocks. At this point the banker sells his Government securities (which he bought with his "idle" promises), and re-lends these promises to industry - thus flooding the empty markets with the means of exchanging goods and so inflating the prices of such goods as remain in the markets. Prices having risen, everyone sees a profit and wants to borrow money in order to get that profit by manufacturing goods. And so a new boom begins and continues until, once more, all the available promises have been lent to industry and a halt must once more be called. Thus, again, slump succeeds to boom and boom to slump.

Now, it is obvious that one of the weak places in this system is the necessity of ceasing to lend at a point unrelated to the needs of production or consumption. So long as goods are being produced and so long as people exist who need these goods money ought to be available to enable the goods to be bought and used. If such extra money is not made available one of two things must happen: either the goods will have to be destroyed or the price level will have to fall so as to enable the new goods as well as the old goods to be disposed of within the existing buying power of the markets.

But, evidently, this inherent weakness of the credit system may be made to serve the private ends of those who administer it. For the power to lend or not to lend is the power to increase or decrease the quantity of money in the market, and so to raise prices or to lower them; and that is the power of life or death, seeing that every man is burdened with fixed costs, such as rent, which cannot be reduced immediately when prices fall.

The lender of promises-to-pay, however, is compelled by law to make good these promises of his whenever and by whomsoever asked to do so. Here is his chief anxiety. Having lent promises-to-pay ten times the quantity of money in his possession, he must so arrange matters that the largest actual demand on him for fulfilment of his promises, that is to say for real money, shall never exceed one-tenth part of the possible demand. He achieves this purpose by inducing people to use "credit instruments" instead of money. Thus, a cheque may be drawn against a loan from a bank (an overdraft). The person who receives the cheque will pay it into his bank, where it will become a ledger entry in his favour. He himself, in his turn, will write cheques against his "money in the bank." Obviously no real money is required for such transactions.

This is but one example of the many "credit instruments" known to the financial system. Those, on the other hand, who ask for actual money - being a small number as against those who use "credit instruments" - are readily and easily suppnea with it. Let the reader ask himself how much of his own money he spends in actual coin or notes and how much he spends by means of cheques. He will find that his use of real money is, probably, far less than one-tenth of his use of credit instruments (cheques). There is the inner secret of the bankers' power. Like a juggler who can keep four balls in the air by means of the activities of two hands, the banker is able to meet all the demands on him for real money, and so to create the illusion that he has enough real money to pay all the demands that could conceivably be made.

History, however, shows that any strong "run" on a bank - that is to say any large demand that the promises-to-pay shall be honoured in real money - has always broken it. If the "run" becomes nation-wide and many banks are involved, the Government comes to the rescue. This happened in England in 1847, 1857 and 1866, and, later, in 1914. It happened in America in March last year, 1933. The breaking of a bank means, of course, that all the people who have entrusted their savings to it lose these savings. For their savings are not represented by real money but only by bankers' promises-to-pay that real money. And bankers possess only one-tenth of the real money they have promised to pay.

In England, after the Napoleonic Wars, the farmers and industrialists tried to break the fetters of this credit system which, without rhyme or reason, so far as they could see, refused the money necessary to the exchange of their goods after a certain fixed quantity of money had been issued. These Farmers and industrialists accused the bankers of being stupid and short-sighted. Why, it was demanded, must every expansion of trade be brought to a standstill before there was any real need for contraction? Why not, as more goods came into the market, put out more money to buy them? And so on. The people who argued in this way were unaware that no banker dared to accede to their demands, however much he might wish to do so. They did not know that bankers were lending promises-to-pay money which they did not possess and that, consequently, come what might, they must avoid being caught out by any sudden demand for real money.

How is such a sudden demand likely to arise? It has already been pointed out that the time chosen by bankers to expand their loans to industry is the time when, stocks having been depleted, markets are more or less empty of goods. If a market in which goods are scarce is suddenly flooded with money, prices must rise, for there will be more buyers than sellers. As soon, however, as goods begin to come to these empty markets prices will tend to fall unless more money is kept flowing in. This is, of course, a vicious system, because it is putting the cart before the horse. The time when more money is needed is not when a market is empty of goods but when it is too full of goods. If the money appears before the goods have appeared, prices must rush up. But if the money appears at the same time as the goods, prices will not rise and will be prevented from falling.

Why, then, do the bankers adopt this system of flooding empty markets with money? The answer is that their system demands that prices shall be made to rise sharply, or, in other words, that what they call "inflation," when anybody else performs it, shall take place. The reason why a sharp rise of prices is necessary is that a sharp rise offers the chance of a big profit, and so tempts large numbers of people to borrow promises-to-pay from the bankers and to pay good rates of interest on these promises. This is what bankers speak of as "Confidence."

Confidence - that is to say, the rise of prices and so of profits - continues so long as money is being pumped into the markets in excess of goods (in the form; for example, of wages paid to people who are employed in building factories from which, ultimately, goods will come). But as soon as the pumping - in of money stops the rise of prices, and with it confidence, will disappear. The bankers, as has been seen, must stop lending when their loans of promises have reached a definite proportion of their holdings of cash, no matter how great may be the quantity of goods in the market at that moment. Consequently, the level of prices will begin to fall just when the newly created goods are becoming most plentiful. Then, as has been seen, producers will be told that there has been "over-production." Booms and slumps, in other words, are inherent in the nature of a system which is based on the lending of promises-to-pay money that the lender of the promises does not possess. If real money - for example, Treasury Notes - was being issued by the King in accordance with the needs of his people, it would be issued only when goods actually came onto the market. No sharp rises of price would occur in such circumstances, nor would any need exist to refuse to produce more money as more and yet more goods appeared. In other words, men would be enabled to produce and to consume as much as they desired.

The artificially produced rise of prices which heralds and accompanies every boom, and which represents a true inflation, imposes a further stress on the credit system. When prices are low wages also are low, and hence less money is needed to pay wages. Wages are paid not by cheque but in actual money. Consequently a rise of prices, which sooner or later means a rise of wages also, imposes a bigger demand for actual money on the banking system. Bankers find that the employers who have borrowed from them want more pounds, shillings and pence each week when pay-day comes round. That demand is an increased demand that promises-to-pay shall be honoured in actual money. Hence the need of stopping the rise of prices.

The credit system, in short, is a fraudulent system. It is based on what are essentially false promises. It professes, falsely, to keep prices stable, whereas, in fact, it cannot operate at all unless prices can be made to rise and fall. It professes to abhor both inflations and deflations, whereas, in fact, it exists by means of inflations (flooding empty markets with money and so raising prices), and of deflations (draining money away from overstocked markets). Bankers may and do defend themselves by saying that the credit system cannot be made to work except by the methods they employ. This is true. But the moral is not that these methods must be employed but rather that the credit system itself must be abolished. Money must serve industry and not industry money. Prices must not remain the playthings of the creators and lenders of promises-to-pay non-existent money. That is another way of saying that the power of life and death over producers and workpeople, the whole nation, must be taken from the hands of private people without any real substance and restored to the hands of the people's representative - namely, the King.

The financial panics which occurred in England in the early years of the Nineteenth Century were due, primarily, to the resistance offered by producers to the bankers. The farmers and industrialists compelled the bankers occasion ally to go on lending promises-to-pay beyond the "limits of safety" of the credit system. Prices and wages were thus forced up and up, until the demands for real money exceeded the bankers' holdings. "Runs" then took place, and banks broke. But instead of these "runs" convincing people that there was something inherently vicious in the system (namely, the issue of money in advance of the arrival of goods on the market) the conclusion was drawn that what was wrong was an excessive prolongation of the booms. It the banks has stopped lending when their promises-to-pay amounted to ten times their holdings of cash, it was argued, the "runs" would not have taken place. Consequently, instead of putting an end to the credit system and regaining the control of money, the Government of the day established the gold standard, a device by which, when prices rose, gold would be caused to flow out of the country, and when gold flowed out of the country home bankers would be compelled to cut down their loans. On the face of it the gold standard seemed to offer a means of abolishing both booms and slumps. Actually, however, it achieved no such result. The credit system remained; indeed, gold gave the credit system a new guarantee and a new prestige. It is simply untrue that, after the gold standard began to operate, booms and slumps ceased. They have never ceased and never can cease so long as the credit system lasts.

All that happened was that the more extreme movements were "ironed out."

"Being on the gold standard," in fact, is a most misleading term. So is the term "off the gold standard." The truth is that so long as the credit system operates every nation, whether "on" or "off" gold, is in the same position. Its price-level remains at the mercy of the world's bankers. Only that nation which abolishes the private ownership of credit will have reached freedom.

Indeed it is true to say that only that nation which abolishes credit will be free - because the term National Credit is meaningless. A national credit system is not a credit system at all but a currency system, seeing that a nation has the power to make its credit instruments legal tender. The King, in other words, does not need to "promise to pay" real money. Any money issued by him, whether in the form of coin or notes or figures in a ledger, is real money for the wood reason that he is the fountain of money.

The English farmers and industrialists were defeated by and subjected to the credit system and passed, in consequence, under the dominion of international finance. If some industrialists and some noblemen were given "plums" by their conquerors, that was only to consolidate the position of these conquerors. England was conquered as effectively as she had been conquered by the Normans, and Englishmen, unhappily, were little better than victims of a Money System which, being founded on false promises, could not be other than a taskmaster, dispensing to all its victims an "inexorable economic law."

The sign and seal of this enslavement was the loss by the English Government of the control of the price-level, which remained, and remains, wholly at the mercy of the financial powers. The credit system and the private control of the price-level are two names for the same thing. (The gold standard is merely a regulator of this private control; it could be used equally well as a regulator of a national currency system. As things stand it is a promise-lender's lure which secures to the owners of gold the power to resist and overcome their opponents.)

Government control of the price-level, therefore, is incompatible with the existing financial system. Stable prices enable producers to get out of debt and so to escape from the promise-lender's clutches. There is the secret of the fury against commodity dollars (i.e., dollars with a fixed purchasing power), which the bankers are now displaying. If a Government determines to fix prices and hold them fixed, it is adopting a course the end of which is the escape of its people from usury and the consequent destruction of usury. Because, once good borrowers have got out of debt, promise-lending becomes too dangerous to be carried on on any considerable scale. As the promise-lenders, perforce, withdraw from the field, the Government must step in with real money - or the price-level will fall. Thus, when the power to move the level of prices up or down is taken out of private hands, a private credit system will inevitably become a currency system, a system, that is to say, not of promises-to-pay non-existent money, but of money itself. If these facts are borne in mind the assault which was made on the American price-level soon after the War will be understood.

The Great War did for America what the Napoleonic Wars had done for England; America became the creditor of Europe and the owner of most of the world's gold. It is explained in the text how this situation gave rise to demands that American agriculture and American industry should at once be brought into subjection to American (and world) finance - that American prices and wages, in short, should be reduced to the world level and made easily movable up and down according to the needs of the lenders of promises-to-pay. It is shown in the text how stubborn was the resistance offered by the American industrialists and farmers to this onslaught; but it is shown also that resistance was gradually being destroyed and broken down by a series of catastrophes not unlike those by which the resistance of Englishmen had been subdued a century before. I ventured to prophesy that the outlook for the World Economic Conference was not very bright, but I feared greatly, nevertheless, that American production, like English production, would go down before the onslaught of the promise-lenders.

That fear grew as the year 1933 advanced. Twelve million hungry and often desperate men walked the streets and highways of the United States. Women and children of these men went uncared for, except by private charity, amid an abundance of goods. Farmers were banding together to beat off the usurers' men from their hearths; workers in some instances actually faced machine guns and tear-gas bombs in order to retain the roofs over their children's heads. Would a people, stripped and stricken, as armies do not strip nor strike, hold out longer against the demands of "sound finance"?

In the middle of these doubtings came the thought that it was indeed miraculous that so long and so stout a resistance had been offered. My reader will judge of that when he comes to the descriptions of the various calamities which the American people suffered. This was the people against whom the promise-lenders had hurled every invective in their vocabulary. This was "Uncle Shylock" glutting himself with gold. This was the land of the "Almighty dollar." These were the "poor boobs" from "way back" who knew nothing and understood nothing, the worshippers of prosperity and of their "inflated" standard of living. The Americans lost their prosperity and their standard of living. But not their courage. They continued to resist the demands that their tariff should be lowered and their gold allowed to run out, and this although all their leaders promised them abundant prosperity if they would only give way. I have heard all the purely materialistic explanations of this resistance and I confess that they do not wholly satisfy me. No doubt Americans are anxious to preserve what they can of their possessions; no doubt they are human beings with the weaknesses of human beings, the greeds and fears and ambitions. But this resistance seems to me to transcend such motives. It may have begun as a protest against loss of trade; it continued when ruin was in full possession and when none could see even a ray of hope. I doubted, then, the materialism of America and began to see, as I thought, another spirit, young perhaps, but heroic and faithful. Could it be that, under the surface of things, the Christian spirit was alive and quick in this great land?

And then, in March, the rumble of a new earthquake, the collapse of the banks, with the promise-lenders croaking dismally, "I told you so," and licking their lips at the thought of final, overwhelming triumph. Across that clamour of downfall the voice of the new President reached Europe and the world, promising a "re-dedication" of the people and asking, in that re-dedication, the help of Almighty God.

I confess that, until that moment, I had had very little hope of President Roosevelt. I thought that he was "a sound money man," pledged to reduce the tariff and extinguish the War Debts. I confess further that since that day in March I have sometimes doubted him. But nothing which followed removed the thrill which his words occasioned. This man, in Ibsen's phrase, possessed "the King-thought."

It became clear very soon that the promise-lenders had good hope of making capital out of the banking crisis. Statements that the crisis indicated merely how right Finance had been and how wrong was the opposition to it began to appear, and the new President was advised to keep the small banks closed and "cut out the deadwood," which means the savings of large numbers of men and women. The banking system, it was demanded, must now be centralized like the English banking system. Prophecies that the tariff would soon be lowered were made freely, and there was a new, jubilant note in all the bankers' talk. The references to "money changers" in President Roosevelt's inaugural address seemed to have been forgotten. After all, he was a politician and, no doubt, had to say something in the very trying circumstances.

This attitude convinced most people that the American resistance was about to come to an end in the way desired by international finance. The eager preparations for the World Economic Conference confirmed that melancholy belief. On all sides financiers described President Roosevelt as a "big man," and foretold how he would break the resistance of Congress, that stubborn obstacle to the fulfilment of their wishes. Even America's sudden abandonment of the gold standard did not suffice to shake this faith, though it occasioned a sharp spasm of alarm and indignation. On the eve of the World Conference, it was everywhere held that a universal return to the gold standard as the prop of the credit system was about to take place. All, indeed, that remained in doubt was the relationship which ought to exist between the pound and the dollar.

It is well to understand what this attitude meant. The international financiers proposed that the "return to gold" should be the signal for a great expansion of credit throughout the world - that is to say, of a great increase in the volume of promise-lending. Prices would undoubtedly have risen sharply under this stimulus, for stocks were exhausted. It would then have been proclaimed to a joyous world that, once again, salvation had come through the banking system and the gold standard.

Incidentally, however, other plans were held in mind. A universal return to gold would have been the signal for a flight to the pound from both the dollar and the franc, for the reason that England was considered a safer place for money than either New York or Paris.

This flight of "short-term money" must have made pounds dear and dollars and francs cheap (for money increases and decreases in value according to the demand for it). President Roosevelt would thus have been assailed by demands for gold with which to buy pounds, or, in other words, people would have changed their dollars into gold and bought their pounds with the gold instead of buying their pounds directly with the depreciated dollars.

Thus, if President Roosevelt had done what it was hoped and believed and expected that he would do, the World Economic Conference would have been followed by a huge, even a torrential, outflow of gold from America to London. London, in consequence, would have regained her dominant position as the holder of the world's stock of gold and the promise-lenders, free at last of the shackles of American resistance, would have triumphed once more.

But President Roosevelt appears to have foreseen this danger. No sooner was the World Conference in being than he refused absolutely to stabilize his dollar. What he was concerned about, he declared, was not stabilization but price raising, and, after that, price fixing. He had made this clear two months earlier in the statement issued by him and by the British Prime Minister:

"The necessity for an increase in the general level of commodity prices was recognized as primary and fundamental... We must, when circumstances permit, reestablish an international monetary standard which will operate successfully without depressing prices..."

The promise-lenders knew of no international monetary standard which would operate successfully without sooner or later depressing prices, nor did they wish to hear about such a standard seeing that fixation of price, as has been shown, is incompatible with the system of promise-lending. Consequently, this plain warning of what was coming was brushed aside. When the blow fell on June 18, 1933, it produced consternation. The Conference had failed. There was to be no return to gold, no outflow of gold from America, no expansion of credit, no inflation in the world's empty markets, no rise of price-level, no boom. On the contrary, the dreadful spectre of fixed prices (the "commodity dollar") loomed before the masters of the credit system. Appeal after appeal was sent to Washington. On July 3, the President cabled his own message:

It would be a "catastrophe amounting to a world tragedy" if the Conference should forsake its great purpose of helping mankind because of the failure to agree upon a "proposal of a purely artificial and temporary expedient affecting the monetary exchange of a few nations only." The demand for a return to gold was a "specious policy" full of "basic economic errors" and "fetishes of so-called international bankers."

Never was challenge spoken in tones of a loftier scorn. All these delegates, it was declared by implication, had been brought to London not to help a broken world to rise again and not to give that world a newer and better system than the system which had ruined it, but only to re-establish promise-lending.

Bewildered British statesmen who, with the best will in the world, had called the Conference, felt hurt that, for some reason not understood by any one of them, the American President had turned his back on them. They tried to keep the Conference in being. When their efforts failed they congratulated themselves that, in any case, they had done what they could.

But the masters of finance were in a very different mood. If they did not, as yet, fear President Roosevelt, they wished to discredit him as statesman and leader. The magicians of all the "cities" and "streets" made ready to cast their darkest spells on this uncomfortable occupant of the White House. What did he know about high finance? They would soon show him that the credit system is greater than the power of a President.

They reckoned without the "King-thought." In these months since his inauguration President Roosevelt had been engaged on a task lying far beyond the comprehension of Wall Street. He had been establishing himself in the love and confidence of the people, using the wireless to this end with astonishing skill. The Press, that greatest invention and engine of finance, by which Kings and peoples had everywhere been separated and held asunder, was circumvented. No matter what the headlines might say, the President could explain quietly, of an evening, what was really in his mind. Nor had he stopped at explanation. He had gone in person to many Christian bodies and delivered to them addresses in which he bade them realize that they were the vanguard of the "New Deal." Thus leader and people become one in the spirit of service which is the spirit of Christ, and thus, once again, were established the pillars of European civilization on their ancient foundations. America received from the hands of her President the spiritual inheritance of Christendom.

And so when the bankers' offensive against the President was launched last November it failed of its object. Had not this American people been spectators of the Senate Banking Inquiry? The scales had fallen from millions of eyes. President and people were one man. Congress knew another master and made ready to serve him. In other words, the essential features of Christian Monarchy had been given to America instead of the greed system of international finance or the fear system of dictatorship. The greed system has ever masqueraded under the name of democracy - a name to which it has no title. It has been maintained by popularly elected chambers of politicians who, whatever their qualities, have seldom, anywhere, so much as questioned the right of a private monopoly to control price-levels, create promise-money and take possession of their neighbours' goods, by the mere process of writing figures in ledgers. Politicians who permit and support a system whereby the power of life and death over every citizen is given to a private monopoly cannot reasonably be described as upholders of popular rights, of liberty or of democracy. They are more truthfully described as the ignorant functionaries, even the lackeys, of a wholly irresponsible and entirely unrepresentative dictatorship, the aims and objects of which are everywhere opposed to those of the citizens who elect the politicians. Financial democracy is a system of pillage disguised under a cloak of philosophical liberalism which, unhappily, has deceived many honest men, including creative artists, lovers of peace and lovers of freedom.

In these circumstances the idea that the gold standard, or any other standard by which the credit system may from time to time be bolstered up, can offer the smallest protection against the rapacity of "politicians" is illusory. "Politicians" and the credit system are part and parcel of the same financial "democracy." It is not the peculations of a few rogues that signify, but the wholesale annexation of the work and goods of nations which power to change the level of prices bestows. The bankers make much capital of the fear of politicians which infects many honest minds, and so are enabled to carry out operations of their own on the most gigantic scale without a word of criticism. Any politician who possessed enough knowledge of the secrets of finance to offer an effective resistance would soon discover what the public has been taught to believe about politicians when they dare to trespass on the consecrated ground of monetary policy.

But the politicians, certainly, are in no position to criticize the dictators. Who can exert a dictatorship more absolute than that by which the prices men shall obtain for their labour and goods can be determined? Dictatorship has many forms; the most powerful and probably the most evil form of dictatorship is that secret form known as the credit system, whereby, under a veneer of political liberty, men are divided and ruled by the fear of hunger. All dictatorship is hateful; but if a choice of evils must be made, most men would prefer to face bayonets rather than to be compelled and coerced by the spectacle of the undernourishment of their children.

I shall have failed utterly in the purpose of this book if I do not make it clear that Christian Monarchy has as little resemblance to dictatorship as it has to financial democracy. Greed and fear can have no part in loyalty. Christian Monarchy took centuries to build up and make perfect. It represents, as I believe, the last word which has so far been spoken in political wisdom. I know of no substitute for it nor can I conceive of any substitute.

But in saying that I am not setting out to prove that Kings are invariably good men. Many a rogue and many a fool has sat on a throne. Many a King has sold himself to money-lenders. Many a King has denied or attacked that Christian faith on which his throne was built. Such instances can be matched from any kind of government which men have ever found. What I am insisting upon is that the Christian religion affords a basis for a kind of government, Christian Monarchy, which more than any other kind of government enables men to realize the chief end of man - namely, that he may know the Lord his God and so order his life that time and eternity become one event in the love of the Lord Jesus Christ. Christian Monarchy is not only not irreconcilable with democracy; it is the only conceivable guarantee of democracy, of liberty, and of an ordered progress whether in the production of goods or in the development of mind and spirit. Such institutions as parliaments regain at once their true function when the union of King and people affords them protection against private interests and the secret assaults of money. But there cannot, as has been said, be a consecrated King without a consecrated people. Christian Monarchy, therefore, is always leadership by consent. It is always leadership by love - in the first instance, love of the Lord Jesus Christ and one's neighbour. It is my personal belief that the resistance to finance today springs from an outpouring over the world of the spirit of Christianity - that, in short, we are witnessing a real renaissance. The love-song of Christ rises once more above the din of the merchants of money and power.

It is worth noting that, already, President Roosevelt has embarked on policies the aim of which is the nationalization of money and of land but not of private enterprise. The Christian King held both land and money (the means of production and exchange) in trusteeship for his people. His people were free to serve one another in any individual enterprise and to take for themselves the products of such enterprise. The doctrines of Socialism and Communism have their origin in a misunderstanding of the nature and power of the credit system. They represent attempts to achieve the impossible - namely, to adapt the system of private credit to the uses of mankind. It is significant that many bankers and financial leaders speak well of Socialism, of "National Socialism," of Fascism, of Nazism, and even, occasionally, of Bolshevism. It was from the financiers that the world heard first about the blessings of "rationalization." The world is hearing now about "planned economy," which, it is to be feared, means a regimentation of men and women in the interest of the credit system. Christian Monarchy stands far away and far above all these devices for perpetuating the rule of the promise-lenders. The dictatorship of finance with its false liberalism flows over easily into the dictatorship of bayonets, which, again, can be re-converted at will into the dictatorship of finance. Christian Monarchy has no part in this tragic kaleidoscope.

It remains to ask what is the purpose behind the financial policy which President Roosevelt put into operation on February 1 of this present year. I speak with diffidence because I speak without any special knowledge; but I believe that what we are now witnessing is an attempt to give to the world the blessing of national control of the price-level. If the nations of the world agreed to maintain a stable price-level then exchanges would automatically be stabilized and the gold standard could be turned from the uses of the private monopoly of credit to the uses of mankind. It may be that the President feels that his new gold standard cannot succeed until the old gold standard has been abandoned by all the nations. It is reasonably clear that, if the old gold standard can be defeated in open conflict with the new, the masters of the monopoly of credit will have suffered what must, sooner or later, prove to be a mortal blow. A stable price-level, as has been said, means the use by men of all their powers of production and the enjoyment by men - of all the goods produced by them. I am far from feeling assured of victory. But this, at any rate, is sure. If the Roosevelt policy succeeds humanity will have been rescued from the power both of greed and of fear. That is the prospect of a new world. I beg my readers to realize that salvation, if it comes, will have come from consecration and not from force or any orgy of aggression. "God," said President Roosevelt, "is marching on." The sole guarantee which men can have of their civilization is the spirit which, in the beginning, called that civilization into being, and gave form, in the first instance, to its lively organs. We in England possess still the inestimable blessing of a Christian Monarchy. How much we owe to that Monarchy is but little understood by the mass of the people, for the truth about the Nineteenth Century has not yet emerged. Englishmen, today, who are seized of the nature and extent of the struggle in progress must pray, as perhaps they have not prayed before, "God save the King."

TURGOT AND THE ANCIEN RÉGIME IN FRANCE

BY DOUGLAS DAKIN,

LECTURER IN HISTORY, BIRKBECK COLLEGE, UNIVERSITY OF LONDON

HERE is the gist of the interview as Véri had it from Turgot's own lips. 'All that I have told you is a little confused, said Turgot, because I am still not at my ease. - I know that you are nervous, but I know also that you are constant and honest and that I could not have made a better choice; I called you to the Marine for a little while to have the opportunity of knowing you. - It is necessary, Sire, that you should give me permission to put in writing my general opinions and, I may venture to add, my conditions, concerning the manner in which you ought to support me in this administration, for, I assure you, the superficial knowledge that I have of affairs causes in me some misgivings. - Yes, yes, said the King, just as you wish; but I give you my word of honour in advance, he added, taking Turgot's hands, to follow all your ideas and to uphold you always in the courageous course that you have taken.'

Véri's account has not come down to us in its entirety. But Mlle de Lespinasse, who was in close touch with Turgot and his friends, no doubt completes the story when she writes to her lover, Guibert, as follows: '... He had some difficulty in accepting the Finances for which M. de Maurepas proposed him.

When he went to thank the King, Louis said to him, "You do not wish, then, to become Comptroller-General?" "Sire," answered M. Turgot, "I assure Your Majesty that I would have preferred the Marine because the office is less precarious and I am sure that I should do more good there; but at this moment it is not to the King I give myself: it is to an honest man." The King took Turgot's hands and said to him, "You will never be deceived." M. Turgot added: "Sire, I ought to mention to Your Majesty the necessity of economies, of which you must give the first example. All this, no doubt, the Abbé Terray has already told Your Majesty." "Yes," replied the King, "he has told me, but not as you have."

That same day Turgot put in writing - in his famous letter of 24 August - the general outline of his programme. It is a long letter, and it probably took him the remainder of the day to write; it is one mass of erasures and interpolations. When reading it - and this applies to all the letters that he wrote to Louis - one must remember the extreme youth of the King. Turgot was endeavour ing to descend to his level, and his words have the ring of a kindly pedagogue. The language of reason is translated into sentiment, for no other appeal to Louis could have been effective. Yet it was not without some misgiving that he availed himself of the Abbé de Vermond's strategy. In later days he told the Abbé de Véri that, afraid of abusing the confidence of so young a monarch, he decided to confine innovation to a barest minimum, being content to wait until Louis could be convinced in a rational way of the necessity for radical reform. And it was therefore with great difficulty that he wrote a letter which would appeal to Louis's conscience and yet satisfy his own.

1774 August 24,
Anne-Robert-Jacques Turgot to
Louis XVI, King of France

Having just left Your Majesty's room, still full of the anxiety produced by the immensity of the burden you place upon me, overcome be the touching kindness with which you have deigned to encourage me, I hasten to convey to you my respectful gratitude and the absolute devotion of my whole life.

Your Majesty has been good enough to authorize me to put in writing the promise you have made to uphold me in the execution of those plans for economy that are at all times, and to-day more than ever, of an absolute necessity... At this moment, Sire, I confine myself to recalling to you these three phrases:

No bankruptcy;
No increase of imposition;
No borrowing.

No bankruptcy either avowed or disguised by arbitrary reduction (of interest on public stock).

No increase of impositions; the reason for this lies in the plight of your subjects, and still more in Your Majesty's heart.

No borrowing; because every loan always diminishes the unanticipated revenue and necessitates, in the long run, either bankruptcy or an increase in taxes. In time of peace it is perhaps permissible to borrow, but only in order to liquidate old debts, or to redeem other loans contracted on less advantageous terms.

There is only one way of fulfilling these three aims: that of reducing expenditure below receipts, and sufficiently below to ensure each year a saving of twenty millions (*livres*) with a view to the redemption of long-standing debts. Failing this, the first gunshot will drive the State to bankruptcy.

It will be asked, "On what can we retrench?" and all officials, speaking for their own departments, will maintain that every particular item of expenditure is indispensable. They will be able to put forward very good reasons; but since the impossible cannot be achieved, all these must yield to the absolute necessity of economy.

It is, then, highly essential for Your Majesty to insist that the heads of all departments should act in concert with the Minister of Finance. It is imperative that he should discuss with them in the presence of Your Majesty the urgency of proposed expenses. Above all it is essential, Sire, that, as soon as you have decided what amount is strictly requisite for each department, you should forbid the officials concerned to order any new expenditure without first arranging with the Treasury the means of providing for it. Without this regulation each department will load itself with debts, which will always become Your Majesty's debts, and your Minister of Finances will be unable to answer for the discrepancy between income and expenditure.

Your Majesty is aware that one of the greatest obstacles to economy is the multiplicity of demands by which you are constantly besieged, and which have unfortunately been sanctioned too indulgently by your predecessors.

It is necessary, Sire, to arm yourself against your kindness by a greater kind-heartedness, by considering whence comes this money which you are able to distribute to your courtiers, and by comparing the wretchedness of those from whom it is extracted (sometimes by the most rigorous methods) with the condition of those people who have the greatest call upon your liberality.

There are certain favours which, it is thought, you can readily grant, because they do not immediately bear upon the Royal Treasury.

Of this kind are profit-sharing in revenue collections (*intérêts* and *croupes*) and privileges; they are the most dangerous and the most open to abuse. Every profit made on imposition which is not strictly necessary for their collection should be devoted to the relief of the taxpayer and the needs of the State.

Besides, these participations in the rewards of the tax-farmers are a source of corruption for the nobility and of vexation to the people, since they afford all such abuses secret and powerful protectors.

It may be hoped that, following an improvement in husbandry and also the suppression of irregularities in the collection of taxation, and as a result of more equitable assessments, a substantial relief for the people may be obtained without diminishing greatly the public revenue; but unless economy is the first step, no reform is possible, because every readjustment entails the risk of interrupting the collection of taxation, and because increasing difficulties, caused by the manoeuvres and protests of those interested in perpetuating abuses, are only to be expected, there being no abuse upon which someone does not thrive.

So long as the finances are continually subject to the old expedients in order to provide for State services, Your Majesty will be at the mercy of the Financiers, who will always be able by their stratagems to frustrate reforms. No relief will be possible either by way of lightening the burden of the taxpayer or through legislation and changes in administration. The Government can never feel at ease, because it cannot ever win affection, and because the discontent and impatience of the masses are always the means utilized by intriguers and disaffected persons to excite disturbances. It is, then, upon economy that, above all, the prosperity of your reign depends; upon it, too, hangs the tranquillity of your kingdom, its reputation among foreign Powers, the happiness of the nation and your own.

I must impress upon Your Majesty that I take office at a serious time when disquietude is widely prevalent respecting the sustenance of the people - a disquietude aggravated in the public mind for several years by the want of uniformity in the principles of administrators, by a number of imprudent operations on their part, and above all, by a harvest below average. On this matter, as upon other, I do not ask Your Majesty to adopt my principles without first having them thoroughly examined and discussed, as well by yourself as by your counsellors in your presence. But should you recognize the justice and the necessity of these principles, I implore you to maintain with firmness their application, showing no fear for the clamours which are absolutely certain to arise, no matter what system you adopt or policy you pursue.

These are the matters that I have been permitted to recall to Your Majesty. You will not forget that in accepting the office of Comptroller-General, I have felt to the full the value of the confidence with which you favour me; I have felt that you entrust to me the happiness of your people, and, if I may be permitted to say so, the mission of promoting among your people the love of your person and of your authority. But at the same time I am aware of all the dangers to which I expose myself. I foresee that I shall be alone in fighting against abuses of every kind, against those who profit by them, against the many prejudiced persons who, opposed to all reforms, are such powerful instruments in the hands of vested interests intent on perpetuating the existing disorder. I shall have to battle even against the natural goodness and generosity of Your Majesty and of persons who are most dear to you. I shall be feared, hated even, by nearly all at Court, by all who solicit favours; they will attribute refusals to me; they will call me a hard man because I advise Your Majesty not to enrich even those you love at the loss of your people's sustenance. And these very subjects, for whom I shall sacrifice myself, are so easily deceived that perhaps I shall arouse their hatred of the very measures I take to save them from exactions. Appearances being against me, I shall be subject to calumny, the aim being to deprive me of Your Majesty's confidence. I shall never regret losing an office which I never expected. I am ready to resign it to Your Majesty as soon as I can no longer hope to be useful in it; but the esteem, the reputation for integrity, the desire to promote the common good, all of which have led you to favour me, are more dear to me than life, and I run the risk of losing my reputation even though meriting in my own eyes no reproach.

Your Majesty will remember that it is my faith in your promises which leads me to shoulder a burden perhaps beyond my strength, and that it is to you personally, to an honest, just, and good man rather than to the King, that I give myself.

I venture to repeat here what you have already been kind enough to hear and approve. The affecting kindness with which you condescended to press my hands within your own, as if accepting my devotion, will never be effaced from my memory. It will sustain my courage. It has for all time welded my personal happiness with the interests, the glory, and the welfare of Your Majesty.

Such was Turgot's plan. It contained the promise of the barest minimum of reform; it nowhere departed from the principles of sound business and common sense; and yet, as he himself was well aware, his was a colossal undertaking, in view of the difficulties that he would encounter - the bewilderment and timidity of his master, the sinister influences of those around him, the ease with which vested interests could turn popular dis affection against the Crown, making even a moderate reform the most hazardous of ventures.

Yet Turgot's following were more elated than ever and the kingdom at large hoped for better times. Mlle de Lespinasse wrote to Guibert, 'Every one was intoxicated with joy, my friend... I repeat to you: you missed a great deal here.' Paris and the provinces celebrated vociferously the disgrace of Maupeou and the Abbé Terray, and the fishwives of Compiègne, under cover of a time-old custom of the day of Saint-Louis, congratulated the King upon his good 'bag'. 'Men of all ranks', declares Stormont, 'vie with each other in demonstrations of joy.' Bonfires were lighted, the streets were decorated, and the fallen Ministers were burned in effigy. Terray was fortunate not to be personally assaulted. The crowd at the ferry at Choisy le-Roi were for throwing him into the river, and only by bribing the watermen, who pulled him quickly from the bank, did he manage to escape from the grasp of his ferocious pursuers.

Far away at Limoges a touching and most appropriate ceremony was organized. The municipal assembly sent to Turgot a letter of congratulations, and on 8 September held a public fête which ended with a firework display, the final effect being the lighting of a

Catherine-wheel upon which were the words, *Vive Turgot*.

At the Court Turgot's appointment caused very little stir. Opinion had not changed much during the short period that he had been at the Marine, and it was still the *dévots* who denounced him because of his former associations with the encyclopaedists. But, as the King had overlooked the indiscretions of his early years, they must grudgingly forgive him also. They must be thankful that he was not a Choiseuliste. On the other hand, the Choiseulistes must console themselves that he was not a *dévot*. Neither party was then fully aware that as a result of their struggles they had advanced a common enemy. Disappointed though the various factions were, they must remember that things might have been much worse. The Queen's interest was most sanguine. Was not Turgot the Abbé de Vermond's friend? Might he not use his influence to promote the Queen's favourite, Sartine, to the Royal Household? Might he not improve the Queen's financial position? Such were the arguments that Mercy unfolded to the Empress; and Marie-Antoinette wrote once again to tell her mother that Turgot was a very honest man.

No less satisfactory was Turgot's reception from the magistracy. There was, of course, a vague uneasiness among them, and Nicolai, who received him at the *Chambre des comptes* on 31 August, while lavishing praise and fine words upon him, hinted that systems were dangerous and implored him to ' avail himself of simple and facile methods in his financial administration'. But this was hardly the time to voice open discontent. Turgot and Miromesnil were to be preferred to Terray and Maupeou. Indeed, the Ministerial changes promised well for the magistracy, for it was known that Turgot favoured the reversal of Maupeou's *coup d'état*. It mattered little for the moment that he also held other ideas which the magistracy held in abhorrence. For the time being he must be welcomed: old scores could wait for another occasion.

THE ASSIGNATS

BY HARRIS, SEYMOUR EDWIN

CHAPTER XI - SUMMARY

THE Assignats were primarily a financial resource: the nominal amounts issued, reduced to the values of 1790 by a table of depreciation, were equivalent to seven years of ordinary revenues of the pre-Revolutionary era. The Assignats were freely disbursed for the payment of the Government's obligations in the early years of the Revolution; and they contributed most of the public revenue during its later years. Taxation contributed a small but not negligible proportion of the total revenues, and, it is to be emphasized, this proportion varied, increasing notably in 1792. Both the value of the later issues of paper money, and the importance of tax receipts suffered because of the depreciation. Only the system of price control saved the country.

The maintenance of the land security unimpaired was an indispensable condition for the retention of confidence in the paper money. Regardless of the validity of the contention that the Assignat and a parcel of land of equivalent value were identities, the general assent to that contention did help to instill confidence in the paper money. The people believed in the land security; it transformed the Assignat in their eyes into circulating land. Redemption was a reality. Land sales absorbed large quantities of Assignats, especially in the first three years of their history. A more provident policy on the part of the Government - a policy of security, of protection to purchasers of lands instead of a policy of terrorism for all with visible means of wealth, and of non-interference with agricultural prices - would doubtless have resulted in larger and more profitable sales of lands. But, of course, the system of price control is justified on other grounds.

The undiscriminating use that has been made of the various measures of depreciation, is lamentable. We ought not only to be aware of the attributes of the measures we employ, but also to be wary of unconscious shifting from one measure to another. The movement of the prices of commodities provides us with the most acceptable of all measures, in spite of weighty theoretical objections. The prices of the foreign exchanges and of gold and silver were affected by independent forces, with the result that they deviated appreciably from the corresponding values for the prices of commodities. Insufficient attention has been given to the problem of the selection of the most appropriate measure of depreciation. The depreciation of the Assignat in 1790-1791 that writers discuss, probably did not occur. A premium on the price of gold and of the foreign exchanges emerged, but the general price level remained undisturbed.

The differences in the value of the paper money between the eighty or more departments of France constitute a curious aspect of the history of the Assignat.[3] The variations (according to the local tables of depreciation) attained large proportions: the Assignats in circulation were depreciated from 20 to 80 per cent in different places at the same time. Part of these differences was genuine: thus one section of the country suffered from the lack of supplies, especially of subsistence; in another section, the Assignat had to compete with metallic money; one section of the country had more confidence in the paper money than another. The wide discretion allowed to local officials in the construction of the tables, no doubt, accounted for some part of the vast differences: the apparent discrepancies were in part fictitious. The extremely high values of the Assignats circulating in Vendée, the center of the anti-Revolutionary agitation - in almost every month of the paper money period, an Assignat circulated there that apparently maintained a value above its value in any other department - a noticeable scattering (geographically) of extreme values (both high and low), the large proportion of the discrepancies accounted for by the two extreme deciles - all of these facts substantiate the contention that part of the difference was fictitious. A more gradual tapering off to

---

[3] A. Wagner observed similar discrepancies in Russia in the sixties of the last century; and Subercaseaux observes them in South American experiences. See G. Subercaseaux, op. cit., pp. 204-205.

extreme values might be expected if the variations were wholly genuine. But real differences of large proportions were present; the wide scattering (geographically) of a few sporadic variables, which may be attributed to idiosyncrasies of construction, is not inconsistent with the presence of genuine differences evident from an examination of the geographical concentration of similar values.

The radical members of the Convention, refuting the doctrines of the Economists and borrowing largely from the doctrines of Rousseau, carried through a system of price control and rationing in May, 1793 that endured until December, 1794. The result of the system was that the purchasing power of the Assignats at the disposal of the Government was greatly increased. But with diminished supplies on the markets as a result of the Revolution and wars, as well as of this artificial reduction of the price levels, the buying propensities of the public had to be curbed. The public was prevented from disbursing all of its Assignats; hence it is an error to assume that the value of the Assignat increased during this period merely because maximum prices were depressed. Since a large proportion of all of the Assignats at the disposal of the public were hoarded, it is probably nearer to the truth to say that the value of the *average* Assignat fell. No writer on the Assignats has observed that the increase in the value of the Assignats during this period was in the main a fictitious one. No writer (with the possible exception of Marion and Hawtrey) has even considered the system of maximum prices in relation to the changes in the value of the Assignats; writers have merely observed and commented on the increased value of the Assignat, which was evident in the Treasury figures. Hawtrey advances further than other writers in pointing out that the price of gold was artificially depressed during this period, and, therefore, that the gain of the Assignat was not as great as appeared on the surface. But he is in error to concentrate his attention on the price of gold; and he unknowingly quotes the price of the exchanges and not of gold. Marion attempts to demonstrate that the Maximum was ineffective and hence could not affect the value of the Assignat.

The system of maximum prices encountered innumerable obstacles of an administrative nature; but at least for one year of its existence - notably during the Terror - the maximum was tolerably effective in spite of many violations. The system prevented the farmers from profiting from the curtailed supplies at the expense of the Government and the residents of the cities. The benefits derived by the Government and the urban elements by the increased purchasing power of the Assignats expended, were, without doubt, in part offset by the reduced supplies sent to the markets by the farmers. At any rate, the system enabled the Government to issue additional supplies of paper money without paying the penalty of higher prices, and thus enabled the Government to support fourteen armies, as well as Paris.

Depreciation cannot be understood without a consideration of the many forces at work. The condition of the subsistence market was of fundamental significance. Periods of scarcity were accompanied by depreciation. With the fear of starvation ever present, any deficiency in the normal supplies might cause a wholesale dumping of Assignats. Periods of inadequate subsistence synchronized closely with periods of depreciation.

The Revolution was a period of curtailed production, and, therefore, of reduced supplies. Not only did the Revolution witness increased issues of paper money, but it was accompanied also by a reduced demand for money. The latter factor in itself would have caused a very large fall in the value of the livre. Especially during the latter part of the Revolution, when the cumulative effects of the Revolution, of the extensive warfare, and of maximum prices began to be felt, are the reduced supplies to be considered. An explanation of depreciation without a consideration of the curtailment of production and circulation of products, is of doubtful value. Although the demand for money decreased during the Revolution, in at least one direction the demand increased. Speculation was rampant, which tended to keep prices down when no turnover of commodities and bills was involved.

Gold and silver were in circulation in varying amounts during the Revolution. Before the terrorist policies were successfully enforced, the Assignats had to compete with gold and silver to an appreciable extent. With the weakening of these policies, and finally with the repeal of the discriminatory legislation against gold and silver, the metals offered renewed competition to the Assignats. No final significance is to be attached to the statistics of paper money in circulation so long as an unknown quantity of gold and silver circulated in addition to the paper money.

Four factors that influenced the value of the paper money have been outlined above, viz., the land security, the state of the subsistence market, the supplies of commodities, and the competition of gold and silver. But I considered several other factors in Chapters VII and VIII: political, military and financial conditions, public discussions of depreciation, demonetisation practices (including "au cours" payments with its increased demands on the currency and the loss of confidence resulting from an official recognition of depreciation), and counterfeiting.

Three problems that owed their origin to the introduction of Assignats have been discussed - the problem of coping with depreciated exchanges, of adjusting creditor-debtor relations after and during the period of extreme depreciation, and of bringing back gold and silver. The movement of the exchanges, however, was not exclusively an effect of the issues of the Assignats; for such factors as capital movements, public control of gold movements, trade and the exchanges, and the inelastic demand for necessities on the part of the Government, all had independent effects. Of much interest today are the attempts of the Government to support the exchanges: control of imports and exports, the confiscation of all foreign credits, payment abroad with gold, silver and precious stones instead of by the purchase of foreign exchange, borrowing from foreign banks, payment abroad in Assignats, and requisitioning of luxuries for export purposes.

The Assignats were replaced first by gold and silver, then by the Mandats, and finally by gold and silver again. The attempt of the French Government to revise the contracts made during the period of paper money, forms a fascinating chapter in paper money history. Two problems were involved: first, the Government had to prevent attempts (during the periods of rapid depreciation) to repay in a worthless paper money for debts contracted in a more valuable money; and, second, it had to save debtors who had incurred obligations during the paper money regime from the unfair demands for metallic reimbursements. Payments to the Government, farm leases and the like also had to be revised.

The third problem was how to return to a metallic standard. A protracted period of hardships resulted from the failure of the precious metals to return from abroad and from private hoards as quickly as was expected. The stable value of the paper money fell to approximately one hundred million livres at the end of 1795. The more rapid consumption of monetary balances, the partial return of gold and silver, and a reduced demand for money scarcely offset this reduction of the pre-Revolutionary circulating media by 95 per cent. Prices fell; the Government found it difficult to collect its revenues; and a heterogeneous collection of new paper substitutes appeared.

CAUSES OF DEPRECIATION

The Convention, occupied in the summer and early fall with the new constitution, devoted comparatively little time to the pressing needs of finance. There is no evidence of a single significant success for the many plans put into operation in 1795. The administrative machinery of the Government was weak. The Convention relied on Assignats more than ever, with some aid from continued requisitions. Legislation against the evil speculators, responsible for this depreciation in the opinion of many, was enacted repeatedly during the second half of 1795. The Convention attempted to dispose of the houses in Paris owned by the Government, requiring payment within a few weeks. On October 25 the Convention approved an extraordinary war tax of twenty livres for each livre of assessment for the Foncière. The Legislature approved several other extraordinary measures on November 15: some taxes to be collected in numeraire; a pronouncement once more in favor of the collection of public receipts "au cours"; a 3 per cent loan to be paid, principal and interest in numeraire; a milliard of Cedules d'hypothèque for extraordinary expenses; and a sale of forests and "mobilier" in metals or "au cours". The Government soon recognized the folly of issuing a loan, payable in gold and silver, but receivable in Assignats of a market value of 1 per cent of their nominal value. The final decree on the Cédules, voted on November 25, authorized the conversion of Assignats into Cédules at the market value of the Assignats and the expropriation of the Government from any parcel of land at any offer to pay the "prix d'estimation" in Cédules.

When the value of the Assignat was reduced to less than 1 per cent of its nominal value, proposals to demonetise were made almost daily. Lafon-Ladébat suggested that all notes lose their monetary values in four months, for the announcement of such a program would cause people to hurry to pay off their debts, and hence the value of the Assignat would increases He did not divulge whether the demonetisation was to be in effect only temporarily. De Valence proposed virtually a complete demonetisation in suggesting a compulsory exchange for a government bond which was to yield 1½ per cent.

A measure, enacted on November 20, to suspend the sale of lands, "to assure the holders of the Assignats that they will invariably have the portion of security which is legitimately due them", helped to impart the final blow. I have considered elsewhere the forced loan of six hundred millions that was voted at this juncture. It was not a striking success. Who can doubt, after considering the nature of these many attempts to resuscitate the Assignats, that they only accelerated their depreciation?

The political situation - especially on the frontiers - did not warrant this unprecedented loss of confidence in the Assignat. The increase of speculation was not a negligible factor in helping it to retain its value longer. The state of the subsistence market, the disorganization of the productive processes, the deplorable financial conditions resulting from the lax administration and the inability to concur on a definite program, the reduction of and loss of confidence in the security, the proposals to demonetise, and, finally, the renewed competition of gold and silver, all detracted from the confidence in the Assignat and contributed to the headlong depreciation. Depreciation proceeded much more rapidly than would be expected from a mere consideration of the issues:

the depreciation by the end of this period was at least twelve times as great as might be expected from a survey of quantities in circulation. The lack of confidence in the paper money, as evidenced by the desire to be rid of it, reflected the composite effect of all of these forces, and is of much greater significance than mere quantities.

Summary

No comprehensive and systematic treatment of the depreciation of the Assignat has yet been made. Many writers on the subject take depreciation for granted. Why stop to explain the depreciation of a paper money issued to excess? An uninterrupted fall, in the opinion of some, was inevitable. Hawtrey's emphasis on speculation is helpful, although he does not consider speculation in all its ramifications. The most serious deficiency in Hawtrey's treatment - to be expected in a brief essay - is his failure to consider the many forces that affected depreciation. Falkner makes a brilliant contribution in pointing out the necessity of considering the availability or unavailability of the metals for satisfying the demand for money.

One explanation of the depreciation was and is fully appreciated. The economists, the writers on public finance, and the monetary theorists have all expressed (or implied) an adherence to the quantity theory. Their allegiance to that theory often explains a neglect to inquire further into the process of depreciation. As has been indicated, however, the writers and thinkers of the

Revolution found much that was not explicable in terms of quantity. Lavoisier, for example, considered the moral effects of additional issues; Johannot commented on the depreciation, incomprehensible on a consideration of quantities alone, when Doumouriez betrayed his country. A brilliant essayist, Boislandry, formulated a comprehensive list of the causes of depreciation that a writer of today, better versed in monetary theory, might well be proud of. The man in the street did not miss an opportunity to scoff at the quantity theory; he pointed out, for example, that in May, 1796, the price of the louis was 9000 livres, whereas when the money in circulation had been three times as great, the price was but 2000-4000 livres. A police reporter made note not only of the fact that prices fell with the capture of Amsterdam early in 1795, but that the populace expected that a fall in prices would follow a great victory.

Wagner and Mitchell have made familiar the thesis that changes in the value of money are caused in large part by changing political fortunes. But Ferraris, whose treatise on paper money still remains one of the great works in the field, was critical of Wagner's position. Mises observes that military success was accompanied by final depreciation during both the French and American revolutions.

Wagner and Mitchell employed exchange and gold quotations as measures of depreciation. These markets are speculative and reflect the changing military and political situation well; in fact, one is easily misled by appreciable movements that are not easily explained by changes in fundamental conditions. But perhaps the most important explanation of the differences between Wagner and Mitchell, on the one hand, and Ferraris and Mises on the other, is that the former dealt with periods in which the depreciation was moderate, or at least not extreme. They did not have in mind periods in which the financial strain was so great that the creation of artificial purchasing power became the dominating factor in the situation. I agree with Wagner and Mitchell that a favorable political event would have an advantageous effect; but Wagner, and especially Mitchell were inclined to overemphasise the effects of the changing political situation.

What has been neglected in the explanations of the depreciation of the Assignat? There has been unquestionably a failure to consider adequately the problem of the supply of commodities, or, more comprehensively, of the demand for money. War, internal insecurity, and misguided public policies, all contributed to the reduction of supplies. But the effects of these forces varied so that the demand for money was not constant during this period. A careful consideration of the demand for money is indispensable for an estimate of the residue of damage caused directly by the Assignat.

Closely related, and yet a problem that requires special analysis, is the problem of subsistence. The Economic Federalism, the disorganized conditions of transportation, the effects of the public control and of the warfare, all require analysis. The singular synchronization of the periods of rapid depreciation and of lack of subsistence, forces the writer to the conclusion that the unhappy state of the subsistence market was a factor of fundamental importance for the value of the Assignat. An Assignat that could not buy bread was indeed worthless and the holder was willing to offer an increasing number of paper livres until he could procure the necessary subsistence. That the French expended perhaps two-thirds of their incomes on bread, is significant.

The purchase of subsistence required a large proportion of the resources of the Treasury. A writer estimated the monthly cost of the distribution of bread at 546 million livres in 1794-95. The cost of feeding Paris in 1795 equalled one-tenth of the total expenditures of the Government. Dubois Crancé, a well informed contemporary, estimated that two-thirds of the daily expenditures of the Government in the spring of 1795 were consumed in the purchase of subsistence, and by that time the circulation had been enriched by 6 milliards (more than one-half of the total) as a result of governmental expenditures for subsistence.

Thirdly, consider the effect of the land security, which received some attention in Chapter III. The study of the Assignats demands more than an acquaintance with present-day monetary theory: it requires an insight into the conditions during the Revolution. A study of the daily life of the Revolution confirms the impression that the fundamental source of the confidence in the Assignat lay in the land security that strongly supported it. The man in the street believed that the waste of these resources was equivalent to a demonetisation of the Assignat. Does any one suppose that the crafty legislators of the Revolution persistently advertised the abundance of the land security for the mere joy of the computation? We may not go all the way with D'Ivnerois who said that " The confiscations in 1793-94 kept the Assignat at its high value during the Terror", but we cannot doubt either the purpose of the confiscations of the possessions of the Émigrés and of the condemned, or the aid rendered the Assignat by these additions to the security. A minute study of all the specifics, suggested or carried through from 1794 to 1796, reveals that very few of them were not proposals to increase the receipts from the sale of lands. Can we give full confidence to the many writers on the Assignats who either neglect or dogmatically dismiss the very important influence of the land security on the value of the Assignats? So much for the more important sins of omission.

I have not intended to make this chapter on depreciation either a refutation of the quantity theory, or an encomium of it. I hold only that a discussion merely on the basis of quantities leads us nowhere. Subsistence, supplies, security, taxation, and the other factors at work, all finally affect the value of money through changes in the quantity of paper money thrown on the market or through any of the other variables in the equation of exchange. Quantities issued are of little significance without a consideration of the varying haste with which they are disbursed. The most effective way of paying homage to the quantity theory is to disregard it in its superficial form; but in apparently disregarding it, to study the forces at work - forces that finally become effective through changes in the supplies of and demand for money.

Criticisms of the quantity theory have been numerous in recent years. One of the by-products of this criticism has been a change in emphasis from quantities to balances. Aftalion points out that large variations in prices in the war and post-war period were accompanied by small variations in the supplies of money issued. Gide observes that the countries of the greatest inflation were not those of the highest prices. Bonnet observes that inflation remained inoperative because the public was unable to dispose of its large balances. Hahn points out that individuals who received additional cash were more likely to save than spend. They are all seeking for an explanation of the failure of the rigid quantity theory. Herrmann expresses the difficulty well: depreciation does not necessarily follow inflation, for inflation may be latent.

www.ingramcontent.com/pod-product-compliance
Lightning Source LLC
Chambersburg PA
CBHW050124170426
43197CB00011B/1708